•

The Europeanisation of Citizenship Governance in South-East Europe

This book looks at how Europeanisation affects the link between citizenship and governance in and across the new states of South-East Europe. Contributors unpack the intimate relationship between the European Union, national governments and citizens through a tripartite model that captures the uneven and diversified effects of Europeanisation on the governance of citizenship-related policy areas. Reflecting on the meaning of governance in different contexts, this book invites the readers to reconsider the terms and concepts that are commonly used for studying the consolidation of new states. By doing so, it directs attention to the transformative power of European integration not only on modes of governance, but also on practices and experiences of citizenship. Individual chapters are 'paired' to examine three policy areas that are to a different degree affected by the requirements of European Union accession. Combining analysis of policy frameworks with assessment of their impact, the contributors highlight that the impact of Europeanisation can be located on a continuum stretching from 'strongest' in matters regarding justice and home affairs, to 'moderate' in general issues of social policy, to 'weakest' in transforming citizenship through education policies. This book was originally published as a special issue of *European Politics and Society*.

Jelena Džankić is a Marie Curie Fellow at the European University Institute. She holds a Ph.D. in International Studies from the University of Cambridge, UK.

Simonida Kacarska is Research Coordinator at the European Policy Institute in Skopje, Macedonia. She holds a Ph.D. in Politics and International Studies from the University of Leeds, UK.

Nataša Pantić is a Chancellor's Fellow at the School of Education of the University of Edinburgh, UK. She holds a Ph.D. in Education Sciences from Utrecht University, The Netherlands.

The Europeanisation of Citizenship Governance in South-East Europe

Edited by
Jelena Džankić, Simonida Kacarska and Nataša Pantić

LONDON AND NEW YORK

First published 2016
by Routledge
2 Park Square, Milton Park, Abingdon, Oxon, OX14 4RN, UK

and by Routledge
711 Third Avenue, New York, NY 10017, USA

Routledge is an imprint of the Taylor & Francis Group, an informa business

© 2016 Taylor & Francis

All rights reserved. No part of this book may be reprinted or reproduced or utilised in any form or by any electronic, mechanical, or other means, now known or hereafter invented, including photocopying and recording, or in any information storage or retrieval system, without permission in writing from the publishers.

Trademark notice: Product or corporate names may be trademarks or registered trademarks, and are used only for identification and explanation without intent to infringe.

British Library Cataloguing in Publication Data
A catalogue record for this book is available from the British Library

ISBN 13: 978-1-138-18506-7

Typeset in Times
by diacriTech, Chennai

Publisher's Note
The publisher accepts responsibility for any inconsistencies that may have arisen during the conversion of this book from journal articles to book chapters, namely the possible inclusion of journal terminology.

Disclaimer
Every effort has been made to contact copyright holders for their permission to reprint material in this book. The publishers would be grateful to hear from any copyright holder who is not here acknowledged and will undertake to rectify any errors or omissions in future editions of this book.

Contents

Citation Information   vii

1. Introduction: The Governance of Citizenship Practices in the Post-Yugoslav
States: The Impact of Europeanisation   1
Jelena Džankić, Simonida Kacarska, Nataša Pantić and Jo Shaw

2. The Unbearable Lightness of Europeanisation: Extradition Policies and the
Erosion of Sovereignty in the Post-Yugoslav States   11
Jelena Džankić

3. Losing the Rights along the Way: The EU–Western Balkans
Visa Liberalisation   27
Simonida Kacarska

4. Welfare State Change and Social Citizenship in the Post-Yugoslav States   43
Marija Stambolieva

5. Citizenship and Social Welfare in Croatia: Clientelism and the Limits of
'Europeanisation'   59
Paul Stubbs and Siniša Zrinščak

6. Citizenship and Education in the Post-Yugoslav States   75
Nataša Pantić

7. Dissatisfied Citizens: Ethnonational Governance, Teachers' Strike and
Professional Solidarity in Mostar, Bosnia–Herzegovina   93
Azra Hromadžić

8. Conclusion: Citizenship and the Practice of Governance in South-East Europe   111
Andrew Geddes

Index   119

Citation Information

The chapters in this book were originally published in the *European Politics and Society*, volume 16, issue 3 (September 2015). When citing this material, please use the original page numbering for each article, as follows:

Chapter 1
Introduction: The Governance of Citizenship Practices in the Post-Yugoslav States: The Impact of Europeanisation
Jelena Džankić, Simonida Kacarska, Nataša Pantić and Jo Shaw
European Politics and Society, volume 16, issue 3 (September 2015) pp. 337–346

Chapter 2
The Unbearable Lightness of Europeanisation: Extradition Policies and the Erosion of Sovereignty in the Post-Yugoslav States
Jelena Džankić
European Politics and Society, volume 16, issue 3 (September 2015) pp. 347–362

Chapter 3
Losing the Rights along the Way: The EU–Western Balkans Visa Liberalisation
Simonida Kacarska
European Politics and Society, volume 16, issue 3 (September 2015) pp. 363–378

Chapter 4
Welfare State Change and Social Citizenship in the Post-Yugoslav States
Marija Stambolieva
European Politics and Society, volume 16, issue 3 (September 2015) pp. 379–394

Chapter 5
Citizenship and Social Welfare in Croatia: Clientelism and the Limits of 'Europeanisation'
Paul Stubbs and Siniša Zrinščak
European Politics and Society, volume 16, issue 3 (September 2015) pp. 395–410

Chapter 6
Citizenship and Education in the Post-Yugoslav States
Nataša Pantić
European Politics and Society, volume 16, issue 3 (September 2015) pp. 411–428

CITATION INFORMATION

Chapter 7

Dissatisfied Citizens: Ethnonational Governance, Teachers' Strike and Professional Solidarity in Mostar, Bosnia–Herzegovina
Azra Hromadžić
European Politics and Society, volume 16, issue 3 (September 2015) pp. 429–446

Chapter 8

Conclusion: Citizenship and the Practice of Governance in South-East Europe
Andrew Geddes
European Politics and Society, volume 16, issue 3 (September 2015) pp. 447–454

For any permission-related enquiries please visit:
http://www.tandfonline.com/page/help/permissions

Introduction

The Governance of Citizenship Practices in the Post-Yugoslav States: The Impact of Europeanisation

JELENA DŽANKIĆ*, SIMONIDA KACARSKA**, NATAŠA PANTIĆ† & JO SHAW††

*Robert Schuman Centre for Advanced Studies, European University Institute, Italy; **European Policy Institute, Macedonia; †Institute for Education, Teaching and Leadership (ETL), University of Edinburgh, UK; ††The Institute for Advanced Studies in the Humanities, University of Edinburgh, UK*

ABSTRACT *This Introduction explains the origins of the project of exploring citizenship and citizenship-related issues in the framework of Europeanisation in the new states in South East Europe. It defines the terminology used in the contributions and explains the conceptual underpinnings of the project and the structure of the edited collection. Finally, these introductory remarks also give an overview of the contributions to the special issue of Perspectives on European Politics and Societies entitled, 'The governance of citizenship practices in the post-Yugoslav states: The impact of Europeanisation.'*

Introduction

This special issue examines the governance of citizenship and citizenship-related issues in the context of complex and sometimes contested processes of Europeanisation in and across the new states of South East Europe. The basic premise for the research was the centrality of the construction and governance of its citizenship regime for each new state that emerged during the course of the progressive breakup of the Socialist Federal Republic of Yugoslavia (SFRY) from 1991 onwards. Each new state established the laws and policies necessary to determine not only who were the initial citizenry of the state, but also how citizenship was acquired (and sometimes lost) at birth, through residence (or non-residence), via descent, and through other recognised connections such as 'special qualities'. However, the study of citizenship necessarily goes beyond these narrow boundaries, looking at other types of 'quasi' statuses such as permanent residency as well as informal ideational and ideological aspects of citizenship policies. And while the starting point for such citizenship studies may be the status elements of membership, it quickly becomes

THE EUROPEANISATION OF CITIZENSHIP GOVERNANCE

evident that the enjoyment of citizenship can never fully be dissociated from its rights and identitarian elements.

The preliminary mapping of the formal and informal elements of these new regimes through detailed country case studies was the primary focus of a first phase of work by the team working on the project *The Europeanisation of Citizenship in the Successor States of the Former Yugoslavia (CITSEE)*.[1] One task of the work (Shaw & Štiks, 2012a) was that of highlighting for scholars of citizenship more generally the importance of mainstreaming the cases of new state formation in Europe within the body of scholarship which attempts to understand the functions and structure of citizenship laws and practices, and to provide typologies which explain the main currents. In fact, as Shaw and Štiks (2012b, p. 309) have argued:

> The post-Yugoslav landscape offers a unique situation when it comes to citizenship. It is simultaneously a post-socialist, post-partition and post-conflict region which has witnessed, over the last 20 years, multiple processes of disintegration, successful and unsuccessful attempts at secession, and a huge variety of internal political and territorial arrangements.

Thus, the case of the former Yugoslavia is an important complement to comparative studies of citizenship regimes, even though it is hard to shoehorn these cases into simple typologies of civic or ethnic, restrictive or liberal approaches to citizenship acquisition and loss.

At the same time, the work of CITSEE has demonstrated to scholars of the former Yugoslavia, and of Balkan studies more generally, the importance of the citizenship dimension – that is, the formal question of who is included and who is not included both at the moment of state formation and on an ongoing basis as well as the reasons behind the grant or denial of citizenship status. This forms an important baseline for polity and demos building not only around issues such as voting, elections and political parties, but also for the purposes of immigration and refugee issues (Krasniqi, 2012; Džankić, 2014; Djordjević, 2015; Sardelić, 2015). It also has state security dimensions. It can be shown to have had important influences upon the process of disintegration and gradual re-integration of these states within a broader European frame (Štiks, 2012). Citizenship status may not exhaust the conceptual resources of 'membership', but it provides an important baseline reference point.

The seven new states adopted very different approaches to developing their citizenship regimes even though all of them – with the exception of Kosovo – shared a common root in the sense of having been a republic within the SFRY. To put it another way, the citizenship regimes that were put in place by subsequent governments and legislatures drew in different ways upon former elements of the two-level Yugoslav framework of federal-level 'national' citizenship and republican citizenship, based on registers of citizens at that level. As the federal-level citizenship represented a legal and symbolic umbrella of the Yugoslav unity, at the time of the disintegration of this multinational state, the republican citizenship clearly took precedence in constituting the new states' citizenship regimes. Since the territorial borders of many of the new states coincided with those of the former republics that constituted Yugoslavia, the sub-federal citizenship better articulated new ideas of *belonging*.

These new ideas of *belonging* were central to constructing the tissue of new states and societies in the post-Yugoslav space. The strong group attachments, revivals,

2

THE EUROPEANISATION OF CITIZENSHIP GOVERNANCE

transformations and developments of ethno-national identities all contributed to the central-ity of citizenship policies in *constructing* and *governing* new states. Citizenship policies determined which group or groups had the claim to the state, which would have a special status, and which would be marginalised in or completely excluded from the con-struction of the demos. The definition of the demos in this regard was not only a symbolic expression of the state's constitutional identity, but also a more pragmatic tool for regulat-ing who would be included in or excluded from such an identity. Hence citizenship, as a symbolic and a pragmatic manifestation of what the state is intended to be, reinforced pol-itical processes in the newly established post-Yugoslav states.

Definition of Terms

The governance of citizenship examined in this special issue is not only related to the citi-zenship policy that is encapsulated in a country's nationality law. Rather, it refers to broader policies that regulate the distribution of rights across the demos, including mobi-lity, participation, social policy, and education. In other words, the governance of citizen-ship spreads across multiple overlapping arenas within which individuals make claims and exercise duties that they have by virtue of being members in a state. Such practices of citi-zenship take place within 'wider political settlement, reflecting, for example, contestations between, for instance, titular "national" and minorities, among "constitutive peoples", pol-itical and ideological groups or simply citizens over citizenship and related rights, especially rights of political participation' (Shaw & Štiks, 2012b, pp. 312–313).

However, one of the most important geographical and geopolitical facts about this region is that the states that remain outside the European Union (EU) (Bosnia–Herzegovina, Kosovo, Macedonia, Montenegro and Serbia) represent, along with Albania, an enclave surrounded by the EU. Moreover, only Slovenia joined the EU in the first tranche of central and Eastern European states in 2004, and Croatia had to wait until 2013 to take its place. Hence, it is clear that almost throughout the territory of the former Yugoslavia, the processes of Europeanisation have been retarded and contested, not least as the conse-quence of the troubled history of this region and as a result of the presence of several unconsolidated states with rigid citizenship regimes (Džankić, 2015).

While as a preliminary effort, Europeanisation may be defined as 'domestic adaptation to European regional integration' (Vink & Graziano, 2007, p. 7), in practice this special issue tries to dig deeper into the concept. The articles collected here permit a deep study of the transformations of citizenship governance triggered by the interaction between the national governments and the EU. This thus helps us to build on and reformulate Radaelli's (2000, p. 4) seminal view of the concept as:

> processes of (a) construction, (b) diffusion and (c) institutionalisation of formal and informal rules, procedures, policy paradigms, styles, 'ways of doing things' and shared beliefs and norms which are first defined and consolidated in the EU policy process and then incorporated in the logic of domestic (national and subnational) dis-course, political structures and public policies.

A broader approach to the concept of Europeanisation is essential here, as the process that occurs between national governments of countries that are Member States of the EU differs significantly from that in those aspiring to EU membership. While the EU

THE EUROPEANISATION OF CITIZENSHIP GOVERNANCE

Member States have an opportunity to affect the policies at the EU level, thus feeding directly into the process, the post-Yugoslav countries are subject to unidirectional domestic adaptation to the accession requirements (Schimmelfennig & Sedelmeier, 2005; Schimmelfennig et al., 2006).

This adaptation requires not only the direct absorption of the *EU acquis*, but also the acceptance of the norms and values enshrined in international human rights norms and promoted by other international organisations such as the Council of Europe (CoE), the Organisation for Security and Cooperation in Europe (OSCE), and the World Bank. These have become complementary tools for ensuring the key guarantees of rights and freedoms for the citizens of the newly established states, and as such have become integrated in the process of EU accession indirectly through Europeanisation, rather than through formal *acquis* requirements.

Yet, in the context of the governance of citizenship, we need to be aware of the limits of the transformative power of the EU, as the regulation of membership statuses is the prerogative of the Member States. Indeed, while some mechanisms of policy convergence of nationality laws, such as the CoE's European Convention on Nationality, exist, they are commonly understood as standard setting rather than legally binding. Hence while the impact of Europeanisation on the matters of status is rather limited, it has had a significant effect on the rights associated to membership. International instruments and standards, including the European Convention on Human Rights and Fundamental Freedoms (ECHR), the Framework Convention for the Protection of National Minorities (FCNM), the European Charter for Regional and Minority Languages, but also judgments of the European Court of Human Rights and recommendations of other CoE bodies (such as the Venice Commission, parliamentary committees) have become an essential component of the governance and practices of citizenship across the post-Yugoslav states. Specific examples of these effects are to be found across the papers in the special issue.

Special Issue: Conceptualisation and Structure

This special issue, which also draws on the CITSEE work, explores the governance and practices of citizenship in innovative ways, in the interests of bringing the citizenship-based material to a broader European/EU studies audience interested in the complex phenomenon of Europeanisation. It draws on an emerging body of citizenship studies across different disciplines which have dealt with the construction, regulation and practices of citizenship in Europe's new states, many of which are to be found in South East Europe. Legal scholars have examined how the formal links between the individual and the state have been created when states come into being, and have explored the legal consequences of the boundaries of inclusion and exclusion especially for minority or vulnerable groups such as Roma. Sociologists and anthropologists have looked at citizenship practices in a broader context, often focusing on how people articulate claims against institutions, how they behave and what broader societal reactions their activities trigger. Political scientists explored the different levels and dimensions of citizenship in their attempts to unveil the nature of the relationship between the individual and the newly established polities and the strategies of states often under pressure from both the inside and the outside.

Yet only a handful of these works have been devoted to the study of how the spaces for citizenship practices are shaped, governed and transformed in the multi-level governance context of Europe. These spaces, which demand study from the perspective of many

THE EUROPEANISATION OF CITIZENSHIP GOVERNANCE

different academic disciplines, encompass the status, rights and identity dimensions of citizenship, but concern not just the formal institutional elements of citizenship understood as a top-down phenomenon (imposed and restricted by states). On the contrary, they are experienced or lived by the people on a day-to-day basis, and it is possible also to see how individuals and groups negotiate aspects of their memberships (often plural) with states and – in certain respects – with the EU, which has had an increasing direct and indirect impact upon citizenship regimes.

Thus the spaces for lived citizenship are shaped, governed and transformed both internally and under external influences such as EU accession processes. In the post-Yugoslav states, which have been for the first time experiencing independent citizenship regimes, the creation, management and change of these spaces is not affected only by the tendencies of the domestic actors to consolidate the governance of citizenship with their political objectives in mind. Rather, it is also subject to the pressures stemming from the external environment and above all the EU, since these states are (or aspire to become) Member States of the EU. In this context, the post-Yugoslav states are required to adapt to the conditions of membership. To reiterate, these conditions are broader than the *acquis*. Hence as a preliminary condition of accession to the EU, the post-Yugoslav states have become members of the CoE and acceded to the ECHR. Meanwhile, some of the states have also experienced direct intervention in their affairs in the context of conflict prevention and peace-keeping activities, with impacts upon their citizenship regimes (Shaw, 2011).

This special issue takes a closer look at the conditions of EU membership against the backdrop of a broader field of European and international-level norms (e.g. relating to human rights). It does so by distinguishing between different dimensions of citizenship, where the requirements of EU accession (or pathways towards accession such as Schengen visa liberalisation) according to the regulatory character of the various fields. For while these conditions are stipulated clearly in some areas through the EU's *acquis* (hard governance), in other cases they are only vaguely or scarcely defined (soft governance). The more regulated these areas are through the EU's *acquis*, the greater is the potential for a 'misfit' of the policy or laws at the national level with the conditions of accession. Thus, the effect of EU-driven rule transfer is likely to have a more profound effect upon the transformation of citizenship in those spaces of citizenship governed directly through the *acquis*, as this will become embedded in the domestic modes of governance. On the other hand, the subtler effects of norm transfer in other fields where the EU's governance is confined to 'softer' approaches can have notable impacts upon the scope of citizenship, especially the rights of citizenship and the capacity of individuals to enjoy full membership.

Hence, this special issue explores how the lived spaces of citizenship are governed in the context of three areas of public policy which are, to a different degree, affected by the EU. The freedom of movement, examined here through the focus on visa liberalisation and extradition, is a key part of the EU's *acquis* and represents an example of hard governance; social policies and welfare are only partly included in the EU's regulation, and as such reflect a mixed mode of governance, while education policies lie predominantly with the national authorities at different levels and the EU sets only the general principles and contributes through complementary policies. The latter, soft modes of governance, include principles such as promotion of social inclusion in education and training, and some education-relevant provisions from within other fields such as minority rights in the field of education. In the context of EU studies, the approach taken in this special issue will contribute to a better understanding of (a) the types of competence and (b) the modes of

THE EUROPEANISATION OF CITIZENSHIP GOVERNANCE

governing – from the traditional 'community method' (supranational, hard law) to the 'open method of coordination' (intergovernmental, soft law). It helps to unveil the export of the EU's modes of governance to acceding countries, while simultaneously looking at how these countries adapt to the transfer of competences to the EU in various policy areas.

It helps to build a more nuanced picture of the Europeanisation process, especially in the context of accession and pre-accession, going beyond the classic descriptive or interpretative theories of Europeanisation which largely see this, in pre-accession contexts, as a top-down process of adjustment for the purposes of acquiring membership of the EU. However, given the different disciplinary starting points of the papers, the special issue does not work with a single imposed description or theory of the Europeanisation process, but encourages the various authors to develop complementary frames of reference that draw on a variety of overlapping literatures.

In order to analyse how different nuances of Europeanisation are articulated in the governance and practices of citizenship in the post-Yugoslav space, the papers in this special issue are organised in pairs. What all papers have in common is their focus on the effects of the evolution of citizenship in the new states as these implement their aspiration to join the EU. However, the effects of Europeanisation on the governance and practices of citizenship differ. They can be positive or negative for the construction of the demos. While Džankić's paper clearly highlights the positive impact of Europeanisation on driving states away from 'constitutional nationalism' (Hayden, 1992, p. 655), Kacarska's highlights the negative and exclusionary effects of the process of visa liberalisation on the exercise of human and minority rights. Equally, if the three sets of papers indicate, the impact of Europeanisation can be located on a continuum from 'strongest' in matters regarding justice and home affairs (Džankić and Kacarska), to 'moderate' in general issues of social policy (Stambolieva and Stubbs and Zrinščak), to 'weakest' in transforming citizenship through education policies (Pantić and Hromadžić). The broader scholarly implication of these conclusions is that the consequences of Europeanisation are different in nature, character and scope. As such, while generally having a positive effect, they may produce as much contestation, convolution and conflict along the different arenas in which citizenship is governed and exercised.

Examining these issues through the lenses of extradition policies and visa-free travel of third country nationals as key segments of the *EU acquis* is the main objective of the first set of papers in this special issue. Although operating within similar conceptual boundaries of Europeanisation in the area of justice and home affairs, the papers provide a differing, even contrasting view of this process using diverse methodological tools. In her paper *The Unbearable Lightness of Europeanisation: extradition policies and the erosion of sovereignty in the post-Yugoslav states,* Jelena Džankić analyses vertical (legal adaptation) and horizontal consequences (conclusion of bilateral agreements) of Europeanisation on citizenship in the post-Yugoslav states. Specifically, the paper examines the evolution of the different states' policies related to extradition of their own nationals in the context of the implementation of the European Arrest Warrant Framework Decision in conjunction with the requirements for regional cooperation and good neighbourly relations implemented in the Western Balkans. Methodologically, the paper looks at three categories of states: EU members, candidate countries, and potential candidates and contested states. In contrast to (dominant) arguments of fake compliance in the region under examination in this special issue, Džankić supports the line of deep transformative effect of Europe in this specific issue under examination, including a spillover on other policy areas. Yet, she

THE EUROPEANISATION OF CITIZENSHIP GOVERNANCE

emphasises that the major constitutional and legal adaptations to the requirements for accession relation to justice, freedom and security, that is, Chapter 24 in the EU negotiating structure, are more likely however in the last stages of accession, judging by the experiences of Croatia and Slovenia.

A contrasting view of the operation and outcome of the Europeanisation of candidate countries is presented in Simonida Kacarska's paper, *Losing the rights along the way: the EU-Western Balkans visa liberalisation,* that studies the transformation of fundamental rights during the Schengen visa liberalisation process. As a potentially powerful tool for transformation, Kacarska approaches the visa talks as a parallel process to the regular EU accession mechanisms. Operating within the conceptual boundaries of Europeanisation by conditionality, the paper studies whether and how the EU has managed to incorporate fundamental rights requirements in a security-dominated and politically significant process as the visa liberalisation. It adopts a before and after approach in relation to 2009/2010 when the visa requirements were lifted. Analysing both the formal benchmarking process and data from stakeholders' interviews, the paper illustrates the securitisation and side-lining of fundamental rights during and in the aftermath of the visa negotiations. Contrary to Džankić's work, this paper demonstrates the potential for unwanted effects of conditionality and questions the role of the EU in promoting fundamental rights. As such, it raises significant questions on the impact of the visa liberalisation project upon the governing of the citizenship regimes in the region.

While the first pair of papers deals with policy areas which are under a direct influence of the EU, the second pair deals with welfare policies, which are only partly included in the EU's regulation, reflecting a mixed mode of governance. Although present, the Europeanisation paradigm in the latter is of secondary importance, that is, these papers foremost operate in the context of the post-communist transformations. In this vein, Marija Stambolieva in her paper *Welfare state change and social citizenship in the post-Yugoslav states* discusses the interaction between social citizenship and the welfare state. She examines the relationship between changing political institutions and notions of citizenship, on the one hand and changing welfare policies on the other. She attributes the welfare diversity to inherited legacies and the transitional context, and particularly the political responses to it. Moreover, the paper locates the welfare reforms in the context of democratisation processes, which have on the other hand also affected both the notions of citizenship. The largely uneven role of the EU in these processes is a segment of the multitude of international influences that challenged existing structures and offered new perspectives. Based on the combined effect of these influences in the post-Yugoslav space, she discerns four social citizenship types: neo-corporatist (Slovenia), accommodating (Croatia), paternalistic (Serbia and Montenegro) and neo-liberal (Macedonia and Kosovo).

While Stambolieva looks horizontally at a set of countries, the next paper of the special issue zooms in on the case of Croatia, the most recent EU Member State. In their paper *Citizenship and social welfare in Croatia: Clientelism and the limits of 'Europeanisation'*, Paul Stubbs and Siniša Zrinščak explore issues related to the governance of welfare through the lens of 'clientelism' in the context of transition, war, nation state building and political settlements in Croatia. Clientelism is described as a complex structure that has an impact on social welfare which may be explicit, when particular political elites trade directly favours for votes, or institutional or hegemonic, defining an informal political common-sense. Stubbs and Zrinščak consider the relationship between governance, citizenship and social welfare and illustrate how these relationships have been shaped internally with

THE EUROPEANISATION OF CITIZENSHIP GOVERNANCE

limited external influences of the EU accession processes. The paper explores how politicisation of governance and dominance of nationality over territorial-based citizenship claims helped shape the development of clientelistic welfare, focusing on the practices of privileging the rights of war veterans and of those of Croatian ethnicity particularly from neighbouring Bosnia–Herzegovina. The authors argue that an asymmetric redistribution of resources and an ethnicised nationalism consolidated through the clientelistic welfare in the 1990s have remained largely unchallenged by the EU's regulation. Although the EU accession process impacted on and reconfigured economic, political and social arrangements, there was no radical 'break' with the social and political circumstances which had produced and consolidated these clientelistic welfare arrangements. The authors also consider the prospects for changes in these arrangements in the context of the current economic and financial crisis and in the light of EU membership. They suggest that after gaining the membership on 1 July 2013, and with the translation of EU-led austerity politics, ideas of social citizenship may be unravelling once more in Croatia.

The last two papers in this special issue explore how citizenship is lived and governed in relation to education as an area of policy and practice that is predominantly in the charge of local authorities. In her paper *Citizenship and Education in the post-Yugoslav States*, Nataša Pantić explores interactions between citizenship and education policies in six post-Yugoslav contexts. The paper maps out policies that shape the intended spaces for experiences of citizenship by the young people which encompass the status, rights and identity dimensions. The paper explores how elements of ethnocentric, multicultural and civic citizenship regimes reflect in education governance structures and language policies. It exemplifies the ways in which relevant provisions of the FCNM and other international norms protecting group and individual rights are adopted and adapted through their partial implementation driven by the local, by and large ethnocentric education agendas. The author considers how both universal and consociational education systems promote ethnocentric and exclusive conceptions of citizenship reflected in the context-dependent status of different minorities, and in the language policies that perpetuate dominant ethnic groups, while inclusive elements have been identified in the anti-discriminatory measures for inclusion of Roma students in mainstream education. Multicultural approaches to linguistic and cultural rights are reflected in the provision of minority language instruction options, although ethnocentric motives can be discerned behind their territorial implementation. The author argues that while observance of the EU membership criteria and relevant norms have been an important driving force for adopting social inclusion and minority rights in education-relevant legislation and policies, their domestic consolidation and limited implementation created tensions between ensuring group rights and protection of individual rights and non-discrimination. The interactions between citizenship and education policies in the post-Yugoslav states have been summarised as the rise of *ethnocentric,* on the pretext of ensuring *multicultural* education of young citizens in line with the European ideals of respecting cultural and linguistic diversity.

The final paper in this special issue entitled *Dissatisfied citizens: Ethnonational governance, teachers' strike and professional solidarity in Mostar, Bosnia–Herzegovina* and authored by Azra Hromadžić presents an ethnographic and anthropological study which documents how citizenship is experienced by people in their daily life, focusing on a case of professional solidarity among teachers in Bosnia–Herzegovina. This paper illustrates how the intended governance structures and policies only partly contribute to the

THE EUROPEANISATION OF CITIZENSHIP GOVERNANCE

shaping of citizens' identities. The paper describes how ethnically divided Croat and Bosniak teachers at the first 'reunified' school in postwar Bosnia and Herzegovina came to strike together to voice their professional citizen-demands. Administrative reunification of Mostar Gymnasium exemplifies the international influence over local governance mentioned earlier in this introduction. The school's reunification was celebrated by the OSCE – the main international body in charge of reunification – and some local politicians as the most powerful symbol of the city's reunification, while ethnic segregation was preserved through separate national curricula for the students of the two ethnic groups. The case illustrates how ethnic governance of the Mostar gymnasium could be at least temporarily disrupted if not completely transformed through teacher-citizens' actions. A teachers' protest group was formed across the ethnic when the feelings of citizens' dissatisfaction combined with a loss of social status and being left out of administrative procedures, which enable access to rightful entitlements. These teachers frequently referred to themselves as 'dissatisfied citizens', stressing the generational, moral and economic aspects of their predicament. Their joint actions generated a shift in the teachers' political subjectivities and probed the horizon of ethnic politics in postwar Bosnia. The author argues that these actions cannot be simply glorified as a form of cross-ethnic solidarity or as an expression of professional ethic, nor dismissed as supportive of an ethno-national regime, since these practices are never monologic, oppressive or liberatory. Rather, they illuminate the blurred distinctions between the state and citizens, the professional and personal, and the hegemonic and sincere.

Read in conjunction with the concluding remarks of Andrew Geddes, who highlights the contextual and conceptual contributions of the special issue to the wider studies of citizenship and Europeanisation, as well further avenues for research, the papers in this special issue aim to illuminate the nuances of balance and contradiction between the international (EU) and domestic factors for change. At a time when the EU is faced with major economic, political and societal challenges, it is of central importance to understand how it affects transitional societies, and what effects its accession requirements may have in different countries and across different policy areas. The two case studies examined in this special issue – those of clientelism in Croatia and the teachers' strike in Bosnia and Herzegovina – show the potential and limitations of Europeanisation to affect social citizenship and citizens' identities in two post-conflict, post-partition countries that have had a different experience of requirements and rewards of EU accession.

Acknowledgements

The editors of the special issue and individual authors are thankful for the insightful comments of the anonymous reviewers.

Disclosure statement

No potential conflict of interest was reported by the author(s).

Funding

The financial support of the European Research Council (CITSEE, ERC 230239) in the preparation of this special issue is acknowledged with gratitude. The support of the

THE EUROPEANISATION OF CITIZENSHIP GOVERNANCE

Robert Schuman Centre for Advanced Studies for organising a one-day workshop is acknowledged with thanks.

Note

[1] Details of the CITSEE project can be found on its websites: www.citsee.ed.ac.uk (which includes the text of working papers which present the raw findings of the CITSEE research) and www.citsee.eu (the Web Magazine *Citizenship in South East Europe*).

References

Djordjević, B. (2015) Whose rights, whose return? The boundary problem and unequal restoration of citizenship in the post-Yugoslav space, *Ethnopolitics*, 14(2), pp. 121–139.

Džankić, J. (2014) Citizenship between the 'image of the nation and 'the image of politics': The case of Montenegro, *Southeast European and Black Sea Studies*, 14(1), pp. 43–64.

Džankić, J. (2015) *Citizenship in Bosnia and Herzegovina, Macedonia and Montenegro: Effects of Statehood and Identity Challenges* (Alderidge: Ashgate).

Hayden, R. M. (1992) Constitutional nationalism in the formerly Yugoslav republics, *Slavic Review*, 51(4), pp. 654–673.

Krasniqi, G. (2012) Overlapping jurisdictions, disputed territory, unsettled state: The perplexing case of citizenship in Kosovo, *Citizenship Studies*, 16(3–4), pp. 353–366.

Radaelli, C. M. (2000) Whither Europeanization? Concept stretching and substantive change, *European Integration online Papers (EIoP)*, 4(8), pp. 1–28.

Sardelić, J. (2015) Romani minorities and uneven citizenship access in the post-Yugoslav space, *Ethnopolitics*, 14(2), pp. 159–179.

Schimmelfennig, F., Engert, S., & Knobel, H. (2006) *International Socialization in Europe: European Organizations, Political Conditionality, and Democratic Change* (Basingstoke: Palgrave Macmillan).

Schimmelfennig, F. & Sedelmeier U. (Eds.) (2005) *The Europeanization of Central and Eastern Europe* (Ithaca, NY: Cornell University Press).

Shaw, J. (2011) The constitutional mosaic across the boundaries of the European Union: Citizenship regimes in the new states of South Eastern Europe, in: N. Walker, J. Shaw & S. Tierney (Eds) *Europe's Constitutional Mosaic*, pp. 137–170 (Oxford: Hart).

Shaw, J. & Štiks, I. (Eds.) (2012a) *Citizenship after Yugoslavia* (London: Routledge).

Shaw, J. & Štiks, I. (Eds.) (2012b) Introduction: Citizenship in the new states of South Eastern Europe, *Citizenship Studies*, 16(3–4), pp. 309–321.

Štiks, I. (2012) A laboratory of citizenship: Shifting conceptions of citizenship in Yugoslavia and post-Yugoslav states, in: J. Shaw & I. Štiks (Eds) *Citizenship after Yugoslavia*, pp. 15–37 (London: Routledge).

Vink, M. P. & Graziano, P. (2007) Challenges of a new research Agenda, in: P. Graziano & M.P. Vink (Eds) *Europeanization: New Research Agendas*, pp. 3–20 (London: Palgrave).

The Unbearable Lightness of Europeanisation: Extradition Policies and the Erosion of Sovereignty in the Post-Yugoslav States

JELENA DŽANKIĆ

Robert Schuman Centre for Advanced Studies, European University Institute, Italy

ABSTRACT *This research analyses the effect of Europeanisation on sovereignty in the post-Yugoslav states by examining the evolution of the different states' policies related to extradition of their own nationals. Extradition is an important aspect of these countries' political transformation, because the rule of law and regional co-operation are enshrined in the set of conditions these countries have to meet to enter the European Union. The research thus looks at how the different post-Yugoslav states approach the extradition of their own nationals, and whether they have altered them in view of the requirements of the accession process. By doing so, this paper looks at the dynamics between the duty of the state to protect its citizens and the transformative power of Europeanisation in the Western Balkans.*

Introduction

On 1 July 2013, Croatia became the 28th European Union (EU) Member State. The Croatian 'accession party' was not attended by the German Chancellor Angela Merkel, who thus expressed her discontent with the change in Croatia's approach to EU legislation at the dawn of EU membership. Two days before the country became an EU Member State, the Parliament of Croatia adopted the amendments to its Law on Judicial Cooperation in Criminal Matters with the Member States of the EU, preventing the extradition of its own nationals to the EU Member States for crimes committed prior to 7 August 2002. The time limitation in the Croatian law corresponded to the date of the enforcement of the European Arrest Warrant (EAW) (Framework Decision 2002/584/JHA), which has established common rules for surrender and extradition among the EU Member States. Previously, the Croatian Law, similar to the laws of another 22 EU Member States, did not contain a temporal limitation on extradition and the country changed its Constitution in 2010 in order to be able to implement the EU's legislation. The abrupt legislative

THE EUROPEANISATION OF CITIZENSHIP GOVERNANCE

changes followed Germany's request of June 2013 for the extradition of Josip Perković, a former security agent, charged for the assassination of a Croatian political émigré in 1983. The underlying amendments, commonly referred to as *lex Perković*, reveal the underpinning questions of the paper. How far does Europeanisation reach when transforming the state-citizen link? How do the different countries respond to the challenges produced by the external requirements for adaptation and the domestic sovereignty concerns?

Starting from the above questions, this paper examines the interplay between the processes of Europeanisation and transition that the post-Yugoslav states are faced with. Contrary to some recent work on the nature of compliance in the Western Balkans (Freybourg & Richter, 2010; Noutcheva, 2012),[1] it argues that policy transfer in constitutional matters, although the adaptation period is longer, has a deep transformative effect both through the institutional lock-in and the spillover on other policy areas. In other words, compliance in areas requiring the change of the constitutional identity of the state directly related to the state-citizen link is progressive and intensifies in the years immediately preceding the accession. Hence the impact of Europeanisation on the constitutional protection of nationals against extradition is transformative. This however does not imply that extradition will cease to be politically controversial. As the case of *lex Perković* illustrates, the tension between the legal and political dimensions of extradition is likely to persist in the Western Balkans, as has also been the case in high-profile cases in the old EU Member States.

To elucidate this argument, the paper analyses vertical (legal adaptation) and horizontal consequences (conclusion of bilateral agreements) of Europeanisation on citizenship in the post-Yugoslav states. It does so by examining the evolution of the different states' policies related to extradition of their own nationals. The research puzzle revolves around three key issues, including (a) the consequences of the change in the nature of political conditionality of the EU; (b) the tension between the internally impermeable and externally porous character of sovereignty in newly established states; and (c) horizontal manifestations of vertically derived norms as catalysts of the aspiration of the post-Yugoslav states to meet the accession requirements.

The criteria for EU accession have evolved so as to ensure not only a stable democratic political environment, but also regional cooperation and good neighbourly relations. In the aftermath of 9/11, the establishment of an area of freedom, security and justice in the EU has given birth to the EAW, which has become a part of the EU *acquis* that the new Member States have to comply with. The EAW abolishes the political dimension of the traditional approach to extradition, and transforms it into a judicial process. By eliminating dual criminality in a number of areas and by allowing the surrender of nationals,[2] the EAW dilutes the prerogative of the sovereign state in regulating the state-citizen link (nationality in international law); it curtails the state's jurisdiction to prescribe (surrendering state); but expands the territorial exclusivity of jurisdiction to enforce (requesting state).

The different successor states of the former Yugoslavia have different policies on extradition of their own citizens, and some (e.g. Slovenia in 2003, Croatia in 2010) have altered them in view of the requirements of the accession process. On the one hand, the state has the duty to protect its citizens, which is reflected in the constitutional order of the successor states of the former Yugoslavia (general prohibition of extradition of its own citizens – nationality exception). On the other hand, in the context of the Balkans, where facing the past, regional cooperation, and the reduction of trans-border crime are all conditions

THE EUROPEANISATION OF CITIZENSHIP GOVERNANCE

for entering the EU, extradition of the country's own citizens becomes an important tool for democratic consolidation and reconciliation among countries.

Changes in the constitutional and legal norms related to the extradition of the country's own nationals in the post-Yugoslav states are examined through the lenses of Europeanisation. To best compare the effects of Europeanisation on citizenship in the context of extradition, this research classifies the countries in line with their proximity to integration into the EU. This is also methodologically important, because different incentives and factors operate in the aspiring members at different stages in the accession process.

In terms of structure, this paper is divided in three sections. The first two explore the conceptual issues surrounding the transformation of Europeanisation and sovereignty in the post-Yugoslav space, and thus offer a contribution to the general political science literature. The third section is empirical and presents an analysis of the nationality exception in three categories of post-Yugoslav states – EU members, candidate countries, and potential candidates and contested states, with the aim of helping the understanding of the vibrant and transforming post-Yugoslav space.

The Changing Nature of Europeanisation

Writing about the traditional understanding of Europeanisation, Börzel and Risse (2012, p. 192) defined the concept as a set of 'causal mechanisms through which EU policies, institutions and political processes impact upon the domestic structures of the member states'. As acknowledged by a number of contemporary Europeanisation scholars (Börzel & Risse, 2012; Elbasani, 2013; Sedelmeier, 2012), the Eastern enlargement induced the need to apply the concept to the states that are required to adapt to the demands of accession by aligning their policies and institutions with the ones of the EU. Unlike the process of Europeanisation of the Member States, which is also affected by the bottom-up policy transfer from the Member State to the EU, Europeanisation of the aspiring members draws heavily on conditional incentives due to the asymmetry that is inherent to the process (Sedelmeier, 2012). The states that are not EU members do not have the same leverage in affecting the development of EU's policies and institutions. Rather, driven by the final incentive of membership the aspiring members 'download' EU's policies and institutions and integrate them into their domestic political contexts. According to Europeanisation scholarship (Noutcheva, 2012; Sedelmeier, 2012), the dynamics of these domestic political contexts, the degrees of requirement of institutional adaptation, and the effects thereof on the power balance among the domestic political actors will be crucial determinants of the 'lock-in' of EU policies in the acceding states. However, in the case of the post-Yugoslav space, several context-based specificities should be taken into account when attempting to understand the impact of Europeanisation (for further details, see Kacarska, 2015).

Different from Europeanisation that took place at the time of the Eastern enlargement, the process in the post-Yugoslav space entails the creation of regional transnational ties as a mechanism of stabilisation (Börzel & Risse, 2012; Börzel, 2012). While the development of transnational cooperation is somewhat inherent in the dynamics of Europeanisation in general, it gains particular salience in the Western Balkans, as it has clearly been enshrined in the accession conditions (Council of the European Union, 2003). Consequently, the erosion of the state-citizen link does not occur only through compliance with the EAW, thus reinforcing the logic of consequences (incentives as the main driver of EU norm adoption). Rather, it also depends on the horizontal spillover through the conclusion of bilateral extradition agreements. This brings logic of appropriateness (socialisation as the main driver of EU norm adoption) to the context, as the reduction of transnational crime becomes a mechanism for strengthening regional cooperation.

In the context of Europeanisation in the post-Yugoslav states, it is also important to account for is process variation, which has two dimensions – the EU's adaptation and the local variation. First, the EU's stance towards enlargement has significantly changed after the entry of Bulgaria and Romania in 2007, thus making the final incentive of membership rather blurry for the Western Balkan states. While the promise of membership exists, no clear timeframe is available to these countries, which has been considered one of the major obstructions to the effectiveness of Europeanisation (Trauner, 2012). Second, the local variation is largely attributable to the different 'state of state-building' in the respective countries (Bieber, 2013), the divergence in their absorption capacities, their party politics (including inter-ethnic competition), and their institutional stability. Therefore, the effects of Europeanisation will not depend only on the degree of misfit between the EU and domestic policy and the adoption costs in terms of bargains among actors. They will also be affected by the degrees of clarity of the condition, the feasibility of its implementation, as well as the tangibility of the incentive(s) and reward(s) for compliance.

A further factor affecting Europeanisation in the post-Yugoslav states is wavering sovereignty. As Noutcheva (2007) argues, the compliance with EU policies depends on how actors shape their goals in spaces that are sovereign and non-sovereign. Unlike the Central and East European (CEE) states, whose sovereignty was firmly established after the fall of communism and gradually surrendered to the EU in the accession process, the post-Yugoslav states were faced with a different dynamic. In Slovenia and Croatia, which are already EU Member States, the nature of sovereignty has been similar to the CEE states. However, in Bosnia and Herzegovina, Serbia, Montenegro, Macedonia and Kosovo, the issue of sovereignty is a more complex one, due to the domestic and external challenges that these states are faced with and the multiple disintegrations that they have undergone since the break-up of the former Yugoslavia. In particular, in the contexts of limited sovereignty, the domestic political actors shape their political preferences in line with the sovereignty priorities, rather than with the requirements of EU accession. As has been shown in a number of recent studies of conditionality in the Western Balkans (Bieber, 2013; Džihić, 2013; Freyburg & Richter, 2010; Noutcheva, 2012), sovereignty concerns have often hampered the compliance of these states with EU rules, either by creating obstacles to the adoption of policies, or by inducing fake compliance through formal policy transfer accompanied by the failure to implement such policies. As a consequence, the absorption of EU policies and institutions in the post-Yugoslav space faces more obstacles than in the 2004 and 2007 enlargements. However, contrary to the findings of Freyburg and Richter (2010), sovereignty concerns are eventually relinquished in order to comply with EU's policies as regards extradition. This is largely due to the external and internal benefits from such compliance.

Europeanisation and the Porousness of Sovereignty: Extradition vs. Citizenship

With the development of distinct channels of communication, followed by the spread of globalisation and the emergence of international, intergovernmental and transnational

THE EUROPEANISATION OF CITIZENSHIP GOVERNANCE

organisations, sovereignty has lost its central role in the study of international affairs (see Ong, 2006; Krasner, 1999; Sassen, 1996). In the context of Europeanisation, the dynamics of policy transfer from the EU level into the domestic arenas of the underlying countries entail a surrender of various aspects of the states' competences. Kostakopoulou (2002, p.148) notes that the character of sovereignty is 'floating', that is,

> sovereignty is neither a thing to be possessed nor an addition of competences whose successive removal, like the leaves of an artichoke, could be constitutionally tolerated until it reached its heart, that is a hard core of the state's powers in the areas of 'high politics' (e.g. immigration policy, fiscal policy, foreign policy, defence matters).

It is precisely this hollow nature of sovereignty that allows for its porousness in the EU integration process, even regarding the issues of citizenship that lay at the very heart of sovereign states.

According to Rogers Brubaker, 'citizenship is a last bastion of national sovereignty' (2009, p. 180). That is, the regulation of the link between territory and population is a prerogative of sovereign states and international legal instruments have only a marginal effect on that link. Contrary to Brubaker (2009), this research asserts that the process of Europeanisation has had a transformative effect on the legal link between the state and the citizens not only in the post-Yugoslav space, but also beyond it, in the Member States of the EU. This is due to two interrelated factors that operate under the umbrella of the process of Europeanisation.

First, the introduction of the EAW Framework Decision in the acquis has required the change of national constitutions as regards the contractual relationship between individuals and the state. Writing about the link between the nature of the polity and its constitutionalisation, Rubenstein and Lenagh-Maguire (2011, p. 1) noted that '[c]itizenship is a prime site for comparisons between different constitutional systems, for the idea of citizenship, and the ideals it is taken to represent, go to the heart of how states are constituted and defined'. Citizenship became particularly significant in those states which sought to establish the link between their (often new and contested) borders and the population living therein. Moreover, in the post-conflict and post-partition polities, the definitions of citizenship were 'associated with a traumatic social, political or constitutional event', and hence were 'seen as protective against particular kinds of feared abuse' (Rubenstein & Lenagh-Maguire, 2011, p. 148). The provision on non-surrender of the state's own nationals (the nationality exception) has thus been entrenched in the constitutional frameworks of the post-Yugoslav states, as a consequence of the conflicts that consumed this region throughout the 1990s.

In addition to being a mechanism for protecting the citizens of the state, the provisions forbidding the extradition of nationals have a deep normative dimension in terms of citizenship. Citizenship is defined as the 'right to have rights' (Arendt, 1951, pp. 294–295). This also entails the state's duty to protect those who are legally linked to it, which has been applied in public international law since the 1555 Declaration of the Parliament of Paris (Manton, 1936, p. 12). Accordingly, 'rights in this manner entail of course both ideas of membership (who has rights to the state) and the *étatisation* of the understanding of one's relation to authority (which needs constitute rights and who is responsible for them)' (Eckert, 2011, p. 311). Hence, the state has the responsibility for enforcing the rights stemming from the contractual link between the individuals and the polity. Consequently, by relinquishing such responsibility through the transposition of the EAW Framework Decision, states surrender elements of their sovereignty in citizenship matters to the EU level.

Second, the EAW changes the dynamics of citizenship between national and international law. In the domestic context, the legal link between the individuals and the state epitomises the rights and duties that the citizens have vis-à-vis the state, and vice versa – the ones that the state has towards its citizens. In the international law, the purpose of citizenship (i.e. 'nationality' in international law) is to 'enable states to exercise clear jurisdiction over individuals' (Blackman, 1998, p. 1149). It is precisely this balance between the domestic conception of citizenship rooted in rights and duties, and the international focus on jurisdiction over individuals that has introduced the nationality exception in constitutional orders of many states. In international law, the nationality exception has traditionally been defended on grounds of four arguments, including:

> 1. the fugitive ought not be withdrawn from his natural judges; 2. the state owes its subjects the protection of its laws; 3. it is impossible to have complete confidence in the justice meted out by a foreign state, especially with regard to a foreigner; 4. it is disadvantageous to be tried in a foreign language, separated from friends, resources and character witnesses. (Deen-Racsmány & Blekxtoon, 2005, p. 317)

Against the traditional defence of the nationality exception, the EAW has transformed extradition from a political into a judicial process in the EU's Member States, which is where it changed the link between national citizenship and international law. That is, no formal extradition agreement is required in the areas covered by the EAW, which completely dilutes the political dimension of extradition in the EU context. In cases of post-Yugoslav states, in most of which the EAW is yet to become in force (apart from Slovenia, which is an EU Member State since 2004 and Croatia, which entered the EU in mid-2013), the changing dynamic between the domestic and international law is mirrored in the constitutional changes that have taken place during EU accession.

Transformation of Sovereignty: The Post-Yugoslav Experience with Citizenship and Extradition

Changes in extradition policies of the post-Yugoslav states resulted from requirements of the accession process, particular as regards Chapter 24 – Justice, Freedom and Security, of which the EAW Framework Decision is an integral component. The following analysis shows the degrees of approximation of the constitutional and legal provisions related to extradition to the EU's requirements. By arguing that Europeanisation erodes the link between the citizens and the state, this section shows that sovereignty, even in the most sensitive areas of the domestic policy fades away in light of EU accession even if states seek to preserve some of its elements. To better understand the variations in institutional adaptation, the countries analysed are divided in three groups – those that are already Member States of the EU (Slovenia and Croatia), those that are candidate countries (Montenegro, Serbia, and Macedonia), and those that are potential candidates and at the same time contested states (Bosnia and Herzegovina and Kosovo).

THE EUROPEANISATION OF CITIZENSHIP GOVERNANCE

Post-Yugoslav EU Members: Slovenia and Croatia

Slovenia has been a Member State of the EU since 2004. In line with the need of the state to protect its citizens from the wars ravaging its surroundings, the December 1991 Constitution of Slovenia posited a ban of extradition of the country's nationals in article 47, stipulating that 'Citizens of Slovenia may not be extradited to a foreign country. Foreigners may be extradited only in cases foreseen by international contracts which obligate Slovenia'. Hence in the period preceding the accession of Slovenia to the EU, extradition matters were governed by international agreements which the country signed pursuant to its national law.

The screening of the Slovenian legislative framework for extradition showed that it was not in compliance with the requirements for the adoption of the EAW. As the latter required mutual recognition of the court judgements as pertaining to both foreigners and nationals, the transposition of the EAW decision was premised on changing the existing provisions related to extradition. This triggered a political debate on the mechanisms required for the Slovenian legislative framework to transpose the EAW Framework Decision, either as a special statute or through amendments to the Criminal Code, as the latter – in addition to the Constitution regulated extradition matters. Šugman (2009) notes that the decision to adopt the special act 'The European Arrest Warrant and Surrender Procedures between Member States Act' (EAWSP) (*lex specialis*) in March 2004 was guided by the existing national extradition legislation (*lex generalis*), whose provisions were to be retained for cases of extradition to third countries. Yet this act was also conditioned with constitutional amendments as it was not in conformity with the nationality exception enshrined in the 1991 Constitution of Slovenia.

The March 2003 Constitutional Act Amending the First Chapter and Articles 47 and 68 of the Constitution of the Republic of Slovenia changed article 47 of the highest legal act of this country. While retaining the general prohibition of extradition following the amendments to the Constitution, Slovenia now allows extradition arising from obligations by a 'treaty by which, in accordance with the provisions of the first paragraph of Article 3a, Slovenia has transferred the exercise of part of its sovereign rights to an international organisation' (article 47). Pursuant to article 3a, adopted through the same constitutional amendments introducing changes to article 47, Slovenia may transfer part of its sovereignty to international organisations 'based on respect for human rights and fundamental freedoms, democracy and the principles of the rule of law and may enter into a defensive alliance with states which are based on respect for these values'. The way in which the EAW has affected the state-citizen link in Slovenia is indicative of the effects of Europeanisation on sovereignty, in that the general prohibition of extradition of the state's nationals has not been abolished. Rather, the constitutional provisions make an explicit reference to sovereignty transfer to international organisations which become the beholders of a part of this country's sovereignty. Therefore, while retaining the general nationality exception, Slovenia did not limit the extradition of nationals only to the EAW.

In a similar fashion, the post-Yugoslav constitution of Croatia, adopted in December 1990, also stipulated that '[a] citizen of the Republic of Croatia may not be banished from the republic, neither can he be deprived of his citizenship, nor can he be extradited' (article 9). This provision was highly contentious in the case of Croatia, which was actively involved in the wars of Yugoslav disintegration, thus implying that some of the country's nationals could be indicted for war crimes. In order to facilitate the cooperation with the

17

THE EUROPEANISATION OF CITIZENSHIP GOVERNANCE

International Criminal Tribunal for the Former Yugoslavia (ICTY), in 1996 Croatia adopted a Constitutional Law on the Cooperation of the Republic of Croatia with the International Criminal Tribunal, which allowed the surrender of individuals domiciled in Croatia to the court. In the Croatian legal context, the adoption of this law implied a significant change, as it differentiated two procedures related to criminal proceedings – surrender and extradition. While the former was reserved for the transfer of the indicted individuals to the ICTY and thus was applicable to the Croatian nationals, the latter applied in cases of extradition to other countries and contained the nationality exception. In other words, Croatian nationals could only be surrendered to the ICTY.[3] Hence, the EU accession process required major constitutional changes in Croatia.

The Screening Report for Chapter 24 revealed that the Croatian legislation does not allow the transposition of the EAW Framework Decision due to the nationality exception. Similar to Slovenia, the adoption of any legal act allowing the transposition of the EAW decision into the national legal framework would have been unconstitutional (Andrassy, 2007). In order to comply with the requirements of accession, Croatia amended its Constitution in 2010. An important aspect of this constitutional change has been the amendment to article 9, defining Croatian citizenship and the nationality exception in the context of extradition. Until 2010, Croatia had a full prohibition of extradition of its own citizens. Following the constitutional change of 12 June 2010, Croatia retained the general prohibition of extradition, but it now can extradite its citizens 'when a decision on extradition or surrender has been adopted in line with an international agreement or in line with the legal practice of the European Union' (article 9). Accordingly, the constitutional change in Croatia is a clear example of the effects of Europeanisation on the country's legislative framework. This is further confirmed by Croatia's eventual compliance with the EAW in the *lex Perković* case, described in the introduction.

In addition to this, Croatia has retained the nationality exception with respect to extradition to the third countries, whereby matters of criminal justice are regulated through the international legal framework. Since 1994, Croatia has been a party to the European Convention on Extradition and its additional protocols, which enabled the country to conclude bilateral extradition agreements with a number of countries, including the post-Yugoslav states. In light of the requirements of the EU to enhance regional cooperation and reduce transborder crime, in 2010 Croatia concluded an Agreement on Extradition with Serbia. The first extradition on these grounds took place in August 2010, when Croatia extradited to Serbia Srecko Kalinić, convicted of conspiracy in the murder of the Serbian Prime Minister Zoran Djindjic in 2003 (B92, 2010). In this respect, we can notice the differential impact of Europeanisation as pertaining to the Member States and the one pertaining to the diffusion of the process. That is, while the EAW requirement changed the legislation of this country and significantly affected the state-citizen link through constitutional changes, it did not change the country's legislation vis-à-vis third countries. Still, the EU's requirement for regional cooperation, including cooperation in criminal matters, intensified the conclusion of bilateral extradition agreements between Croatia and the other post-Yugoslav states thus showing that Europeanisation does have horizontal spillover effects.

Post-Yugoslav EU Candidates: Montenegro, Serbia and Macedonia

After the break-up of the former Yugoslavia, Serbia and Montenegro established the last Yugoslav federation – the Federal Republic of Yugoslavia (FRY) – in 1992. The

THE EUROPEANISATION OF CITIZENSHIP GOVERNANCE

Constitution of the FRY, adopted in April 1992, also contained the nationality exception in article 17, which stipulated that '[a] Yugoslav citizen may not be deprived of his citizenship, deported from the country, or extradited to another state'. Equally, the constitutions of the constituent republics of the FRY – Serbia and Montenegro – had different provisions related to the extradition of their own nationals. While the 1992 Constitution of the Republic of Montenegro contained no explicit nationality exception, the 1990 Constitution of the Republic of Serbia provided that '[a] citizen of the Republic of Serbia may not be deprived of his citizenship, exiled or extradited' (article 47). The provisions in the federal and the Serbian legislation were created as a mechanism for protecting the citizens of the FRY who took part in the wars of Yugoslav disintegration. As in the case of Croatia, a number of FRY citizens who took part in conflicts were indicted for war crimes before the ICTY. The most notable example is the former president of the FRY – Slobodan Milošević – who was extradited to the ICTY in 2001. The decision was adopted on grounds of the Decision on cooperation with the Hague Tribunal, although the FRY constitution at the time contained the nationality exception. The extradition of Milošević was executed under significant international pressure on the new FRY authorities to affirm their democratic orientation (Vreme, 2001).

The FRY was transformed in the common state of Serbia and Montenegro in 2003, and finally dissolved in June 2006 following the Montenegrin independence referendum on 21 May the same year. Following their independence, both Serbia and Montenegro have confirmed their aspiration to join the EU. Due to the specificities of their domestic contexts and the particular requirements of accession, the post-independence extradition policies of Serbia and Montenegro have played out differently than in their republican constitutions within the FRY.

Particular to the case of Serbia, cooperation with the ICTY has been emphasised as a precondition for the country's progress in the EU accession process (Mäki, 2008, p. 51). As a result, the new Constitution of Serbia has introduced a change in the relationship between citizenship and extradition compared to the 1990 Constitution (article 38). That is, the new Serbian Constitution does not provide an explicit prohibition of extradition, as did its predecessor. However, the matters related to the nationality exception are found in the Law on International Legal Assistance in Criminal Matters, which stipulates that the condition for extradition is that the individual whose surrender is requested is not a national of Serbia (article 16, para. 1, pt 1). The same provision nonetheless allows for the surrender of the Serbian nationals to the 'international court that has been recognised through an international agreement' (Law on International Legal Assistance in Criminal Matters (article 3, para. 3). The implications of these provisions are twofold. As regards the practical issues, the nationality exception does not apply in the context of cooperation with the ICTY. Additionally, extradition in Serbia is a legal rather than a constitutional matter. This means that although the Law on International Legal Assistance in Criminal Matters (2009) is not in line with the EAW decision, the adaptation of the law to the requirements of accession will be smoother than the adaptation of the constitution would have been. On top of this, the fact that as a consequence of the requirement for cooperation with the ICTY in the context of EU accession Serbia has already abolished the constitutional provision on the nationality exception reveals the effects of Europeanisation on the state-citizen link in this post-Yugoslav state.

Unlike in the case of Serbia, the EU has not been as persistent in requiring Montenegro's cooperation with the ICTY. The most likely reason for that is that, following the split in the

THE EUROPEANISATION OF CITIZENSHIP GOVERNANCE

ruling Democratic Party of Socialists in 1997, the Montenegrin elite sought to distance themselves from Milošević and the wartime activities in the former Yugoslavia that they themselves incited throughout the 1990s (Morrison, 2013). However, unlike the 1992 Constitution of Montenegro, which did not contain a prohibition of extradition of its own nationals, the post-independence constitution does (article 12). The reason for such a reversal of the state-citizen link in the case of Montenegro is largely attributable to the domestic political context. Namely the wars of Yugoslav disintegration, and the economic embargo to the FRY, generated 'the schemes the elites in the Yugoslav republics used to develop and stimulate smuggling operations' (Hajdinjak, 2002, p. 5). As the profits increased, their major share was retained by the people involved in smuggling, which included the top level politicians in Montenegro (Ivanović, 1999). Among these politicians, the Prime Minister of Montenegro – Milo Đukanović – was indicted by the Anti-Mafia Bureau in Naples (Italy) for cigarette smuggling. In 2004, the Anti-Mafia Bureau requested the arrest of Đukanović, and the question was raised whether at the time he enjoyed diplomatic immunity since Montenegro was not an independent state, or whether he could be prosecuted. Even though the charges against Đukanović were dropped in March 2008, the possibility of extraditing high-profile politicians motivated the domestic legislators to introduce the constitutional prohibition of extradition. However, the most recent screening of the legislative framework in the context of Montenegro, which has started its EU negotiations in July 2012, confirms that constitutional changes will be required as regards the transposition of the EAW (Screening Report Chapter 24, 2012, p. 21).

Indeed, while article 12 of the 2007 Constitution of Montenegro stipulates the general prohibition of extradition, it also allows handing over of the Montenegrin citizens 'in line with the international obligations of Montenegro'. At present, Montenegro has concluded agreements with Macedonia, Croatia, Serbia, and Bosnia and Herzegovina, while the agreement with Kosovo is being negotiated at present. Given the EU's requirement for enhanced regional cooperation, all of these agreements now include a provision on the extradition of the country's own nationals, although the original agreement concluded with Serbia in 2009 contained the nationality exception. According to Milošević (2012), the conclusion of these agreements has been positively assessed by the European Commission in the context of 'good neighbourly relations', which is indicative of the transformative power of Europeanisation.

A very similar dynamic took place in Macedonia, whose 1991 Constitution contained the most restrictive provision related to extradition to the country's nationals. In fact, article 4 of the 1991 Macedonian Constitution prescribed that '[c]itizens of the Republic of Macedonia may not be deprived from their citizenship, exiled or extradited to another country'. This made Macedonia the only successor state of the former Yugoslavia that had a full nationality exception engrained in its Constitution. In the context of regional relations, the most manifest consequence of the Macedonian nationality exception was the impossibility of the country to conclude bilateral extradition agreements that would allow the extradition of Macedonian citizens. This fact has been raised as an important concern in the case of the Western Balkan states, where 'dual citizenship is an obstacle in the implementation of criminal justice' (Manasiev & Djokic, 2010). This issue became highly contentious in the case of criminals, who would use their dual nationality in order to avoid extradition and prosecution.

As a result of the EU's pressures to reduce transnational crime networks in the Balkans, the Macedonian Parliament embarked on the process of constitutional reform, justified by

THE EUROPEANISATION OF CITIZENSHIP GOVERNANCE

the 'increase of transnational organised crime and the fact that the perpetrators of these crimes are able to avoid sanctions thus misusing the nationality exception' (Комисија за уставни прашања, 2011, p. 1). Explaining the need to reconsider the nationality exception in the Macedonian Constitution, the then Minister of Justice of Macedonia – Mihajlo Manevski – stated that 'several states in the region have amended their constitutions and introduced the European Arrest Warrant, while also allowing the possibility to sign bilateral agreements for extradition of their own nationals in the area of organised crime' (Manevski in Комисија за уставни прашања, 2011, p. 1).

The direct consequence of this motion, primarily driven by the EU's requirement to enhance regional cooperation has been the 2011 XXXII Amendment to the Constitution of Macedonia regarding the nationality exception. While the exception has not been completely abolished, article 4 (para. 2) provides that 'a citizen of the Republic of Macedonia cannot be surrendered to another state, except on grounds of a ratified international agreement, following a court decision'. This constitutional amendment allowed Macedonia to sign bilateral extradition agreements that do not contain the nationality exception with Montenegro, Serbia, Croatia, and Bosnia and Herzegovina, which has positively been assessed in the EC's progress reports as regards bilateral regional cooperation (European Commission 2013). However, once it opens the accession negotiations, which have been at a stalemate due to the name issue with Greece, Macedonia is likely to face difficulties in transposing the EAW as the latter does not constitute an international agreement. Adopting a law that would transpose the EAW into the Macedonian legislation may be deemed unconstitutional on grounds of article (para. 2) of the Constitution. Hence the screening of compliance of the Macedonian legislation is likely to result in observations similar to the ones in the case of Montenegro – the requirement for further constitutional changes in the context of EU accession.

The above examples indicate that in cases of those post-Yugoslav states that are candidates for EU membership, the dynamics of Europeanisation are slightly different to those in Slovenia and Croatia. Indeed, both Slovenia and Croatia had to introduce constitutional amendments in order to implement the EAW, but this did not happen in either of the countries until one year before the accession was scheduled. As Serbia, Montenegro and Macedonia are faced with a yet unclear accession timeline, the fact that two of the three states concerned have amended some aspects of their constitution in the context of EU's requirements highlights the transformative power of Europeanisation in this region. Similar forces are at work in the post-Yugoslav potential candidates and contested states – Bosnia and Herzegovina and Kosovo.

Post-Yugoslav Potential Candidates and Contested States: Bosnia and Herzegovina and Kosovo

From among the post-Yugoslav states, Bosnia and Herzegovina and Kosovo are the only 'potential candidate countries' for EU accession. In addition to this, these two states have had the experience of direct conflict in their territories, and their statehood is largely unconsolidated. Given that these two post-Yugoslav states are under international supervision (Shaw, 2010), their legislative frameworks contain a looser approach to the state-citizen link.

The Constitution of Bosnia and Herzegovina does not contain a prohibition of extradition for the country's own nationals. This is due to the fact that the Constitution of Bosnia

THE EUROPEANISATION OF CITIZENSHIP GOVERNANCE

and Herzegovina has been adopted as Annex IV of the Dayton Peace Agreement, which implies that it contains a number of internationally enforceable principles. As a consequence, the Constitution stipulates an obligation for the country to cooperate with international mechanisms and bodies established for Bosnia and Herzegovina (article 2, pt. 8). Moreover, article 203 of the Criminal Code of Bosnia and Herzegovina stipulates an obligation of extradition to the International Criminal Tribunal. However, in terms of extraditing its own citizens to other countries, the legislation of Bosnia and Herzegovina appears more complex, because the article 415 of the Criminal Procedure Code of Bosnia and Herzegovina stipulates the nationality exception in that extradition will be allowed provided 'that a person whose extradition has been requested is not a citizen of Bosnia and Herzegovina'. As in the case of Serbia, which does not have a constitutional, but a legal ban on extradition, it is likely that this provision of the Criminal Procedure Code of Bosnia and Herzegovina will need to be amended.

Notwithstanding, in the context of regional cooperation, the provision in article 415 allowing the conclusion of international agreements overriding the nationality exception has permitted Bosnia and Herzegovina to conclude full extradition agreements with Serbia, Macedonia, Croatia and Montenegro. Given that Bosnia and Herzegovina has not recognised the independent statehood of Kosovo, no agreement is being negotiated at present. Hence similar to the other countries analysed, the erosion of the state-citizen link in the context of extradition in Bosnia and Herzegovina, has been driven by this country's aspiration to progress in the EU accession process by enhancing regional cooperation and good neighbourly relations.

Unlike Bosnia and Herzegovina, the 2008 Constitution of Kosovo also establishes a relationship between extradition and citizenship. Kosovo has a general prohibition of extradition, but may extradite their own citizens in line with bilateral agreements, or international treaties (article 35). So far, Kosovo has concluded an extradition agreement with Macedonia, but article 6 of the Agreement on Extradition between the Republic of Kosovo and the Republic of Macedonia foresees the nationality exception. However, under the pressures for enhancing regional cooperation and reducing trans-border crime, coupled by the concerns that Kosovo 'remains a haven for fugitives dodging surrender requests in the region' (Jovanovska, 2011), Kosovo is currently negotiating extradition agreements with other countries in the region. Hence it is likely that the state-citizen link in this new post-Yugoslav state will be further eroded under the aegis of Europeanisation.

Conclusion

This paper examined the interaction between the processes of Europeanisation and political transition in the post-Yugoslav states by focusing on the transformation of the nationality exception in extradition procedures. The analysis focused on three interrelated questions, including the effects of the change in the EU's approach to accession to the Western Balkans compared to the CEES; the transformation of sovereignty in the new states under the effects of Europeanisation through EAW and Chapter 24 (vertical effects on sovereignty); and the conclusion of bilateral extradition agreements not containing the nationality exception as a mechanism for ensuring regional cooperation and good neighbourly relations (horizontal effects of Europeanisation). The study of these issues proves

THE EUROPEANISATION OF CITIZENSHIP GOVERNANCE

to be important not only for understanding the post-Yugoslav political space, but also for unveiling the changing nature of Europeanisation.

The first part of the paper highlighted the changing nature of the concept of Europeanisation and four particular traits that are characteristic for this process in the post-Yugoslav space, and its relevance for understanding the deep effects of the EU's extradition policies. The differences in the manifestation of Europeanisation in this region compared to the old Member States, the CEES states, and other countries affected by the process, is vested not only in the specificities of the region, but also in the transformation of the EU's approach to enlargement and accession. Indeed, the first characteristic of Europeanisation is to stabilise this post-partition and post-conflict region. The second trait of Europeanisation of the post-Yugoslav states is the tension between the newly acquired sovereignty in these states (and the domestic actors' tendency to retain it) and the aspiration of the EU to use the accession process to build states that are able to surrender elements of their sovereignty as a price for membership. The third characteristic of Europeanisation in the post-Yugoslav states is its multivalence, as the process depends not only on the formal criteria for EU accession, but also on a wide array of complementary effects including the suggestions and recommendations of the CoE and other organisations. The fourth aspect of Europeanisation in this region is its two-tiered nature, composed of the dynamic of learning and adaptation between EU accession as a process, and the local variation in the 'state of state-building' in the post-Yugoslav space (Bieber, 2013). Understanding the different traits of Europeanisation in the post-Yugoslav space helps us to delve into the transformation of the state-citizen link in the context of adapting to the EU's extradition policies, which in the post-Yugoslav political space had both vertical and horizontal consequences.

The second part of the paper looked in more detail in the state-citizen link through the lenses of the porous nature of sovereignty in the EU. By exploring the changes in the prerogative of the sovereign state to regulate its citizenship, this paper has asserted – contrary to many contemporary studies of citizenship – that the multivalent nature of Europeanisation has induced significant changes to the state-citizen link in both the EU Member States and in the candidate countries. While the broad changes to the regulation of citizenship have been induced through the state's accession to instruments such as the ECN and the ECtHR rulings, the EAW has substantially changed the nature of membership in a polity. That is, while the citizens have transferred a part of their sovereignty in constituting the state in return for the rights and duties of membership, the state no longer offers them exclusive protection through the nationality exception.

The final part of the paper offered an empirical analysis of the transformation of extradition policies in the post-Yugoslav space. Methodologically, the section looked at three categories of states – EU members, candidate countries, and potential candidates and contested states. This helped us to look at pre-accession compliance with the EU's requirements in the field of justice, freedom and security as regards the implementation of the EAW Framework Decision in conjunction with the requirements for regional cooperation and good neighbourly relations implemented in the Western Balkans. The study unveiled that the initial constitutional changes to allow extradition may be limited, but that in the pre-accession period these suffice to conclude bilateral extradition agreements that do not contain the nationality exception. In turn, these agreements are seen as a commitment of the post-Yugoslav states to regional cooperation and good neighbourly relations, thus revealing the diffusive effects of Europeanisation. Major constitutional and legal adaptations to the requirements for accession in Chapter 24, containing the EAW, are more

THE EUROPEANISATION OF CITIZENSHIP GOVERNANCE

likely in the last stages of accession due to its implications on state-citizen link and the very recent experience with state sovereignty in the studied countries. Even so, these changes may contain 'last minute' provisions that seek to preserve the state-citizen link, as seen by the recent Croatian experience. In summary, however, the combination of the vertical and the horizontal effects of the EU accession on extradition and citizenship in the post-Yugoslav space shows that Europeanisation is indeed marked by an 'unbearable lightness' – the capacity to transform and be transformed.

Acknowledgements

This is the first of two academic articles coming out of my project 'The Unbearable Lightness of Europeanisation: Extradition Policies and the Erosion of Sovereignty in the Successor States of the Former Yugoslavia', which I conducted as a Jean Monnet Fellow at the Robert Schuman Centre for Advanced Studies at the European University Institute between 2011 and 2013. The research project is largely based on the knowledge and understanding of the notion of citizenship I gained at the CITSEE project at the University of Edinburgh. I thank Professor Jo Shaw and Professor Rainer Bauböck for their useful feedback.

Disclosure statement

No potential conflict of interest was reported by the author.

Notes

[1] The term Western Balkans includes the post-Yugoslav states (Slovenia, Croatia, Bosnia and Herzegovina, Serbia, Macedonia, Montenegro and Kosovo) minus Slovenia plus Albania.
[2] For a full list of the areas covered by the EAW, see EAW Framework Decision 2002/584/JHA.
[3] Europeanisation in the context of surrender has had the deepest effects in terms of the capture and transfer of general Ante Gotovina, a general of the Croatian army indicted for crimes against humanity in operation 'Storm' in 1995, to the ICTY in 2005.

References

Andrassy, I. (2007, April) Constitutional implications of EU membership: An overview of constitutional issues in the negotiating process – the Croatian perspective. Paper presented at conference 'Constitutional Implications of EU Membership', Zagreb, 20 April 2007.

Arendt, H. (1951) *The Origins of Totalitarianism* (New York: Harcourt Brace Jovanovich).

B92 (2010) *Sretko Kalinic izrucen Srbiji, B92.* Available at http://www.b92.net/info/vesti/index.php?yyyy=2010&mm=08&dd=25&nav_category=120&nav_id=454009 (accessed 22 January 2013).

Bieber, F. (2013) Building impossible states? State-building strategies and EU membership in the Western Balkans, in: F. Bieber (Ed.) *EU Conditionality in the Western Balkans*, pp. 9–29 (London: Routledge).

Blackman, J. (1998) State successions and statelessness: The emerging right to an effective nationality under international law, *Michigan Journal of International Law*, 19, pp. 1141–1191.

Börzel, T. (2012) When Europeanization hits limited statehood. The Western Balkans as a test case for the transformative power of Europe, in: A. Elbasani (Ed.) *EU Enlargement and Europeanization in the Western Balkans*, pp. 173–185 (London and New York: Routledge).

Börzel, T. & Risse, T. (2012) When Europeanisation meets diffusion: Exploring new territory, *West European Politics*, 35(1), pp. 192–207.

THE EUROPEANISATION OF CITIZENSHIP GOVERNANCE

Brubaker, R. (2009) *Citizenship and Nationhood in France and Germany*, 2nd ed. (Cambridge, MA: Harvard University Press).

Constitution of Bosnia and Herzegovina (1995) Annex 4 to the General Framework Agreement for Peace in Bosnia and Herzegovina Criminal Code of Bosnia and Herzegovina.

Constitution of the Federal Republic of Yugoslavia (1992) Official Gazette of the Federal Republic of Yugoslavia 1/92.

Constitution of the Republic of Croatia (1990) Official Gazette of Croatia 55/90.

Constitution of the Republic of Kosovo (2008) Official Gazette of the Republic of Kosovo 1/08.

Constitution of the Republic of Macedonia (1991) Official Gazette of the Republic of Macedonia 1/91.

Constitution of the Republic of Serbia (1990) Official Gazette of the Republic of Serbia 1/90.

Constitution of the Republic of Serbia (2006) Official Gazette of the Republic of Serbia 1/06.

Constitution of the Republic of Slovenia (1991) Official Gazette of the Republic of Slovenia 1/91.

Constitutional Act Amending the First Chapter and Articles 47 and 68 of the Constitution of the Republic of Slovenia (2003) Official Gazette of the Republic of Slovenia 24/03.

Council of the European Union (2003) Presidency conclusions of the Thessaloniki European Council (19 and 20 June 2003). Available at http://www.consilium.europa.eu/uedocs/cms_data/docs/pressdata/en/ec/76279.pdf (accessed 14 August 2014).

Criminal Procedure Code of Bosnia and Herzegovina (2003) Official Gazette of Bosnia and Herzegovina 3/03.

Deen-Racsmány, Z. & Blekxtoon, R. (2005) The decline of the nationality exception in European extradition? The impact of the regulation of (non-)surrender of nationals and dual criminality under the European Arrest Warrant, *European Journal of Crime, Criminal Law and Criminal Justice*, 13(3), pp. 317–364.

Džihić, V. (2013) Incentives for democratisation? Effects of EU conditionality on democracy in Bosnia and Herzegovina, in: F. Bieber (Ed.) *EU Conditionality in the Western Balkans*, pp. 29–53 (London: Routledge).

EAW Framework Decision (2002) Official Journal of the European Communities 2002/584/JHA.

Eckert, J. (2011) Introduction: Subjects of citizenship, *Citizenship Studies*, 15(3–4), pp. 309–317.

Elbasani, A. (2013) Europeanization travels to the Western Balkans: Enlargement strategy, domestic obstacles and diverging reforms, in: A. Elbasani (Ed) *European Integration and Transformation in the Western Balkans: Europeanization or Business as Usual?*, pp. 3–22 (Abingdon: Routledge).

European Commission (2013) EU Enlargement. Available at http://ec.europa.eu/enlargement/index_en.htm (accessed 14 August 2011).

Freyburg, T. & S. Richter. (2010) National identity matters: The limited impact of EU political conditionality in the Western Balkans, *Journal of European Public Policy*, 17(2), pp. 263–281.

Hajdinjak, M. (2002) Smuggling in Southeast Europe: The Yugoslav wars and the development of regional criminal networks in the Balkans. Available at http://pdc.ceu.hu/archive/00001572/01/Smuggling_in_SE_EU.pdf (accessed 24 June 2015).

Ivanović, Ž. (1999) Speedboats, Cigarettes, Mafia and Montenegrin Democracy, Institute for War & Peace Reporting Balkan Crisis Report 83. Available at: http://www.iwpr.net/index.pl?archive/bcr/bcr_19991012_3_eng.txt (accessed 24 June 2015).

Jovanovska, S. (2011) Net closing in on fugitive Balkan criminals, *BIRN*. Available at http://www.balkaninsight.com/en/article/net-closing-in-on-fugitive-balkan-criminals (accessed 11 January 2013).

Kacarska, S. (2015) Losing the rights along the way: The EU-Western Balkans visa liberalisation, *European Politics and Society* 16(3). doi: 10.1080/23745118.2015.1061773

Комисија за уставни прашања (2011) Predlogot za pristapuvanje kon izmena na Ustavot na Republika Makedonija, podnesen od Vladata na Republika Makedonija, Vlada na Republika Makedonija 09 – 284/1.

Kostakopoulou, D. (2002) Floating sovereignty: A pathology or a necessary means of state evolution, *Oxford Journal of Legal Studies*, 22, pp. 135–156.

Krasner, S. (1999) *Sovereignty: Organized Hypocrisy* (Princeton, NJ: Princeton University Press).

Law on International Legal Assistance in Criminal Matters (2009) Official Gazette of the Republic of Serbia 20/2009.

Mäki, J-M. (2008) EU enlargement politics: Explaining the development of political conditionality of 'full cooperation with the ICTY' towards Western Balkans, *Politička misao*, 14(5), pp. 47–80.

Manasiev, A. & Djokic, B. (2010) With two passports, Balkan criminals go free, *EU Observer*. Available at http://euobserver.com/news/29862 (accessed 22 January 2013).

Manton, M. T. (1936) Extradition of nationals, *Temple Law Quarterly*, 12, pp. 12–24.

Milošević, M. (2012) Montenegro, Bosnia sign extradition deal, *Balkan Insight*. Available at http://www.balkaninsight.com/en/article/montenegro-and-bosnia-sign-extradition-agreement (accessed 14 February 2013).

THE EUROPEANISATION OF CITIZENSHIP GOVERNANCE

Montenegro: Screening Report Chapter 24 (2012) European commission. Available at http://ec.europa.eu/enlargement/pdf/montenegro/screening_reports/20130218_screening_report_montenegro_ch24.pdf (accessed 11 March 2013).

Morrison, K. (2013) Montenegro: A polity in flux 1989–2000, in: C. Ingrao and T. Emmert (Eds) *Confronting the Yugoslav Controversies: A Scholar's Initiative*, 2nd ed., pp. 426–456 (West Lafayette: Purdue University Press).

Noutcheva, G. (2007) Fake, partial and imposed compliance: The limits of the EU's normative power in the Western Balkan, CEPS Working Document No. 274. Available at http://aei.pitt.edu/7575/1/Wd274.pdf (accessed 11 March 2015).

Noutcheva, G. (2012) *European Foreign Policy and the Challenges of Balkan Accession* (London and New York: Routledge).

Ong, A. (2006) *Neoliberalism as Exception: Mutations in Citizenship and Sovereignty* (Durham, NC: Duke University Press).

Rubenstein, K. & Lenagh-Maguire, N. (2011) Citizenship and the boundaries of the constitution, in: T. Ginsburg and R. Dixon (Eds) *Comparative Constitutional Law*, pp. 143–169 (Cheltenham and Massachusetts: Edward Elgar Publishing).

Sassen, S. (1996) *Losing Control: Sovereignty in an Age of Globalization* (New York: Columbia University Press).

Sedelmeier, U. (2012). Is Europeanisation through conditionality sustainable? Lock-in of institutional change after EU accession, *West European Politics*, 35(1), pp. 20–38.

Shaw, J. (2010) The constitutional mosaic across the boundaries of the European Union: Citizenship regimes in the new states of South Eastern Europe, CITSEE Working Paper Series, 2010/08 (Edinburgh: University of Edinburgh, School of Law).

Šugman, K. (2009) Country report for: Slovenia. Available at http://www.asser.nl/EAW/countryreports.aspx?country_id=195&site_id=8&level1=10789&level2=10838&level3=10899 (accessed 25 March 2013).

Trauner, F. (2012) Deconstructing the EU's routes of influence in justice and home affairs in the Western Balkans, *Journal of European Integration*, 31(1), pp. 65–82.

Ustav Crne Gore (2007) Službeni List Crne Gore 1/07 [Constitution of Montenegro (2007) Official Gazette of Montenegro 1/07].

Vreme (2001) Haški putnik, *Vreme*. Available at http://www.vreme.com/cms/view.php?id=290982 (accessed 22 January 2013).

XXXII Amendment to the Constitution of Macedonia (2011) Official Gazette of the Republic of Macedonia 49/11.

Losing the Rights along the Way: The EU–Western Balkans Visa Liberalisation

SIMONIDA KACARSKA

European Policy Institute, Macedonia

ABSTRACT *This paper examines the conditionality in relation to fundamental rights during and after the visa liberalisation dialogues that took place between the European Commission and national governments of the Western Balkans countries in 2009 and 2010. Conceptually, this paper uses the visa liberalisation to study the interactions between the conditionality mechanism and securitisation paradigm in the context of the European Union (EU) justice, freedom and security area. Analysing both the formal benchmarking process and data from stakeholders' interviews, this paper demonstrates the securitisation and side-lining of fundamental rights during and in the aftermath of the visa negotiations. As a result, this paper informs of unwanted effects of conditionality and questions the role of the EU in promoting fundamental rights.*

Introduction

Visa liberalisation dialogues took place from 2008 to 2010 between the European Commission and the following countries of the Western Balkans: Macedonia, Serbia, Montenegro, Albania, and Bosnia and Herzegovina. The objective of the dialogues was the removal of these countries from the so-called *Schengen black list* registering the third countries whose nationals must be in possession of visas when crossing the external borders and those whose nationals are exempt from that requirement in line with the Council Regulation (EC) No. 539/2001.[1] The compliance with the stipulated benchmarks was determined through written responses by the national governments and several on-the-ground assessments. Ultimately, after satisfactory progress was determined in the dialogues, the visa requirements were lifted for Macedonia, Serbia and Montenegro at the end of 2009, and in the following year for Albania, and Bosnia and Herzegovina.[2]

According to the above-mentioned Regulation, the exemption from the visa requirement is based on 'an assessment of a variety of criteria relating *inter alia* to illegal immigration, public policy and security, and to the European Union's external relations with third countries, consideration also being given to the implications of regional coherence and reciprocity'.[3] In the case of the Western Balkans, the criteria from the Regulation (EC) No. 539/2001 were streamlined in road maps with benchmarks prepared by the European

Commission. These roadmaps were organised in four blocks: document security, illegal migration, public order and security, and external relations and fundamental rights linked to the movement of persons.[4] The benchmarks of the first three blocks of the liberalisation road maps are related to the justice, freedom and security *acquis* and reflected the content of Regulation (EC) No. 539/2001. The last, fourth, block concerning external relations and fundamental rights has more recently been included in the context of visa liberalisation and was not a subject of discussion for the removal of the visa requirement for Bulgaria and Romania which took place in 2001 (See Guild, 2003). The benchmarks in this novel block concern freedom of movement, conditions and procedures for issuing identity documents, adopting and enforcing anti-discrimination legislation and implementing policies regarding all minorities, including Roma, that is, core elements of the respective citizenship regimes.[5] For Shaw and Štiks (2010, p. 7),

> citizenship regimes encompass certain key individual and collective rights protected by national and international human rights law, such as minority rights and non-discrimination rights which profoundly impact upon the exercise of full civic membership within a society and a polity.

This paper examines the implementation of these novel fundamental rights benchmarks in the visa liberalisation process and their role in governing the citizenship regimes in the Western Balkans. Its aim is to assess whether and how the EU has managed to incorporate fundamental rights requirements in a security-dominated and highly politically significant process as the visa liberalisation. For this purpose, this paper studies the formal documents related to the visa negotiations and uses data from stakeholders' interviews.[6] This paper argues that fundamental rights were only formally and not substantially the focus of the visa liberalisation dialogues and the post-visa liberalisation monitoring. Moreover, this paper demonstrates that the visa liberalisation process at times contributed to violations, rather than advancement and protection of fundamental rights. As such, it questions the impact of the visa liberalisation project upon the governing of the citizenship regimes in the Western Balkans as a region in the focus of this special issue. Conceptually, this paper informs of unwanted effects of conditionality and challenges the role of the EU in promoting fundamental rights.

This paper is organized into four major sections. The first section provides a background to the conceptual frameworks and their understanding in this research. The following section examines the role of the fundamental rights benchmarks in the visa liberalisation dialogues. The third section examines the implementation of the fundamental rights benchmarks in practice *during* the visa liberalisation dialogues, focusing on anti-discrimination policy. It also reflects on the implications of the process on Kosovo, which was formally included in the visa liberalisation negotiations in early 2012 (European Commission, 2012). The fourth section examines the developments in relation to the fundamental rights benchmarking in the post-visa liberalisation period. Lastly, this paper reiterates its findings and draws its empirical and conceptual conclusions.

The Visa Liberalisation Processes with the Candidate Countries: Intersecting Europeanisation and Securitisation

Theoretically, this paper stands at the intersection of the discussions on the role of conditionality in Europeanisation on the one hand and the securitisation of the justice, freedom

THE EUROPEANISATION OF CITIZENSHIP GOVERNANCE

and security in the EU, on the other. First, the 'visa liberalisation process' for the purposes of this paper is understood as an element of the Europeanisation of the Western Balkans. Europeanisation is here approached as 'domestic adaptation to European regional integration' (Vink & Graziano, 2007, p. 7). In the light of the potential for concept stretching of Europeanisation already identified in the literature (Radaelli, 2000), this paper focuses on the instrument of conditionality as the key element of the Europeanisation of countries aspiring to become members of the EU. Although a widely used term in the literature, a consensual definition of conditionality is missing. While rational institutionalism defines conditionality as a reinforcement by reward focusing on its outcome (Schimmelfennig & Sedelmeier, 2005), this analysis is also interested in the process of its application. Hence, it understands conditionality as a process, which 'includes not only the formal technical requirements on candidates but also the informal pressures arising from the behaviour and perceptions of actors engaged in the political process' (Hughes et al., 2005, p. 2). Analysing not only formal benchmarking, but also the informal guidance the countries received from the EU institutions, highlights the importance of the latter and thus seeks to uncover the unintended and indirect consequences of EU conditionality (Sasse, 2009).

The second dimension of Europeanisation relevant for this paper is the establishment of the area of justice, freedom and security in the EU and the development of associated policies. The creation of a common external border at the EU level has provided the European Commission with the legitimacy of negotiating visa liberalisation. On a general level, EU law and policy have developed a security nexus between irregular forms of human mobility and border security (Carrera & Guild, 2007). Huysmans has pointed that migration is constructed as a security question in the EU (Huysmans, 2000). In fact, securitisation denoting the 'discursive construction of wider categories of persons and practices as threats' has been considered as a key mechanism in the institutionalisation of the EU area of freedom, security and justice (Guild et al., 2008, p. 2). Since the area of freedom, security and justice is driven by a security rationale, it became a very sensitive policy domain in the context of enlargement (Monar, 2001). Similarly, in relation to the visa liberalisation, it has been argued that the decision to lift the visa requirements is mostly based on an assessment potential threat that migratory flows could potentially pose to the internal security of the Union (Bigo & Guild, 2005, p. 245).

Building upon the conditionality mechanism and securitisation paradigm in the context of the EU justice, freedom and security, this paper examines the way in which these two mechanisms have interacted in the visa liberalisation process. Ultimately, the study demonstrates that security concerns have been overarching and as such the visa liberalisation process was not used as a tool for advancing fundamental rights. This security-dominated approach has implications both for the impact on the transformation of the respective countries and has also contributed to exacerbating the existing discrimination of disadvantaged groups in the post-visa liberalisation period. The empirical analysis that follows highlights the unintended and indirect consequences of EU conditionality (Sasse, 2009).

Fundamental Rights During the Visa Liberalisation Dialogue in the Western Balkans

The rationale for studying the role of the visa liberalisation process in the governance of the citizenship regimes by focusing on fundamental rights requirements is multifaceted. First, unlike the first three security-related blocks, the implementation of the fundamental rights benchmarks has not been thoroughly studied, thereby increasing the academic significance of this analysis (for research on the first three blocks see Trauner, 2008, 2011). Second, the visa-free regime was politically the most significant (and tangible) benefit that was offered by the EU to the governments and citizens in this region.[7] Thus, there was high likelihood for substantial policy changes in various aspects of the citizenship regime, including fundamental rights. Third, in terms of the application of EU conditions, the visa liberalisation process was the most detailed benchmarking process employed by the European Commission and as such provides an exceptional example for evaluating the role of external actors in the domestic transformation. The European Commission (2010b, p. 7) in its own assessments considered that 'the visa liberalisation process has demonstrated the effectiveness of an approach which set concrete, specific reform requirements thus allowing the countries to better focus their efforts'. Fourth, the visa liberalisation process was largely evaluated as an effective exercise of conditionality by policy-makers and analysts who brought back the faith in the potential of the EU to bring about change in as turbulent a region as the Balkans. It has been considered an example that 'demonstrates clearly the mechanics of EU soft power. The EU held out an electorally attractive reward and spelled out clearly the conditions required to obtain it' (Grabbe et al., 2010).

In practice, the European Commission channelled its requirements for the Schengen visa liberalisation through the road maps which 'were almost identical, but […] took into account the specific situation in each country, in terms of existing legislation and practice'.[8] Block four consisted of the following benchmarks:

Freedom of movement of nationals

- ensure that freedom of movement of citizens is not subject to unjustified restrictions, including measures of a discriminatory nature, based on any ground such as sex, race, colour, ethnic or social origin, genetic features, language, religion or belief, political or any other opinion, membership of a national minority, property, birth, disability, age or sexual orientation.

Conditions and procedures for the issue of identity documents

- ensure full and effective access to travel and identity documents for all citizens including women, children, people with disabilities, people belonging to minorities and other vulnerable groups;
- Ensure full and effective access to identity documents for refugees.

Citizens' rights including protection of minorities

- adopt and enforce legislation to ensure effective protection against discrimination;
- specify conditions and circumstances for the *acquis*ition of citizenship;
- ensure the investigation of ethnically motivated incidents by law enforcement officers in the area of freedom of movement, including cases targeting members of minorities;
- ensure that constitutional provisions on protection of minorities are observed;
- implement relevant policies regarding all minorities, including Roma.[9]

With topics generally outside of the justice, freedom and security *acquis*, this block was considered as an outlier in the visa liberalisation process by the national stakeholders.[10] The

THE EUROPEANISATION OF CITIZENSHIP GOVERNANCE

EU and national documents confirm this tendency, as there is evident lack of scrutiny and attention to the issues when compared to the other blocks dealing with the security of documents, migration and the fight against organised crime. The lack of attention to these benchmarks was also confirmed in the decision not to perform on-the-ground peer mission assessments in this policy area and assess compliance through reports that the respective governments sent to Brussels. In these missions, experts from the European Commission and the member states went on the ground to verify the progress in terms of the stipulated benchmarks. During the visa liberalisation dialogues, peer missions on the first three blocks of the visa liberalisation road map were organised in all countries concerned on several occasions during 2009 and 2010. The Commission in its Enlargement strategy of 2010 highlighted that in the context of the visa liberalisation 'peer assessment and other missions have been intensified, bringing judges, prosecutors and other experts in law enforcement, border management and migration from the Member States into direct contact with their counterparts' (European Commission, 2010b).

Nevertheless, this form of detailed on-the-ground assessment was limited to the first three blocks of the visa liberalisation road map, reflecting the secondary importance assigned to the fundamental rights in the process. Despite the positive assessment on the usefulness of the peer missions, the Commission did not organise assessments on block four of the visa liberalisation road map. Instead, all of the countries had a one-day meeting with European Commission experts discussing issues primarily linked to the questions of anti-discrimination, which was considered of primary importance in relation to this block.[11] Overall, 'the issues in this block were assessed on paper, as no one went in Roma settlements in the country to really look what it looked like or talked to NGOs about anti-discrimination'.[12] Not surprisingly, the stakeholders involved in the process at the national level considered the block to be irrelevant and with no significance for the outcome of the visa liberalisation process.[13] An interviewee who participated in the visa liberalisation peer missions provided an interesting example of this tendency. Namely, when visiting a town close to the border in Macedonia an expert from an EU member state inquired about the treatment of persons illegally crossing the border. In order to receive a reply to his query, the expert resorted to the following phrase: 'Do not worry I do not come from human rights NGO, hence I am not interested in rights'.[14]

Anti-discrimination Laws as Benchmarks in the Visa Liberalisation Process

According to Joppke, the liberalisation of access to citizenship in the past half century has resulted in its internal diversification along ethnic, racial and religious lines, and in the light of this development, anti-discrimination and multicultural recognition gain importance for the rights dimension of citizenship (Joppke, 2007, pp. 38–39). Moreover, in the context of the EU, rights instruments can be seen as part of the structure of multi-level governance in the Union in which non-discrimination is one of the most developed components (Mabbett, 2005). This component was streamlined through the visa liberalisation road maps in the requirement for these countries to adopt framework laws on anti-discrimination.[15] All of the countries already had anti-discrimination provisions in area legislation; nevertheless, a framework law was a requirement of the visa liberalisation process. In essence, the anti-discrimination legislation was the most precise benchmark stipulated by the Commission in the fourth block dealing with fundamental rights, as was confirmed in all of my interviews conducted for this study.[16]

31

THE EUROPEANISATION OF CITIZENSHIP GOVERNANCE

In most of the countries, however, progress on this benchmark was formal, and was accompanied with problems both in terms of the legal definitions and implementation. The weak compliance has already been identified as a problem at a more general level in the case of the Western Balkans (see Noutcheva, 2007). In the first group of countries that obtained the visa-free travel, Serbia was the only country to adopt a Law on Prohibition of Discrimination in March 2009, prior to the visa liberalisation decision, which came later that year. Even though the passing of a law denotes a formal compliance with the benchmarks from the road map, the interviewees expressed their disbelief in the potential for significant impact of this law. It was argued that the adoption of this law was a box-ticking exercise and its provisions were not put into life because of activities surrounding this legislation that were missing at the time.[17] Some also expressed concerns about the formal harmonisation with EU requirements, which has been confirmed in the EU Progress Reports on Serbia since then. In 2013, the Commission has assessed that 'certain aspects of the anti-discrimination legislation have yet to be aligned with the *acquis*' (European Commission, 2013, p. 36)

Montenegro, on the other hand, did not adopt a Law on anti-discrimination by the time the decision on lifting the visas was endorsed at the end of 2009. The Montenegrin anti-discrimination act was adopted half a year later, in the summer of 2010, and was not fully aligned with the EU directives on anti-discrimination. Thus, in its progress report the European Commission (2011c, p. 19) notes that 'the alignment of antidiscrimination law with the *acquis* remains limited as there are cases in which it still permits direct discrimination and it fails to include an obligation for employers to provide reasonable accommodation for persons with disabilities'. In addition, the Commission highlights that

> the effective implementation of the anti-discrimination law still remains a challenge; Roma, Ashkalis and Egyptians, persons with disabilities and lesbian, gay, bisexual and transgender (LGBT) persons are still subject to discrimination in practice, including on the part of State authorities. (European Commission, 2011c, p. 19)

Still, the most illustrative example of the lack of importance assigned to the anti-discrimination legislation is the case of Macedonia. The country was considered a frontrunner in the visa liberalisation process, and yet was granted visa liberalisation without having formally adopted a framework of anti-discrimination law. For the purposes of the visa liberalisation process in late 2009, the Government proposed but failed to pass a draft law which was largely in line with the EU *acquis* in the area. Following the liberalisation of the visa regime, in early 2010 a new draft law was put forward and later adopted although it did not include sexual orientation or gender identity as an area of discrimination. Upon its adoption, the law was subsequently considered not to be in line with the EU *acquis* and was criticized by numerous human rights organisations. Overall, my interviewees have considered the visa liberalisation to have been a missed opportunity for the changes in the anti-discrimination policy in the country.[18]

Bosnia and Herzegovina adopted anti-discrimination legislation in July 2009, which is criticised in the 2011 EU report as it does not include age and disability and allows for a wide range of exceptions (European Commission, 2011b). Despite the legislative progress, interlocutors from civil society organisations highlighted that the scope for civil society pressure for implementation on issues such as anti-discrimination was limited, since the Commission advised us [the civil society organisations] primarily to provide information to the citizens on the specificities of the visa liberalization process in order to prevent abuse.[19]

At the same time, contacts at the national level expressed doubts in the potential for success of the anti-discrimination legislation in the light of the delayed harmonisation of the Constitution with the decision of the European Court of Human Rights (ECtHR) in the Sejdic-Finci case.[20] The ECtHR judgement established that there is systemic constitutional discrimination of all persons not belonging to the constituent peoples on account of their ineligibility to run for office (See Hodzic & Stojanovic, 2011). The Parliamentary Commission set-up for resolving the issue did not have any success as it was tasked with reconciling the opposing logics of anti-discrimination and multicultural recognition (Jukic, 2012). In this sense, Joppke's (2007, p. 43) concerns were confirmed, since 'anti-discrimination aims at abolishing ethnicity or race as marker of individual and group differentiation, whereas recognition seeks to perpetuate such differentiation. In a nutshell, anti-discrimination is universalistic; recognition is particularistic'.

Lastly, the Albanian Parliament adopted a specific law on anti-discrimination in February 2010, which at the time was considered to be in line with EU requirements. The adoption of this law was included in the unfulfilled benchmarks as part of the letters the European Commission sent both to Bosnia and Albania in the summer of 2009 (De Brouwer, 2009). In addition to the anti-discrimination law, the letter also included the adoption of measures taken to implement the National Strategy for improving Roma Living Standards and the Roma National Action Plan as part of the Roma Decade (De Brouwer, 2009). As in the case of Montenegro, the Commission included reinforcing human rights and implementing anti-discrimination policies as a part of the key priorities for Albania in its opinion on the application for membership in 2010 (European Commission, 2010a). Moreover, in its 2011 Progress Report on Albania, the Commission highlights that in terms of anti-discrimination, 'some important legislative gaps remain, including as regards persons with disabilities, and implementation of existing legislative and policy tools in this field is still inadequate' (European Commission, 2011a, p. 20). In this vein, with respect to Albania the interlocutors highlighted that when dealing with visa liberalisation, the anti-discrimination legislation was of secondary importance as was the fourth block in general.[21]

Overall, the analysis of how conditionality in relation to anti-discrimination played out in practice indicates that this benchmark was not a deal breaker and was inconsistently enforced during the visa liberalisation dialogues. On the one hand, not all countries had adopted the required anti-discrimination legislation prior to the visa liberalisation decisions. On the other, even in the cases where laws were adopted there remain formal questions over compliance, including problems of implementation. The secondary importance assigned to the issue was confirmed in the interviews with the stakeholders as well. On the other hand, studies have concluded that the 'EU succeeded in transforming the leverage that derived from the prospect of visa liberalisation into a major stimulus for successful EU rule adoption in Macedonia's justice and home affairs sector' (Trauner, 2011, p. 148), highlighting the difference between the fundamental rights requirements and the other three security-related blocks.

THE EUROPEANISATION OF CITIZENSHIP GOVERNANCE

Kosovo: A Delayed Road Out of Isolation

Affecting directly the entire region, the visa liberalisation process has also had significant implications for the citizens of Kosovo. With the amendments to the Council regulation 539/2001 Kosovo in 2009, as defined by the United Nations Security Council Resolution 1244 of 10 June 1999, was added to the EU black list.[22] Thus, the visa liberalisation with all the countries in the region exacerbated the already difficult position of Kosovo citizens with respect to their travel possibilities. In 2010, the holders of the Kosovo passport could travel visa-free to only five other states: Albania, Montenegro and Macedonia in its immediate neighbourhood, plus Turkey and Haiti. This effectively makes Kosovo 'one of the most isolated places on earth' (European Stability Initiative, 2009, p. 2). Between 2008 and 2011, the European Commission on a couple of occasions announced the prospect of a visa liberalisation, which was delayed causing frustration in the Kosovan society.[23] The Roadmap was finally approved at the EU level at the end of May 2012 and delivered to the Kosovan authorities on 14 June 2012.[24]

Since the benchmarks in the road map on Kosovo are largely identical to the earlier road maps, the activities planned in the official action Plan of the government for the fulfilment of the requirements resemble the ones of the other Western Balkan countries. Still, prior to the preparation of the official road map, the Kosovan government had adopted its own Action Plan for Implementation of the Roadmap on Visa Liberalisation Regime with the European Union 2009–2011 (Krasniqi, 2010). The Plan was based on a road map prepared by local experts shaped according to the experience of the other countries.[25] However, the plan from the Kosovan government did not contain a section in relation to the fourth block of the road map, in the light of the previous experience of the countries that negotiated (Government of Kosovo, 2009). At the same time, numerous reports from international organisations have pointed to the discrimination and difficulties that Kosovan minorities face especially in terms of their reintegration in society. However, having in mind the experience with block *four* in the other countries and the side-lining of the rights dimension in this process, the likelihood of successful application of conditionality in this area is also weak.

Fundamental Rights in the Post-visa Liberalisation Period

The aftermath of the first wave of visa liberalisation was accompanied by a rise in the number of asylum seekers from these countries, mostly Macedonia and Serbia, to the EU. In the first year after the liberalization, Macedonia was listed as a major country of origin of asylum seekers with the highest relative increase of more than 599 per cent (UNHCR, 2011). As was reported by *Der Spiegel*, in the case of Germany in 2010, asylum requests from Macedonia and Serbia accounted together for 7444 applications, whereas a year earlier, just 690 applicants came from the two countries (Angelos, 2011). Similar trends were noticeable in Sweden and Belgium as well. A rise of asylum seekers on the grounds of 'blood vengeance' from Albania was registered in the summer of 2011, but lasted for a short period of time.[26]

As a result of this increase and pressure from member states affected, the Commission introduced a post-visa liberalisation monitoring mechanism, which is again focused on the developments in the first three security-related blocks of the road maps (European Commission, 2011d). Moreover, in early 2011, the Commission organised post-visa liberalisation missions in Serbia and Macedonia, which did not deal with the block four of the road map. In May

THE EUROPEANISATION OF CITIZENSHIP GOVERNANCE

2011, Belgium sent a letter to the European Commission suggesting a suspension of the visa-free regime with Serbia. The Belgian letter stipulates that 'if Serbia fails to undertake necessary measures, Belgium is ready to request suspension' [of the visa-free regime with Serbia] (Sommo, 2011). Similar messages were sent to Macedonia as well with the Belgian higher officials regularly visiting Macedonia in order to 'warn' the authorities and the local population. The rise of the number of asylum seekers from these countries has instigated further action at the EU level with proposals for introducing a safeguard clause to suspend visa liberalisation (European Commission, 2011e). Overall, in the post-visa liberalisation period, the monitoring has followed the reasoning 'deal with the asylum seekers immediately'.[27]

The possibility of suspending the visa-free travel instigated the national governments in the region (primarily in Macedonia and Serbia) to attempt to restrict the movement of their citizens, which have come in various forms. The proposed measures can be organised into two groups: first, devising legal ways of criminalising the abuse of the visa-free regime and second, pressure on the border police to profile people when exiting the country. In relation to the former, both Macedonia and Serbia have been looking into ways to criminalise the abuse of the visa-free regime. Such legislative solutions were already enforced in the case of Bulgaria and Romania in 2001, which criminalised the violation of the immigration law of any country of the EU. In Romania,

> the entering or leaving a foreign state by the illegal passing of its borders, committed by a Romanian citizen or by a person without citizenship residing on the Romanian territory is considered as an offence and is punished with imprisonment from 3 months to 2 years.[28]

Similarly, in Bulgaria, Tchorbadjiyska argued that the possibility for revoking the passports of those who have infringed on other states' entry and residence rules might be challenged as a limitation to their freedom to move (Tchorbadjiyska, 2007). Despite the human rights concerns already raised in relation to Bulgaria and Romania, the legislative solutions sought in the Western Balkans have followed the same logic. The Commission in its report of December 2011 on the monitoring of the visa-free regime notes the amendments of the Criminal Codes, which have been prepared in these two countries (European Commission, 2011f). In Serbia, the interlocutors highlighted that the amendment to the Criminal Code was done through legal inventiveness, but it will be very difficult to implement it as it requires proving intent.[29] In Macedonia, however, in June 2012 four people were sentenced to four years in prison by a basic court for having abused the visa-free regime with the EU (Mackic, 2012).

Meanwhile, on the ground, both Serbia and Macedonia have been putting pressure on their border police both verbally and in written form to conduct thorough checks on their citizens when exiting the country. In June 2011, Serbia adopted a Directive on determining the manner of performing police duties of the border police officers and the obligations of people crossing the state border instructing the police officers to ask the citizens leaving the country whether they possess the necessary documents for travelling in the EU.[30] In Macedonia, a verbal directive was issued to the border police officers who also regularly report on the number of people who were prevented from leaving the country.[31] The largely bureaucratic disguise for these practices was an EU request to Serbia and Macedonia for help in the implementation of the Schengen Convention (Knaus & Stiglmayer, 2011). In the same vein, since the liberalisation of the visa regime, the Minister of Interior of

THE EUROPEANISATION OF CITIZENSHIP GOVERNANCE

Macedonia has been reporting in European and domestic media on the number of people being prevented from leaving the country. The media was reported that in the course of May and June 2011, 764 people were not allowed to exit from the country by Macedonian border guards upon suspicion of being false asylum seekers (Radio Free Europe, 2011). Commending the authorities on these activities in December 2011, the Commission has determined that 'the number of citizens of the Western Balkan countries who were ident-ified while attempted to leave their countries without meeting the requirements for entering the Schengen area gradually increased' (European Commission, 2011f).

As EU member state officials argued that most of the asylum seekers belong to the Roma and the Albanian communities, the issue very quickly became defined in terms of the ethnic background of the people leaving these countries (see European Stability Initiative, 2013). For example, in 2011 Serbian interior minister Ivica Dačić announced rigorous control by the border police stressing that 'no one from those communities [Albanian and Roma] will be able to leave the country if they do not have a return ticket, means to support their stay and cannot state the reason for the journey' (B92, 2011). As a result of this policy, national stakeholders have argued that what the EU is requesting in the aftermath of the visa liberal-isation is completely opposite to the requirements of block four:

> Whereas in block four they [i.e. the European Commission and EU member states] demanded us to ensure the freedom of movement without any discrimination, what they demand now is basically that if there is an Albanian, Roma or a poor person at the border to treat him/her differently.[32]

While being encouraged to enforce strict controls, the border police officers do not issue any document on the basis of which a person is not allowed to exit, making it impossible to formally appeal against this decision.[33] In Macedonia local NGOs reported that Roma, who were kept from leaving Macedonia, had the letters 'AZ' [short version of asylum] stamped in their passport, indicating a ban for leaving the country (Arka, 2011).

Although mostly limited to the cases of Serbia and Macedonia, the phenomenon also carries a regional dimension due to the intrinsic links between the countries as well as the population movements as a result of the conflicts of the 1990s. For example, in the summer of 2011 there were 400 registered asylum seekers in the EU from Bosnia which was a significant increase in comparison to previous years (Balkan Insight, 2011). The Bosnian authorities, however, have argued that these people are not citizens of Bosnia and Herzegovina, but from the territory of Kosovo and were falsely presenting themselves to be citizens of Bosnia and Herzegovina (Halimović, 2011). Unsurprisingly, the response was to strengthen controls on the country's border posts, and Bosnian security minister Sadik Ahmetović was quoted saying 'we will do everything in our power to solve this problem as soon as possible' (Balkan Insight, 2011). In the light of this pressure on Bosnia by the European Commission, my interlocutors highlighted that it is likely that the authorities will push for these people, again predominantly Roma, to leave the country.[34] In the second report on the post-visa liberalisation monitoring, the Commission also notes that while the number of asylum seekers from Macedonia and Serbia has decreased, the trend is opposite in the case of Albania and Bosnia and Herzegovina, indicating that similar trend is yet to be expected in these two cases (European Commission, 2011f).

Overall, the increased pressure from the European Commission and EU member states to deal with the issue immediately has undoubtedly contributed to a practice of discrimination

THE EUROPEANISATION OF CITIZENSHIP GOVERNANCE

against marginalised groups. This worrying tendency of profiling at the border has been recognised and has also raised concerns in terms of its implications for the protection of human rights by international organisations and more recently by the judicial authorities as well. The Council of Europe Commissioner for Human Rights in a statement in late 2011 highlighted that

> significantly, it is the minorities, and in particular the Roma, who have become targeted. Everyone cannot be checked on exit and the selection is being done on the basis of 'profiling'. The result is another layer of discrimination against this minority. (Hammarberg, 2011)

Similarly, the Meijers Committee of experts on international immigration, refugee and criminal law highlighted that 'the EU pressure on third countries to prevent Roma from entering the EU in order to claim asylum, […] may contribute to a climate of stigmatisation and repression of ethnic minorities in Balkan countries' (Meijers Committee, 2011). Such practices therefore highlight how through the securitisation of the visa liberalisation process, the conditionality mechanism can lead to the unintended consequences such as discrimination of disadvantaged groups in terms of their freedom of movement. On these grounds a basic court in Skopje in 2014 determined discrimination and violation to the right of equality by the Ministry of Interior that prevented a Roma plaintiff to leave the territory of the Republic of Macedonia.[35]

Similar discriminatory practices have also been introduced at the EU level where the asylum seekers from the region have been subject to specific targeted measures in the recipient countries. In 2012, the German Federal Office for Migration and refugees introduced an accelerated procedure for the asylum seekers from the Western Balkans, which has resulted in shorter decision-making processes (European Asylum Support Office, 2013a). As a result, the average length for decision-making in asylum cases from Serbian and Macedonian citizens was reduced to seven days at the end of 2012. While the German government has argued that this is the result of relocating of staff, the length of the procedures has raised questions among human rights defenders that the procedures were superficial and did not allow for a proper assessment of the asylum claim (see European Asylum Support Office, 2013b).

Conclusion

This paper has examined the implementation of EU requirements on fundamental rights during and after the visa liberalisation dialogues that took place between 2008 and 2010 between the European Commission and the countries of the Western Balkans. In this round of visa negotiations, the European Commission for the first time included fundamental rights requirements in addition to the requirements linked to justice, freedom and security. As a result, the Western Balkans countries have become an indicative case for studying how the EU affects fundamental rights through the visa liberalisation process. In this paper, fundamental rights were approached as essential elements of the respective citizenship regimes. The visa liberalisation process was understood as an exercise of Europeanisation by conditionality and an integral segment of the developments in the EU justice, freedom and security area. Relying on an analysis of official documents and data from stakeholders'

THE EUROPEANISATION OF CITIZENSHIP GOVERNANCE

interviews, this paper has studied how the requirements related to fundamental rights have affected the specific policy area both during the negotiations and in their aftermath.

Studying block four of the visa liberalisation process, which dealt with fundamental rights, this paper focused on how its requirements affected this specific policy area. It shows that in all of the countries studied the interest of the European Commission in fundamental rights was formal, without a thorough examination of the on-the-ground situation. Hence, although included in the negotiations for a visa-free regime, in practice fundamental rights were of minor importance than the security-related requirements. In order to illustrate this point, this paper studied the regulation of anti-discrimination as a benchmark for the visa-free regime. The analysis indicates that in the first group of countries including Macedonia, Serbia and Montenegro, the anti-discrimination legislation was not a deal breaker for the visa-free regime. In fact, both Macedonia and Montenegro had not adopted such a law at the time of the liberalisation of the visa regime although they were considered frontrunners of the liberalisation process. Bosnia and Herzegovina and Albania were a group of countries that negotiated for a further year until the end of 2010, where similar tendencies can be noticed. Though formally both of them adopted anti-discrimination legislation prior to the decision to lift their visa requirements, these laws had substantial gaps and were also not implemented in practice.

While the analysis of the visa liberalisation dialogues confirmed the secondary importance assigned to fundamental rights requirements, the study of the post-visa liberalisation period sheds light on backsliding in this policy area as well. The decision to lift the EU visa requirements was accompanied by an increase of the number of asylum seekers from the region. As the asylum recognition rate for this group is very low, the phenomenon has been labelled as 'false asylum seekers'. In response to these developments, both the European Commission and the governments of the affected EU member states have put increasing pressure on the governments in the Western Balkans to take measures in the direction of limiting the freedom of movement of their own citizens by prioritising security concerns. In essence, the border police officers in the region are instructed to do profiling on the basis of ethnic background as well as economic status of the citizens exiting the country.

Conceptually, the paper used the visa liberalisation process to study the interactions between the conditionality mechanism and securitisation paradigm in the context of EU justice, freedom and security. In terms of the former, this paper illustrated the informal nature of conditionality and the significance of unofficial exchanges between the European Commission and national actors for understanding the operation of this mechanism. As to the latter, the study demonstrated that the security-dominated rationale of the visa liberalisation process has undermined its potential as a tool for advancing fundamental rights. In fact, the informal conditionality in combination with the dominance of security-related concerns informed us of potentially polarising outcomes of the visa liberalisation as an instrument of the Europeanisation process.

Disclosure statement

No potential conflict of interest was reported by the author.

Funding

This work was supported by funding from the CITSEE project (The Europeanisation of Citizenship in the Successor States of the Former Yugoslavia), based at the University of Edinburgh, UK. CITSEE is funded by the

THE EUROPEANISATION OF CITIZENSHIP GOVERNANCE

European Research Council under the European Union's Seventh Framework Programme [ERC grant number 230239], and the support of the ERC is acknowledged with thanks.

Notes

1   Council Regulation (EC) No. 539/2001 of 15 March 2001 listing the third countries whose nationals must be in possession of visas when crossing the external borders and those whose nationals are exempt from that requirement in (EC) No. 539/2001: Official Journal of the European Communities.

2   Council Regulation (EC) No. 1244/2009 of 30 November 2009 amending Regulation (EC) No. 539/2001 listing the third countries whose nationals must be in possession of visas when crossing the external borders and those whose nationals are exempt from that requirement in (EC) No. 1244/2009: Official Journal of the European Communities.

   Regulation (EU) No. 1091/2010 of the European Parliament and the Council of 24 November 2010 amending Council Regulation (EC) No. 539/2001 listing the third countries whose nationals must be in possession of visas when crossing the external borders and those whose nationals are exempt from that requirement in (EU) No. 1091/2010.

3   Council Regulation (EC) No. 539/2001 of 15 March 2001 listing the third countries whose nationals must be in possession of visas when crossing the external borders and those whose nationals are exempt from that requirement in (EC) No. 539/2001: Official Journal of the European Communities.

4   The Road maps for visa liberalisation are available at http://www.esiweb.org/index.php?lang=en&id=352.

5   For an overview of all benchmarks in this block, please see the next section.

6   For the purposes of this paper, I have conducted 12 open-ended interviews with civil servants and civil society representatives engaged in the visa liberalisation process during 2012.

7   Its importance was linked also to the visa-free status enjoyed by the citizens of former Yugoslavia during the times of the Federation.

8   The Visa Road maps, Schengen White List project and European Stability Initiative are available at http://www.esiweb.org/index.php?lang=en&id=352.

9   These benchmarks were part of all the road maps for the five countries negotiating the visa-free travel.

10 Author's interview with a representative of the Ministry of Foreign Affairs of Albania, March 2012; Author's interview with a civil society organisation representative in Belgrade, March 2012.

11 Author's interview with a civil society organisation representative in Belgrade, March 2012, Author's interview with a representative of the Ministry of Foreign Affairs of the Republic of Macedonia in Skopje, January 2012.

12 Author's interview with a civil society organisation representative, Brussels October 2010.

13 Author's interview with a representative of the Ministry of Foreign Affairs of Montenegro, March 2012; Author's interview with a civil society organisation representative in Belgrade, March 2012.

14 Author's interview with a representative of the Ministry of Foreign Affairs of the Republic of Macedonia in Skopje, January 2012.

15 In addition, the EU's demands on implementing the Roma Strategies and Action Plans of these countries were at times included, but due to space constraints they were not analysed in this paper. Both the document and interview data point to the low importance assigned to these topics in the process as well.

16 For an assessment of other benchmarks of block four see: Kacarska (2012).

17 Author's interview with a civil society organisation representative in Belgrade, March 2012.

18 Author's interview with a civil society organisation representative in Skopje, January 2012.

19 Author's interview with a civil society organisation representative in Sarajevo, March 2012.

20 Sejdic and Finci v. Bosnia and Herzegovina, Application nos. 27996/06 and 34836/06, 22 December 2009. Council of Europe: European Court of Human Rights.

21 Author's interview with a representative of the Ministry of Foreign Affairs of Albania, March 2012.

22 Council Regulation (EC) No. 1244/2009 of 30 November 2009 amending Regulation (EC) No. 539/2001 listing the third countries whose nationals must be in possession of visas when crossing the external borders and those whose nationals are exempt from that requirement in (EC) No. 1244/2009: Official Journal of the European Communities.

23 Author's interview with a EU expert in Kosovo, May 2012.

24 EU approves the road map for Kosovo, 30 May 2012. *INFO GLOBI* [Online]. Available at http://eng.infoglobi.com/index.php/kosovo/art/4944 (accessed 2 June 2012).

THE EUROPEANISATION OF CITIZENSHIP GOVERNANCE

[25] Author's interview with a EU expert in Kosovo, May 2012.

[26] Author's interview with a representative of the Ministry of Foreign Affairs of Albania, March 2012.

[27] Author's interview with a civil society organisation representative in Belgrade, March 2012.

[28] Art. 1(1), Emergency Ordinance no. 112 Referring to the Punishment of Some Action Committed. Abroad by Romanian Citizens or by Person Without Citizenship Residing in Romania, 30 August 2001.

[29] Author's interview with a civil society organisation representative in Belgrade, March 2012.

[30] Official Gazette of the Republic of Serbia No. 39/2011.

[31] Ministry of Interior of the Republic of Macedonia (2011)

[32] Author's interview with a civil society organisation representative in Belgrade, March 2012.

[33] Author's interview with a civil society organisation representative in Sarajevo, March 2012.

[34] Author's interview with a civil society organisation representative in Sarajevo, March 2012. Author's interview with a civil servant in the Ministry of Human Rights and Refugees in Sarajevo, March 2012.

[35] See Macedonian Young Lawyers Association News, 'The Basic Court Skopje 2 Rendered The First Judgment In Republic Of Macedonia Which Determinates Discrimination', 29 May 2014, available at http://www.myla. org.mk/index.php/en/news/135-press-release-29-05-2014 (accessed 10 September 2014).

References

Angelos, J. (2011) Wave of Roma Rejected as Asylum Seekers, *Spiegel* 26 May 2011. Available at http://www. spiegel.de/international/germany/0,1518,764630,00.html (accessed 20 May 2013).

Arka. (2011) *Monthly Report for the Situation of the Roma Rights in Macedonia, May–June 2011* (Skopje: NGO ARKA).

B92. (2011) Interior Minister Announces Stricter Border Control. Available at http://www.b92.rs/eng/news/ politics-article.php?yyyy=2011&mm=05&dd=08&nav_id=74223 B92 (accessed 20 May 2013).

Balkan Insight. (2011) Bosnian Asylum Seekers in Belgium to be Repatriated, *Balkan Insight*. Available at http:// www.balkaninsight.com/en/article/bosnian-asylum-seekers-in-belgium-to-be-repatriated (accessed 20 May 2013).

Bigo, D. & Guild, E. (2005) Policing at a distance: Schengen visa policies, in: D. Bigo & E. Guild (Eds) *Controlling frontiers: Free movement into and within Europe*, pp. 203–227 (Burlington: Ashgate).

Carrera, S. & Guild, E. (2007) *An EU Framework on Sanctions Against Employers of Irregular Immigrants: Some Reflections on the Scope, Features & Added Value, Policy Brief, No. 140* (Brussels: Center for European Policy Studies).

Council. (2001) Council Regulation (EC) No 539/2001 of 15 March 2001 listing the third countries whose nationals must be in possession of visas when crossing the external borders and those whose nationals are exempt from that requirement, *Official Journal of the European Communities*.

Council. (2009) Council Regulation (EC) No 1244/2009 of 30 November 2009 amending Regulation (EC) No 539/2001 listing the third countries whose nationals must be in possession of visas when crossing the external borders and those whose nationals are exempt from that requirement, *Official Journal of the European Communities*.

De Brouwer, J. L. (2009) Letter with next steps in the dialogue on visa liberalisation between the EU and Bosnia and Herzegovina. Available at http://www.esiweb.org/pdf/schengen_white_list_project_BiH20LETTER20from20THE 20Commission20PLUS20Annex20-201520JULY202009.pdf (accessed 19 March 2012).

European Asylum Support Office. (2013a) Asylum applicants from the Western Balkans: Comparative analysis of trends, push-pull factors and responses. Available at http://easo.europa.eu/wp-content/uploads/EASO-Report-Western-Balkans.pd (accessed 20 June 2014).

European Asylum Support Office. (2013b) National Report Germany. Available at http://www.asylumineurope. org/files/report-download/aida_ _germany_second_update_final_corrected.pdf (accessed 20 June 2014).

European Commission. (2010a) Commission opinion on Albania's application for membership of the European Union. Communication from the Commission to the European Parliament and Council (Brussels: Commission of the European Communities).

European Commission. (2010b) Enlargement Strategy and Main Challenges 2010–2011. Communication from the Commission to the European Parliament and the Council (Brussels: Commission of the European Communities).

European Commission. (2011a) Albania 2011 Progress Report. Commission Staff Working Paper (Brussels: Commission of the European Communities).

THE EUROPEANISATION OF CITIZENSHIP GOVERNANCE

European Commission. (2011b) Bosnia and Herzegovina 2011 Progress Report. *Commission Staff Working Paper* (Brussels: Commission of the European Communities).

European Commission. (2011c) Montenegro 2011 Progress Report. Commission Staff Working Paper (Brussels: Commission of the European Communities).

European Commission. (2011d) On the post-visa liberalisation monitoring for the Western Balkan countries in accordance with the Commission Statement of 8 November 2010. Commission Staff Working Paper (Brussels: European Commission).

European Commission. (2011e) Proposal for a Regulation of the European Parliament and of the Council amending Council Regulation (EC) No 539/2001 listing the third countries whose nationals must be in possession of visas when crossing the external borders and those whose nationals are exempt from that requirement COM (2011) 290 final. Available at http://ec.europa.eu/home-affairs/news/intro/docs/110524/290/1_EN_ACT_part1_v10.pdf (accessed 20 February 2012).

European Commission. (2011f) Second report on the post-visa liberalisation monitoring for the Western Balkan countries in accordance with the Commission Statement of 8 November 2010. Commission Staff Working Paper (Brussels: European Commission).

European Commission. (2012) Commission launches dialogue with Kosovo on visa free travel. *Europa Press Releases.* Available at http://europa.eu/rapid/pressReleasesAction.do?reference=IP/12/32 (accessed 20 February 2012).

European Commission. (2013) Serbia 2013 Progress Report. *Commission Staff Working Paper* (Brussels: Commission of the European Communities).

European Stability Initiative. (2009) Isolating Kosovo? Kosovo vs Afghanistan 5:22. ESI Discussion Paper: European Stability Initiative.

European Stability Initiative. (2013) Saving visa-free travel: Visa, asylum and the EU roadmap policy ESI Discussion Paper. Available at http://www.esiweb.org/pdf/esi_document_id_132.pdf (accessed 17 March 2014).

Government of Kosovo. (2009) *Action Plan for Implementation of Roadmap of Government of Kosovo on Visa Liberalisation Regime with European Union (2009–2011)* (Pristina: Government of the Republic of Kosovo).

Grabbe, H., Knaus, G. & Korski, D. (2010) Beyond wait-and-see: The way forward for EU Balkan policy. European Council on Foreign Relations. Available at http://ecfr.3cdn.net/904dfdc93d6cd42972_vem6iv3c0.pdf (accessed 20 December 2011).

Guild, E. (2003) The border abroad–visas and border controls, in: K. Groenendijk, E. Guild & P. Minderhoud (Eds) *In Search of Europe's Borders*, pp. 87–104 (The Hague: Kluwer Law International).

Guild, E., Carrera, S. & Balzacq, T. (2008) The changing dynamics of security in an Enlarged European Union in *Changing Landscape of European Liberty and Security Papers.* Research paper no. 12. Available at http://www.libertysecurity.org/IMG/pdf_The_Changing_Dynamics_of_Security_in_an_Enlarged_European_Union.pdf (accessed 20 May 2013).

Halimović, Dž. (2011) Bh. vlasti tvrde: Bezvizni režim nije ugrožen [The BH authorities claim that the visa free regime is not jeopardised], *Radio Free Europe.* Available at http://www.slobodnaevropa.org/content/bih_bezvizni_rezim_belgija_azilanti/24337027.html (accessed 25 February 2012).

Hammarberg, T. (2011) *The Right to Leave One's Country Should Be Applied without Discrimination.* Available at http://commissioner.cws.coe.int/tiki-view_blog_post.php?blogId=1&postId=193 (accessed 15 January 2012).

Hodzic, E. & Stojanovic, N. (2011) *Novi-stari ustavni inzenjering u BiH: Kompleksnost presude Evropskog suda za ljudska prava u predmetu Sejdic i Finci protiv BiH i moguci pravci njenog provodjenja* [New/old Constitutional Engineering? Challenges and Implications of the European Court of Human Rights Decision in the Case of Sejdić and Finci v. BiH] (Sarajevo: Analitika Centre for Social Research).

Hughes, J., Gwendolyn, S. & Claire, G. (2005) *Europeanization and Regionalization in the EU's Enlargement: The Myth of Conditionality (One Europe or Several?)* (New York: Palgrave MacMillan).

Huysmans, J. (2000) The European Union and the securitization of migration, *Journal of Common Market Studies*, 38(5), pp. 751–777.

InfoGlobi (2012) EU approves the roadmap for Kosovo, 30 May 2012. Available at http://eng.infoglobi.com/index.php/kosovo/art/4944 (accessed 2 June 2012).

Joppke, C. (2007) Transformation of citizenship: Status, *Rights, Identity, Citizenship Studies*, 11(1), pp. 37–48.

Jukic, E. (2012) Bosnians Fail to Agree Sejdic-Finci Changes, *Balkan Insight.* Available at http://www.balkaninsight.com/en/article/bosnian-leaders-fail-agreement-on-human-rights-ruling (accessed 30 December 2012).

THE EUROPEANISATION OF CITIZENSHIP GOVERNANCE

Kacarska, S. (2012). Europeanisation through mobility: Visa liberation and citizenship regimes in Western Balkans. CITSEE Working Paper 2012/21 (Edinburgh: University of Edinburgh).

Knaus, G. & Stiglmayer, A. (2011) *Balkan Asylum Seekers and the Spectre of European Hypocrisy EUObserver.* Available at http://euobserver.com/7/113807 (accessed 20 March 2012).

Krasniqi, G. (2010) *Country Report: Kosovo, EUDO Citizenship Observatory.* Robert Schuman Centre for Advanced Studies. Available at http://eudo-citizenship.eu/docs/CountryReports/Kosovo.pdf (accessed 20 March 2012).

Mabbett, D. (2005) The development of rights-based social policy in the European union: The example of disability rights, *Journal of Common Market Studies*, 43(1), pp. 97–120.

Mackic, K. (2012) За 2.000 евра до Финска, рај за азилантите [For 2000 Euros to Finland, heaven for asylum seekers], *Nova Makedonija.* Available at http://www.novamakedonija.com.mk/NewsDetal.asp?vest=6712910356&id=12&prilog=0&setIzdanie=22598 (accessed 7 June 2012).

Meijers Committee (2011) Letter to European Parliament: Note of the Meijers Committee on the proposal to introduce a safeguard clause to suspend visa liberalization. Meijers Committee Standing committee of experts on international immigration, refugee and criminal law. Available at http://www.statewatch.org/news/2011/dec/eu-meijers-committee-visas.pdf (accessed 9 January 2012).

Ministry of Interior of the Republic of Macedonia (2011) *Jankulovska and Naumovski on the Border Crossing Tabanovce: Stop for the False Asylum Seekers* [Јанкулоска и Наумовски на ГП "Табановце" Стоп за лажните азиланти]. Available at http://www.mvr.gov.mk/ShowAnnouncements.aspx?ItemID=10007&mid=710&tabId=358&tabindex=0 (accessed 30 May 2012).

Monar, J. (2001) The dynamics of justice and home affairs: Laboratories, driving factors and costs, *Journal of Common Market Studies*, 39(4), pp. 747–764.

Noutcheva, G. (2007) Fake, partial and imposed compliance: The limits of the EU's normative power in the Western Balkans, *CEPS Working Document* (Brussels: Centre for European Policy Studies). Available at http://www.ceps.eu/ceps/download/1357 (accessed 16 June 2010).

Radaelli, C. (2000) Whither Europeanization? Concept stretching and substantive change, *European Integration online Papers (EIoP).* European Community Studies Association Austria (ECSA-A). Available at http://eiop.or.at/eiop/texte/2000-008.htm (accessed 5 November 2009).

Radio Free Europe. (2011) За два месеци 764 обиди за злоупотреба на визното олеснување [In Two Months 764 Attempts for Abuse of the Visa Free Travel] Available at http://www.makdenes.org/archive/news/20110629/428/428.html?id=24250163 (accessed 5 November 2012).

Sasse, G. (2009) Tracing the construction and effects of EU conditionality, in: B. Rechel (Ed) *Minority Rights in Central and Eastern Europe,* pp. 17–31 (London and New York: Taylor & Francis).

Schimmelfennig, F. & Sedelmeier, U. (2005) Introduction: Conceptualizing the Europeanization of central and Eastern Europe, in: F. Schimmelfennig & U. Sedelmeier (Eds) *The Europeanization of Central and Eastern Europe,* pp. 1–28 (Ithaca, NY: Cornell University Press).

Sejdic and Finci v. Bosnia and Herzegovina, Application nos. 27996/06 and 34836/06, 22 December 2009 Council of Europe: European Court of Human Rights.

Shaw, J. & Štiks, I. (2010) The Europeanisation of citizenship in former Yugoslavia: An introduction. CITSEE Working Paper, 2010/01 (Edinburgh: School of Law, University of Edinburgh).

Sommo, L. (2011) *EU Proposes Mechanism to Suspend Visa-free Regime in Balkan Insight.* Available at http://www.balkaninsight.com/en/article/eu-proposes-mechanism-to-suspend-visa-free-regime (accessed 20 January 2012).

Tchorbadjiyska, A. (2007) Bulgarian experiences with visa policy in the accession process: A story of visa lists, citizenship and limitations on citizens' rights, *Regio-Minorities, Politics, Society-English Edition*, 10(1), pp. 88–105.

Trauner, F. (2008) Deconstructing the EU's routes of influence in justice and home affairs in the Western Balkans, *Journal of European Integration*, 31(1), pp. 65–82.

Trauner, F. (2011) *The Europeanisation of the Western Balkans: EU Justice and Home Affairs in Croatia and Macedonia* (Manchester and New York: Manchester University Press).

UNHCR. (2011) *Asylum Levels and Trends in Industrialized Countries 2010-Statistical Overview of Asylum Applications Lodged in Europe and Selected Non-European Countries* (Geneva: United Nations High Commissioner for Refugees).

Vink, M. P. & Graziano, P. (2007) Challenges of a new research agenda, in: M. P. Vink & P. Graziano (Eds) *Europeanization: New Research Agendas* , pp. 3–22 (New York: Palgrave MacMillan).

Welfare State Change and Social Citizenship in the Post-Yugoslav States

MARIJA STAMBOLIEVA

Department of Political Science, Universität Kassel, Germany

ABSTRACT   *This article discusses the interaction between social citizenship and the welfare state in the context of post-communist transformation. It particularly examines the relationship between changing political institutions and notions of citizenship, and changing welfare policies. The welfare diversity can be attributed to inherited legacies and the transitional context, and particularly the political responses to it. They can be best understood in the context of democratization processes which have affected both the notion of citizenship as well as the welfare state reform. Additionally, increasing internationalization challenged existing structures and offered new perspectives. The role of the European Union has, however, been quite uneven in this process. Based on the combined effect of these influences in the post-Yugoslav space, four social citizenship types could be discerned: neo-corporatist (Slovenia), accommodating (Croatia), paternalistic (Serbia and Montenegro), and neoliberal (Macedonia and Kosovo).*

Introduction

The collapse of communism was not the most favorable moment to expect success of communitarian ideas. The social component of public policies was associated with failing socialism and thus widely questioned. In a period when, under the pressures of globalization, the role of the welfare state and its reform became the order of the day in affluent, democratic countries, the former communist states could hardly rely on retaining a comprehensive commitment to welfare provision. The 'transition' thus incorporated the need for adjustment to the new conditions, which nevertheless took different forms in the different states.

Scholars interested in studying particularly the changes in Central and Eastern European countries started testing the application of the existing schools of thought in the post-communist context. Over time, a consensus has been forged around the combination of factors defining welfare state restructuring, such as the existing historical institutional setting, socioeconomic cleavages and the influence of international institutions (cf. Manning, 2004; Orenstein, 2008; Cerami & Vanhuysse, 2009), even if opinions differ regarding the importance of each or the interrelationship between them. Scholars have noted that the transition-related economic downturn and fiscal pressures have affected the playing field in the post-socialist countries; however, economic arguments have played a secondary role, and the focus has been mainly on the specific legacies and actors' choices. Despite severe changes that have shaken institutional structures and decision-making patterns following the collapse of communism, institutionalists have argued that countries' responses have followed a certain path-dependent logic (Inglot, 2008). Actor-centered approaches have explored the role of party politics and interest groups under conditions of political pluralism and have mainly shown that they have not replicated Western patterns (Orenstein, 1998; Tavits & Letki, 2009). An increasing influence of the agenda of international agents – moving between the two extremes: the International Financial Institutions (IFIs) encouraged 'social liberalism' and 'European welfare conservatism' promoted by the ILO (International Labour Organization) – has been observed (Deacon et al., 1997). Furthermore, evidence has suggested that the reluctance for deeper positive integration in Europe have left the 'European Social Model' a rather fuzzy concept. The project of social Europe has been found sidelined by the neoliberal logic of the single market and the monetary union (Whyman et al., 2012). The 2008 crisis and European Union's (EU) answer to it have been seen as particularly hurtful to the possibilities for European convergence (Galgoczi, 2013).

Given the existing welfare diversity, attempts to place the post-communist welfare regimes under Esping-Andersen's typology have proved futile. The most dominant view seems to be the one which regard their welfare models as hybrids, given shared features with different types of the existing Western models as well as the variety among the post-communist states themselves (Baum-Ceisig et al., 2008; Cerami & Vanhuysse, 2009; Schubert et al., 2009). The post-communist countries, which share many common traits with the Bismarckian conservative tradition, complemented by some universal elements of the Beveridgean tradition (cf. Bonoli, 1997), have during the transition faced pressure to adopt a more liberal attitude toward their welfare policies. Consequently, features of both the conservative and liberal models could be discerned, whereas development of social-democratic forms of welfare policy would be most unlikely to emerge (Deacon et al., 1997).

The countries of the former Yugoslavia have been predominantly excluded from these comparative analyses. The emergence of national identity cleavages there put socioeconomic issues on the back burner. The discourse has been for decades dominated by the issues of nationalism and ethnic polarization, although there have been those that have noted that economic grievances have been intentionally converted 'into nationalist rage, leading to a vicious war and sabotaging chances for liberal democracy for years to come' (Ost, 2007, p. 89). This article picks up on this line of reasoning, and by examining the welfare outcomes that came to be two decades after the secession, aims to illuminate the complexities and interactions of economic and political processes in given time and space that accounted for their development. Drawing upon Marshall's concept of tripartite citizenship (Marshall, 2008 [1949]), the article explores how the political and civic components have shaped the social dimension of citizenship, that is, citizens' ability to balance market effects with the state involvement. It tests the explanatory potential of established schools of thought in the context of transition – where political and economic systems have taken various shapes, which have not necessarily followed other models, be it Western or Eastern European. It argues that the nature of the political transformation processes has changed income distribution patterns, and therefore social citizenship should be

THE EUROPEANISATION OF CITIZENSHIP GOVERNANCE

analyzed beyond traditional interpretations known to established pluralist and capitalist societies. Thus, for understanding a welfare state activity in the post-Yugoslav context, a typical analysis of market rules, ideological interpretations and voter's preferences may say less compared to an analysis of how political structures shaped actual practices of social citizenship either as participative or exclusivist, bottom-up or top-down, or deliberative or clientelist. Given the increasing importance of cross-border interconnectedness, internationally diffused ideas as well as European integration also influenced the changing nature of social citizenship.

The article begins by introducing the concepts of social citizenship and welfare state from historical and contemporary perspective. Subsequently, the former Yugoslav states are brought into the picture. The interplay of explanatory factors is illustrated in order to provide a better understanding of the specifics that led to adopting different approaches to social citizenship. Finally, country cases are clustered and explained accordingly.

Social Citizenship and the Welfare State

The concept of social citizenship is closely linked with the understanding of the welfare state. It underscores the role that welfare provisions have for the enjoyment of the citizenship status. It is therefore closely associated with pluralism and capitalism as it facilitates reconciliation of prescribed rights with market forces. The origin of the term 'social citizenship' can be traced back to T. H. Marshall who saw social inequality as a threat to the full realization of political rights and freedoms (Marshall, 2008 [1949]). According to his rights-based framework of tripartite citizenship, the expansion of the scope of democratic rights (from political, through civil to social rights) widened the ground for bottom-up pressures and thus helped turn modern states into welfare states. The intensification of trade union activities, political engagement of social groups, as well as political successes of the labor party challenged the established socioeconomic order and motivated intervention. This interpretation is at the core of the power resources approach, which has focused on the impact of different class-related and interest groups over the shaping of the welfare state, depending on their interests and effective power. Even though, in historical perspective, different welfare states had different traditions – the introduction of the first welfare programs ensued in authoritarian states (such as Bismarck's Germany) as an elite project with the objective to legitimize the regime –suffrage expansion, founding of workers' (socialist) parties and their electoral success have been proportionately related to the extension of welfare programs across a number of European countries, aimed at pacifying workers by addressing some of their social concerns and neutralizing their political mobilization (Alber, 1982, p. 150).

The collapse of communism implied abandonment of the old social contract, which legitimized the given political order in exchange for a basic economic standard and social benefits. Subsequent democratization was meant to pave the way toward a new social contract defined by political participation. This did not necessarily mean that popular demands for better life conditions would vanish, but, under the new political conditions, transform into rights-seeking claims. The social component in Marshall's democratic citizenship concept, which guarantees a

> whole range from the right to a modicum of economic welfare and security to the right to share to the full in the social heritage and to live the life of a civilized

being according to the standards prevailing in the society (Marshall, 2008 [1949], p. 94)

is at the core of the state's welfare functions. Joining the argumentation of Stubbs and Zrinščak (2015), this article explores an extended view of Marshall's linear and straightforward interpretation of citizenship. Particularly, the elements featured by defective systems, such as clientelism and elite capture, create space for alternate interpretations of the notion of citizenship. The focus here lies on the combination of variables that indicate a certain ideological, political and legal relationship between individuals, communities and states. The design of that relationship helps identify the different approaches to social citizenship. The approaches are not to be mistaken with regimes. Although the categorization of the welfare outcomes draws upon existing concepts (Esping-Andersen, 1990; Bonoli, 1997; Bohle & Greskovits, 2007), they are not sufficiently equipped to be able to grasp all the complexities of the systemic transformation.

Hypothesizing the Post-Yugoslav Welfare Trajectories

The country cases of interest here have after two decades of transition demonstrated sufficient distinctive indicators, which allow us to separate them into four types of social citizenship approaches: neo-corporatist (Slovenia), accommodating (Croatia), paternalistic (Serbia and Montenegro), and neoliberal (Macedonia and Kosovo). The framework relies on correlating the dependent variable (the welfare system) with the explanatory variables (domestic and international factors) in order to work out the states' choices of social citizenship. The post-conflict context of Bosnia and Herzegovina makes it especially difficult to classify due to its extreme fragmentation and complexity in a milieu of limited sovereignty. Nevertheless, massive demonstrations across the country in February 2014 showed that citizens shared the concern of Bosnia and Herzegovina's economic backwardness, poor social conditions and the anger against corrupt elites. One comment on the events summarized the predicament well: 'Bosnians are hungry in three languages' (Petritsch, 2014). Still, the system's multiplicity has impeded the targeting of reactions and has left the outcome unclear. Table 1 summarizes the combined effect of the different variables that have contributed to the variation, to which this text turns next.

Welfare Outcomes

The Yugoslav political system was 'authoritarian with limited social pluralism' (Zakošek, 2008, p. 590), which allowed the development of a 'socialist market economy' (Zakošek, 2008, p. 591) with workers' self-management as its economy's distinctive feature. As a country implementing a specific type of socialism, Yugoslavia rejected the soviet model of governance and, as a result, created a welfare system, inspired by the European traditions. A mixed Bismarckian–Beveridgean system, consisting of social insurance (pension and disability insurance, health insurance, social insurance in case of temporary unemployment) and social protection (Stambolieva, 2011), provided wide-ranging benefits, comprehensive coverage and decent standard of living. Still, despite the shared system, inherent differences, related to economic structure and allocation of resources, created discrepancies among the different regions (former republics and provinces). As a result, the commitment to welfare provision could not be equally upheld, which in practice

THE EUROPEANISATION OF CITIZENSHIP GOVERNANCE

Table 1. Summary of findings

Policy-making approach	Neo-corporatist	Accommodating	Paternalistic	Neoliberal
Welfare system	Mixed corporatist conservative (Bismarckian) and social-democratic (Beveridgean) system	Mixed Bismarckian/ Beveridgean system with some liberal elements	Predominantly conservative system	Residual system with some conservative remnants
Variables	Favorable initial conditions; Strong economic base; Solid democratic consolidation; Weak external influence	Favorable initial conditions; Moderate economic base; Moderate democratic consolidation; Strong external influence	Semi-favorable initial conditions; Weak economic base; Defective democratization; Moderate external influence	Unfavorable initial conditions; Weak economic base; Defective democratization; Strong external influence
Post-Yugoslav country	Slovenia	Croatia	Serbia, Montenegro	Macedonia, Kosovo

translated into social programs of varied scope and quality. The welfare models, which ultimately came into existence during the last couple of decades, range between the two extremes of the comprehensive welfare state of Slovenia and the residual welfare regime of Macedonia. Thus, as also suggested by the institutionalist argument, the shape that the welfare systems of the different countries took also seems to reflect the inherited initial differences.

Slovenia's welfare model became an example of mixed corporatist conservative (Bismarckian) and social-democratic (Beveridgean) system. Minor reforms, such as the introduction of a supplementary pension scheme based on individualized savings, voluntary health insurance, active labor market measures, have been undertaken; however, the state retained its stronghold. Similarly, Croatia kept the mixed Bismarckian/Beveridgean model, while introducing some (neo)liberal elements promoted by the IFIs. Despite reforms, various exceptions made to dampen their adverse effects or to preserve privileges have diluted the new elements. Serbia's and Montenegro's welfare systems suffered tremendously during the 1990s when their functionality was brought under question. The overthrow of the previous political regime allowed the two countries to rebuild their systems. Albeit under different administrations,[1] both chose a model based on the features of the previous conservative welfare system – the state preserved a dominant role in social services provision offering porous security. Finally, Macedonia proved most susceptible to the neoliberal trend, as it gradually started abandoning the inherited welfare system and developing a residual welfare model. Expenditure rationalization, privatization and targeting have become its core characteristics. Kosovo's path-departure was even more abrupt and its post-conflict welfare design, constructed as a product of international interventionism, has been typical of the unfinished state-building process (Stambolieva, 2012).

THE EUROPEANISATION OF CITIZENSHIP GOVERNANCE

Changing Citizenship – Overview of the Main Variables

The Yugoslav constitutional reforms during the 1970s enforced greater autonomy of the federal units whose national elites had very different ideas on how to solve the problems of that period consisting of stagnating economy, soaring inflation, rising unemployment and widening regional disparities. Diverging trends particularly came to the fore after the collapse of the federation. For instance, the choices of the national elites in Serbia and Croatia that led to war, Slovenia's war avoidance, Macedonia's own interethnic conflict, and the national post-secession and post-conflict responses significantly impacted the countries' future paths. Subsequent democratic consolidation, political choices, economic progress, social organizing and international (European) integration revealed differences in pace and substance, the combination of which guided the profiling of the individual approaches to social citizenship.

The context of Yugoslavia's violent breakup assisted the creation of 'exclusionary and ethnicized models of citizenship' (Cerami & Stubbs, 2011, p. 21; see also Shaw & Štiks, 2013). Divisions along ethnic and national lines were successful attention diverters and also facilitated the development a web of clientelistic relations among political, economic elites and the dependent population, most visible in the privileged treatment of war veterans, persons disabled by war, their families, or attending to refugees and internally displaced persons (cf. Cerami & Stubbs, 2011; Belogrey et al., 2012). Elite capture continued to impede economic progress and democratic development even after the wars had ended (Džihić et al., 2012).

Socioeconomic indicators, for instance, gross domestic product, employment, and poverty rates, show a straightforward country gradation from the most successful case of Slovenia, followed by that of Croatia, Montenegro, then Serbia, and finally Macedonia and Kosovo (EBRD, 2010a; Stambolieva, 2012). Evidence of transformation from a semi-closed to market economy has not been that straightforward. Economic liberalization, on average, has been most advanced in Slovenia and Croatia, then Macedonia, Serbia, Montenegro, and finally Kosovo (EBRD, 2013). Economic liberalization has failed to yield positive results in those states where resources have been captured to privilege the elites' position in economic and state affairs.

Political transformation indicators demonstrate a reverse pattern when compared to the case of economic achievements. Slovenia transformed early into a 'consolidated' democracy (Freedom House, 2013; Bertelsmann Stiftung, 2014). Democratization has been most 'defective' in Kosovo, Macedonia, Montenegro, and then Serbia in that order (Bertelsmann Stiftung, 2014), whereas Croatia,[2] although not completely freed from the ghosts of the past, has been consolidating a democratic regime. Within the newly opened up democratic space, political elites had to seek political alliances. Public voice had however suffered under the conditions of ethnic conflicts, elite-captured political and economic structures, as well as neutralized labor (cf. Stambolieva, 2013). Dysfunctional state structures mainly served elite interests and have been disruptive to the social component of citizenship.

Dependency on international loans largely attached to a neoliberal agenda (Deacon, 2007) had additionally countered public demands on the state. The penetration of neoliberal ideas, demanding less state involvement in welfare, is not to be mistakenly associated with weak state structures or the triumph of free markets. With elites meddling in state and market affairs, the neoliberal success in some of the post-Yugoslav states can be attributed

THE EUROPEANISATION OF CITIZENSHIP GOVERNANCE

to the phenomena of state capture and clientelism (cf. Stubbs & Zrinščak, 2015), which tend to undermine the welfare state.

The EU has played an uneven role. Countries that underwent faster European integration were exposed more strongly to the EU's influence, in line with its Social Agenda, whose focus has been on adapting systems of social protection and pensions to demographic challenges, stimulating competitiveness, employment and social dialogue, as well as promoting social inclusion of the most vulnerable (Commission of the European Communities, 2005). Conversely, belated European integration has negatively affected the social dimension in the candidate states, not least because of its changing nature on the supranational level itself, as a result of the ongoing economic and financial crisis (also Stubbs & Zrinščak, 2015).

The combined effect of these factors took its toll on social citizenship. Thus, the fact that social partners have been incorporated in the policy-making structures from the beginning of the transition certainly facilitated the neo-corporatist decision-making approach in Slovenia, which preferred gradualist transformation and retention of the welfare state. Deferred democratization in Croatia made social policies contingent on power relations, forcing political elites to accommodate various social needs either to quiesce social groups or to meet their claims. Defective democratization in Serbia, Montenegro and Macedonia hampered already weakened social groups to play a key role in policy-shaping, making their welfare systems mainly contingent on elites' choices. Elites' approaches nevertheless differed, depending on the different traditional and transitional contexts. While Serbia's and Montenegro's elites adopted a paternalistic approach toward social policy, characterized by provision of basic social security for social order preservation, Macedonia's elites embraced the international neoliberal trend of liberalization, retrenchment and privatization. Particularly related to the transition, Serbia and Montenegro's governments have long been skeptical toward international interference, while Macedonian elites have actively sought it out. Kosovo has been the most extreme case in this sense, as, due to its limited sovereignty, it was the international community that set its policy agenda. The new welfare structure, albeit path-departing, enhanced Kosovo's inherent specifics – that of a top-down agenda-setting creating residual and exclusionary policies. The following remarks elaborate the conditions that underpinned these different approaches.

Neo-corporatist Approach: Slovenia

The crisis in Slovenia ensuing after its secession from Yugoslavia was rather short-lived. Ethnic and national cleavages played a less salient role compared to the other former Yugoslav republics, given the relative ethnic homogeneity[3] of the country and prompt closure of the state-building process. Slovenia quickly developed a full-fledged democracy with in-built institutional mechanisms conducive to consensual decision-making (cf. Lukšič, 2010). Faced with the dilemma over how to best proceed under the new conditions, Slovenian decision-makers opted for a gradualist approach toward socioeconomic transformation and rejected the alternative 'shock therapy'[4] (Mencinger, 2004). A strong sense of solidarity and public support to the state's intervention in the interest of decent living conditions for all, strong trade unions and social-democratic party scene were all factors which worked in favor of 'feeding the welfare state'.[5] This approach proved successful for Slovenia, which managed to achieve comparatively favorable macroeconomic indicators and in 2004 joined the EU[6] as one of the economically most successful of the former communist countries. International and European exchanges inspired welfare reform proposals which mainly focused on financial sustainability, economic efficiency and introduction of private elements. However, the corporatist political culture and strong social partnerships prevented deeper reforms and kept social service provision predominantly public as well as based on the solidarity and equality principles. Both center-right and center-left governments' attempts[7] to push reform proposals by circumventing social partners backfired, costing the governments their mandates. 'Slovenians rejected Janša's confrontational style' (Guardiancich, 2011, p. 6) and voted out his center-right government at the 2008 elections. As a first reaction to the global financial crisis and Slovenia's own debt crisis, which threatened colliding with the Euro convergence criteria, Pahor's center-left government extended welfare provisions, simultaneously initiating reform measures, which caused severe reactions from trade unions and students' organizations (Stanojević & Klarić, 2013). After three government reform proposals for the pension system and after the labor market experienced a referendum debacle, the government fell in 2011; however, the relationship between the social partners and future governments remained tense.

Thus, the crisis posed a serious challenge to the country's coordinated market economy approach and reliance on public policies. Slovenia has for a longer period been exposed to criticism over its lack of progress with enterprise restructuring and the sizeable state involvement (cf. EBRD, 2010b), and although a 'radical neoliberal turn' has been consistently resisted (Stanojević & Klarić, 2013, p. 225), the constellation of urgency and fiscal consolidation coercion in times of crisis made Slovenia more vulnerable and opened up possibilities for reexamination of the existing model.

Accommodating Approach: Croatia

Although Croatian political elites have not inherently been inclined toward inclusive decision-making, for any one-sided reform attempts that undermined the public character of the system or the existing social rights, they had to reckon with severe opposition coming from different social groups. While satisfying the needs of the war, veterans and war victims was considered a 'moral obligation' (Stubbs & Zrinščak, 2009, p. 128) during the wars of Yugoslav secession, which, in the aftermath of the ethnicized conflict, spurred clientelist relations between these groups and the political elite (Stubbs & Zrinščak, 2015); other groups had to fight to improve their position. In particular, the delegitimation of the authoritarian leadership that persisted during the 1990s had an empowering effect on social groups. Disillusionment with the nationalist and politicized economic model (Franičević, 2002), whose failing strategy caused an economic crisis in 1998, propelled Croats to depart with the regime. Conversely, the democratizing environment put the demands of different social groups, which consisted mainly of rights and benefits conservation, onto the government's agenda. Internationally driven reforms offset the conservative and clientelist mindset on the Croatian political scene. The new government's pro-reform, neoliberal economic program (Boduszyński, 2010, p. 96) and its inability to bind trade unions and pensioners, however, soon backfired; so the governments after 2003 sidelined the international actors and adopted a more compromising approach. Thus, due to pensioners' pressure, ex post interventions in the pension system watered down the initial reform design (cf. Guardiancich, 2007). Furthermore, a government initiative to introduce mandatory supplementary health insurance was resisted by the opposition, trade unions, medical associations, and the Croatian Pensioners Party, backed by the

THE EUROPEANISATION OF CITIZENSHIP GOVERNANCE

public, which forced the government to yield (Vidović & Pauković, 2011, p. 105). The EU accession process reinforced the position of trade unions and facilitated their profiling into an important decision-making factor on the negotiating table. A new Labor Code adopted in 2009 in order to align Croatian labor legislation with the EU was a product of more than a year of negotiations with the social partners (UATUC, 2010). The adoption of the Joint Assessment of the Employment Policy Priorities of the Republic of Croatia (2008) and the Joint Memorandum on Social Inclusion of the Republic of Croatia (2007) between the EU and Croatia, aimed at preparing Croatia for participation in the open method of coordination in the area of employment and social inclusion, have also been positive examples of consensual decision-making (Stubbs & Zrinščak, 2009).

Thus, Croatian center-right governments, which, with the exception of the short-lived center-left government (2000–03), prevailed throughout the transition, chose to accommodate various social needs and kept public spending, including social spending, high[8] at the expense of increasing the country's indebtedness. Global trends in the direction of economic liberalism narrowed the distance between the parties of the right and the left while the process of European integration 'further strengthened the preference for liberal economic positions of both major parties in Croatia' (Dolenec, 2012, p. 82). As a result, all Croatian governments have had to reconcile international pressures with domestic social groups' demands. While in a period of economic upswing the governments successfully juggled the different forces, the crisis of the last years has made this possibility more difficult. Worsening indicators and tightened external financing conditions motivated rethinking the status quo. The final stage of the EU integration process, which coincided with the global economic crisis, unraveled twofold effects: on the one hand, it exposed detrimental corruption practices and facilitated political change at the 2011 elections, but, on the other hand, also limited the playing field for future policy alternatives to austerity.

Paternalistic Approach: Serbia and Montenegro

For most of the 1990s the regime in the Federal Republic of Yugoslavia tried to artificially keep the old welfare system alive in the midst of international economic and political isolation. It played the card of exploiting state resources, financially exhausting the population, and manipulating nationalist and communist rhetoric to successfully stay in power. It was only after an external intervention (NATO's military operation in 1999) that the oppositional forces could unite and mobilize disillusioned masses seeking change.

Following the regime change, Serbia embarked on transition for the second time (Uvalic, 2010, p. 139); however, deepening political polarization (Spoerri, 2010) held back the process of transformation in political as well as socioeconomic sense. Most reforms, including in the area of social policy, were initiated during the mandate of the first democratic, center-left government (2001–03). The renewal of the membership in the IFIs (the IMF and the World Bank) provided Serbia access to the necessary capital to start restructuring. The reform package was aimed at macroeconomic stabilization, economic liberalization and privatization of socially owned enterprises (Bartlett, 2008, p. 49). The shock therapy approach was moderated by socially sensitive policies, mainly conducted through the maintenance of high public spending, continued subsidizing of loss-making enterprises and introduction of a Social Program that accompanied the privatizations in the period 2002–03 (Pavlović, 2006, p. 269). Interestingly, despite its liberal orientation on the one hand, and the lack of organized social pressure on the other, the government did not blindly follow the recommendations of the international actors, which was most evident in the pension system where Serbia went for parametric reforms and declined the World Bank's proposal of partial privatization. Ensuing center-right governments between 2004 and 2008 slowed down the overall process of reform, partly due to their conservative approach, and partly due to the governments' 'feudalized' organization (Orlović, 2008, p. 174), where each party 'controlled' a certain ministry or public company without much mutual coordination. Additionally, other political issues deprived the government of constructive energy and eventually pushed economic and social policy reforms aside. Open divisive issues related to Yugoslavia's secession and Serbian statehood have been at the forefront of party contestation (Slavujević, 2003; Orlović, 2011). They fed national skepticism toward international involvement and were constant domestic attention diverters. These issues[9] also prevented the EU to play the same integrative role as in Croatia. Thus, also in the arena of welfare, the relationship between Serbia and international actors remained highly contentious, given the international actors' demands for higher fiscal discipline and Serbian governments' reluctance to reform. In principle, Serbian decision-makers reinstated a conservative welfare model in a top-down approach, albeit offering benefits and protection at a very modest level, which have been unable to make up for the transitionally induced social stratification (cf. Orlović, 2008). Therefore, state intervention was used to regulate the poor and buy social peace. Weakened trade unions were unable to assert themselves as a relevant bargaining factor or to mobilize the exhausted citizenry (cf. Stojiljković, 2010). Weak social base and slow democratic consolidation thus enabled the pursuit of paternalistic social policies.

The global economic crisis of recent years coincided with the rule of a center-left government (2008–12), which reinforced the leverage of international feedback. Although the socioeconomic hardship brought the former nationalists, now reformed populists into power at the 2012 elections, it did not reverse the process of growing susceptibility to international influences.

Montenegro pursued own policies in the area in economic and social reform, especially after the Kosovo war in 1999, when the Montenegrin government distanced itself from the policy of the federal state (Vuković & Perišić, 2011). However, similarly to Serbia, also Montenegro chose not to interfere with the established welfare model. Political continuity[10] and the lack of major power shifts averted major disruptions in the existing welfare structures which could have resulted in the loss of electoral support. The economic recovery after 2000 improved the labor market situation and provided the fiscal basis for the social programs which were used by the political elites to retain social peace. The prevalence of the question of statehood and identity issues on the political agenda (cf. Dzankić, 2011) have facilitated the paternalistic attitude in social policy-making, at least until the country's independence. Cooperation with the international organizations was secured by partial acceptance of their proposals, as a result of which, for instance, voluntary pension and health insurance was introduced next to the mainly public systems. With the start of EU accession,[11] the role of the EU started increasing mainly through social dialogue promotion (Dzankić, 2011, p. 215). The faster-paced approximation to the EU thus increased the potential for welfare approach alteration. Aimed at securing EU pre-accession financial assistance, Montenegrin governments focused on enhanced reform of public finances, which had been increasingly affected by the global financial crisis, including a reform of the social system toward greater sustainability and in support of economic growth (Vlada Crne Gore, 2013).

THE EUROPEANISATION OF CITIZENSHIP GOVERNANCE

Neoliberal Approach: Macedonia and Kosovo

Following Yugoslavia's breakup, Macedonia found itself in a downward economic spiral. The loss of the Yugoslav market and of the transfers from the federal development funds, the embargo on the northern neighbor (Serbia), and the embargo imposed from the south (Greece) contributed to weakening of the already fragile Macedonian economy. The transition to market economy turned into a competition over scarce resources. Ever since the early 1990s, Macedonian governments started implementing a policy mix of economic liberalization, privatization of state-owned companies and macroeconomic stabilization, supported by arrangements with the IFIs (Bartlett, 2008). The arrangements with the IFIs became a regular companion to the socioeconomic reform process in the country. During the 1990s, the focus was on 'survival of the welfare system, which was at the same time undergoing transition',[12] whereas, after 2000, reforms intensified with the introduction of cost-containment measures and private elements. Economic liberalization through privatization, tax reforms and slashing of welfare benefits was at the forefront of the first center-right government's agenda (1998–2002). However, after a decade of latent ethnic divisions, an armed conflict materialized in Macedonia as well, which ended with the signing of an internationally facilitated peace agreement, also known as the Ohrid Framework Agreement, introducing a bi-ethnic power-sharing model in the political system (Shaw & Štiks, 2013). Related to this conflict as well as the refugee crisis from neighboring Kosovo (World Bank, 2002), public expenditure increased,[13] which eventually contradicted the government's initial goals. In the conflict's aftermath, subsequent governments continued the course of expenditure reduction and resumed welfare sector reforms with the help of international loans. During the center-left government's mandate (2002–06), Macedonia became a candidate for accession to the EU, which especially welcomed 'the substantial progress made in completing the legislative framework related to the Ohrid Framework Agreement' (Council of the European Union, 2006, p. 7). Despite formally recognized successes, there was little effect on people's lives, as unemployment and poverty remained endemic,[14] which was reflected in the electoral mood at the 2006 parliamentary elections. An aggressive economic liberalization program was announced by the new center-right government, 'spiced up' with a variety of populist measures used in exchange for political support – ranging from instruments of larger scope, such as employment in public administration and awarding agricultural subsidies, to smaller measures, such as free public transport for pensioners on certain days, free spa for certain pensioners, social housing, computer vouchers for students. Given that the anticipated economic progress was not achieved, the center-right governments after 2006 exploited the grim socioeconomic picture to install clientelistic relations with political supporters who expected employment and benefits in return for votes (cf. Dehnert, 2010). Both favors and support were distributed along ethnic belonging and party affiliation lines. The highly divided society and dysfunctional democracy undermined the anyway weak social mobilization capacity. The Macedonia–Greece name dispute and related blockade of Macedonia's Euro-Atlantic integration also undercut the potentially positive role that the EU could play. Still, unlike in Serbia, political elites in Macedonia were not skeptical toward international involvement, quite the opposite. Cooperation with the international factor proved important for the survival of the new state (cf. Gligorov, 2002), and was often sought out by the domestic elites. The receptiveness to the neoliberal agenda in the area of social policy may well be attributed to this. In particular, during

53

the last few years, a residual welfare model started to take shape. Dramatic reductions in benefits and number of beneficiaries in the area of unemployment and social protection, but also health care, started to give the impression that, if the option were there, the governments would completely 'get rid of' social policy.

Interestingly, Macedonian economy was less affected by the global economic and financial crisis than its regional peers (EBRD, 2012). A highly controversial project 'Skopje 2014', consisting of the center-right government's investment in construction of neoclassical buildings and sculptures, may have artificially kept a higher economic growth rate. However, in 2012 the impact of the Eurozone crisis began to affect Macedonia through reduced remittances, lower export demand and lower foreign direct investment (EBRD, 2012). Given the country's fiscal dependence on international financing sources which required more fiscal discipline and the government's irresponsible splashing of public resources without backing in the real economy, it was the welfare sector which suffered most.

Albeit having shared the Yugoslav welfare design, Kosovo's system was underperforming when it came to coverage, benefits and services. During the 1990s, Kosovo's socioeconomic and political situation was defined by the wars that the Federal Republic of Yugoslavia was involved in, its exclusionary policies toward Kosovo, the related UN imposed economic sanctions and finally NATO's military intervention. At the beginning of the 2000s, Kosovo was a collapsed system facing a complete post-conflict political, economic, and social makeover. The moment represented a favorable opportunity to break with the past and start anew. The task of reconstruction was assumed by the international actors (mainly the IFIs) according to their neoliberal agenda, having in mind the long-term goal of gradual handing over competences to Kosovo's authorities. Social policies were not a priority in the international actors' agenda[15] and they failed to use the opportunity to employ them as a tool in the reconciliation process, in particular between the different ethnic communities. The Serbian community kept close ties to Serbia, partly as a result of lack of trust in Kosovo's institutions and political intentions, but also because Serbia, which had a different legacy, namely that of a strong public system, has been providing them with access to benefits, such as pensions and welfare, which have been keeping them out of poverty (cf. Cocozzelli, 2007). Furthermore, international actors overestimated the local administrative capacities responsible for policy implementation. The outcome was the reproduction of weak and unstable emergency welfare patterns.

Conclusion

Having outlined the main variables influencing the way the diverse social citizenship types came to be, namely the initial conditions, the economic and political transformation, and the international exchanges, I briefly summarize the main assumptions. Inherited differences among the former republics, expressed through the different levels of economic development and the national elites' choices at the onset of the secession, survived. Democratic consolidation increased the possibility for active political participation and democratic control of governments' actions. The formation of functional systems of checks and balances proved conducive to a social citizenship approach in favor of the state's redistributive role. Conversely, the IFIs' proposals suggesting less state involvement in the organization and provision of social security found fertile ground in economically less

THE EUROPEANISATION OF CITIZENSHIP GOVERNANCE

viable, financially dependable and democratically defective systems. The process of European integration also increased the likelihood of international exchanges, though its role has been rather uneven. Belated European integration has had an adverse impact on citizenship, including its social component.

The global economic crisis brought inherent systems' shortcomings to the surface. In the light of it, different reactions can be expected. Democratic regimes would find it hard to circumvent interest groups and public discontent when taking decisions, while clientelist policies and state capture in defective regimes may prove to be risky for the welfare structures, reinforce inequality stimulating practices and thus have an adverse effect on social citizenship. On the other hand, global pressures drew attention to the magnitude of international economic interdependencies and thus call for internationally negotiated political responses. As a result, the national playing field and the possibility for isolated decision-making on welfare policies have been restricted, regardless of the regime. Higher degree of policy convergence among countries could be a likely scenario for the future, whose direction would depend on the outcome of internationally competing ideas.

Acknowledgements

I would like to thank the editors of this volume for their guidance and valuable feedback.

Disclosure Statement

No potential conflict of interest was reported by the authors.

Notes

[1] Serbia and Montenegro became part of the Federal Republic of Yugoslavia in 1992, which existed until 2003 when the State Union of Serbia and Montenegro was founded. In 2006 Montenegro and Serbia finally became independent sovereign states. It should be mentioned that Kosovo was an autonomous province within the former socialist Republic of Serbia. Since 1999 it has been under UN administration and in 2008 it proclaimed independence.

[2] The Bertelsmann Transformation Index classifies Croatia together with Slovenia as a consolidating democracy, whereas the Freedom House Nations in Transit reports consider it a semi-consolidated democracy, together with Serbia, Montenegro and Macedonia. Political indicators are worst in Kosovo, which is branded a semi-consolidated authoritarian regime (Freedom House, 2013).

[3] In 1992, citizens of other former Yugoslav republics who failed to obtain Slovenian citizenship were erased from the Slovenian register of permanent residents and consequently stripped off all rights and declared illegal. On two occasions, in 1999 and 2003, the Slovenian Constitutional Court found the act of erasing unconstitutional; however, the issue continued to spark controversy and discrimination persisted (for details, see Mirovni Institut, 2013).

[4] 'Shock therapy' is a term associated with Jeffrey Sachs, a lead advisor on economic liberalization in the aftermath of communism, who also became involved in Slovenia. Sachs later explained that he was an advocate for end-of-price controls and contested being an advocate of shock therapy in its neoliberal sense and for complete dismantling of government intervention in the economy (Sachs, 2012).

[5] Author's interview with Danica Fink-Hafner (28.09.2011).

[6] Slovenia adopted the Euro as its national currency in 2007. Out of the former Yugoslav republics, it has been the only EU member state until recently. In July 2013, Croatia was also admitted to the EU.

[7] It is nevertheless worth mentioning that while the center-right government's reform proposals have been part of their policy agenda, the center-left government's proposals for reform have been closely related to the looming crisis and fiscal pressures.

THE EUROPEANISATION OF CITIZENSHIP GOVERNANCE

[8] Social expenditure in Croatia has been around 20 percent of GDP – average value between 2000 and 2009 (Stambolieva, 2011, p. 352). For more on Croatia's social spending in comparative perspective, see Stubbs and Zrinščak (2015).

[9] The fact that the way to the EU was inextricably linked to cooperation with The Hague and the question of the status of Kosovo reinforced the political split between pro-European forces and nationalists (Orlović, 2011, p. 26). Serbia gained EU candidate status in 2012 upon delivery of the last war suspects to The Hague and series of concessions on Kosovo.

[10] Interesting fact is that one political figure has held the most important offices for the entire period after the collapse of communism: Milo Đukanović has been Prime Minister of Montenegro between 1991–98, 2003–06, and 2008–10 and has come to power again since 2012. Between 1998 and 2002 he served as Montenegro's President.

[11] Montenegro was granted candidate status in 2010 and started the EU accession negotiations in 2012.

[12] Author's interview with Nano Ružin (07.02.2013).

[13] In 2000 general government expenditure was 33.7 percent of the GDP, in 2001 – 40.3 percent, in 2002 – 40.5 percent, while in 2003 it declined again to 34.5 percent (EBRD, 2010a).

[14] Macedonia has continuously registered unfavorable socioeconomic indicators. For instance, both unemployment and poverty rates have remained around 30 percent (cf. Stambolieva, 2011).

[15] Neither the EU-facilitated Belgrade–Prishtina dialogue, which commenced in 2011, referred to social policy issues.

References

Alber, J. (1982) *Vom Armenhaus zum Wohlfahrtsstaat: Analysen zur Entwicklung der Sozialversicherung in Westeeuropa* (Frankfurt: Campus Verlag).

Bartlett, W. (2008) *Europe's Troubled Region: Economic Development, Institutional Reform and Social Welfare in the Western Balkans* (New York: Routledge).

Baum-Ceisig, A., Busch, K., Hacker, B. & Nospickel, C. (2008) *Wohlfahrtsstaaten in Mittel- und Osteuropa-Entwicklungen, Reformen und Perspektiven im Kontext der europäischen Integration* (Baden-Baden: Nomos Verlagsgesellschaft).

Belorgey, N., Garbe-Emden, B., Horstmann, S., Kuhn, A., Vogel, D. & Stubbs, P. (2012) *Social Impact of Emigration and Rural-Urban Migration in Central and Eastern Europe (VT/2010/001)* (Koeln: Gesellschaft für Versicherungwissenschaft und –gestaltung e.V).

Bertelsmann Stiftung (2014) Transformationsindex BTI 2014: Status Index. Available at http://www.bti-project. de/index/status-index/ (accessed 17 March 2014).

Boduszyński, M. (2010) *Regime Change in the Yugoslav Successor States: Divergent Paths Toward a New Europe* (Baltimore, MD: The Johns Hopkins University Press).

Bohle, D. & Greskovits, B. (2007) Neoliberalism, embedded neoliberalism and neocorporatism: Towards transnational capitalism in Cental-Eastern Europe, *West European Politics*, 30(3), pp. 443–466.

Bonoli, G. (1997) Classifying welfare states: A two-dimension approach, *Journal of Social Policy*, 26(3), pp. 351–372.

Cerami, A. & Stubbs, P. (2011) *Post-communist Welfare Capitalisms: Bringing Institutions and Political Agency Back in* (Zagreb, Croatia: The Institute of Economics).

Cerami, A. & Vanhuysse, P. (Eds) (2009) *Post-communist Welfare Pathways – Theorizing Social Policy Transformations in Central and Eastern Europe* (Basingstoke, UK: Palgrave Macmillan).

Cocozzelli, F. (2007) Kosovo, in: B. Deacon & P. Stubbs (Eds) *Social Policy and International Interventions in South East Europe*, pp. 203–220 (Cheltenham, UK: Edward Elgar).

Commission of the European Communities (2005) Communication from the Commission on the Social Agenda. Available at http://eur-lex.europa.eu/LexUriServ/LexUriServ.do?uri=COM:2005:0033:FIN:EN:PDF (accessed 17 March 2014).

Council of the European Union (2006) *Brussels European Council 15/16 December 2005, Presidency Conclusions* (Brussels: European Union).

Deacon, B. (2007) *Global Social Policy and Governance* (London: Sage Publications Ltd).

Deacon, B., Hulse, M. & Stubbs, P. (1997) *Global Social Policy. International Organizations and the Future of Welfare* (London: Sage Publications Ltd).

Dehnert, S. (2010) *Elections and Conflict in Macedonia. Country Analysis* (Berlin: Friedrich Ebert Stiftung).

THE EUROPEANISATION OF CITIZENSHIP GOVERNANCE

Dolenec, D. (2012) The absent socioeconomic cleavage in Croatia: A failure of representative democracy? *Politička misao*, 49(5), pp. 69–88.

Dzankić, J. (2011) Political transformations: Welfare states in transition. Montenegro: A long drive down and tough road, in: M. Stambolieva & S. Dehnert (Eds) *Welfare States in Transition – 20 Years after the Yugoslav Welfare Model*, pp. 202–227 (Sofia, Bulgaria: Friedrich-Ebert-Stiftung).

Džihić, V., Segert, D. & Wieser, A. (2012) The crisis of representative democracy in the post-Yugoslav region. Discrepancies of elite policies and citizens' expectations, *Southeastern Europe*, 36(1), pp. 87–110.

EBRD (2010a) Economic Research and Data. Available at http://www.ebrd.com/pages/research/economics.shtml (accessed 12 December 2010).

EBRD (2010b) *Transition Report 2010: Recovery and Reform* (European Bank for Reconstruction and Development).

EBRD (2012) *Transition Report 2012: Integration Across Borders* (European Bank for Reconstruction and Development).

EBRD (2013) *Transition Report 2013: Stuck in Transition?* (European Bank for Reconstruction and Development).

Esping-Andersen, G. (1990) *The Three Worlds of Welfare Capitalism* (Cambridge, UK: Polity Press).

Franičević, V. (2002) *Politička i moralna ekonomija u prvom desetljeću tranzicije u Hrvatskoj*, *Politička misao*, XXXIX(1), pp. 3–34.

Freedom House (2013) Nations in Transit 2013. Available at http://www.freedomhouse.org/report/nations-transit/nations-transit-2013#.Uym7Vz9dUWY (accessed 17 March 2014).

Galgoczi, B. (2013) *ESM: European Social Model or European Stability Mechanism?* Available at http://www.social-europe.eu/2013/06/esm-european-social-model-or-european-stability-mechanism/ (accessed 28 August 2013).

Gligorov, K. (2002) *Makedonija e se što imame* (Skopje, Republic of Macedonia: Kultura).

Guardiancich, I. (2007) The political economy of pension reforms in Croatia 1991–2006, *Financial Theory and Practice*, 31(2), pp. 96–151.

Guardiancich, I. (2011) The uncertain future of Slovenian exceptionalism, *East European Polics and Societies*, 26 (2), pp. 380–399.

Inglot, T. (2008) *Welfare States in East Central Europe 1919–2004* (New York: Cambridge University Press).

Lukšič, I. (2010) Das politische system Sloweniens, in: W. Ismayr (Ed.) *Die politischen Systeme Osteuropas, 3., aktualisierte und erweiterte Auflage*, pp. 729–772 (Wiesbaden, Germany: VS Verlag für Sozialwissenschaften).

Manning, N. (2004) Diversity and change in pre-accession Central and Eastern Europe since 1989, *Journal of European Social Policy*, 14(3), pp. 211–232.

Marshall, T. H. (2008 [1949]) Citizenship and social class, in: S. Leibfried & S. Mau (Eds) *Welfare States: Construction, Deconstruction, Reconstruction, Volume I: Analytical Approach*, pp. 89–137 (Cheltenham, UK and Northampton, MA: Edward Elgar Publishing).

Mencinger, J. (2004) Transition to a national and a market economy: A gradualist approach, in: M. Mrak, M. Rojec & C. Silva-Jauregui (Eds) *Slovenia. From Yugoslavia to the European Union*, pp. 67–82 (Washington, DC: Word Bank).

Mirovni Institut (2013) The Erased: Information and Documents. Available at http://www.mirovni-institut.si/izbrisani/en/ (accessed 31 October 2013).

Orenstein, M. (1998) A genealogy of communist successor parties in East-Central Europe and the determinants of their success, *East European Politics and Societies*, 12(3), pp. 472–499.

Orenstein, M. A. (2008) Postcommunist welfare states, *Journal of Democracy*, 19(4), pp. 80–94.

Orlović, S. (2008) *Politički život Srbije: Između partokratije i demokratije* (Beograd, Serbia: Službeni Glasnik).

Orlović, S. (2011) Partijski sistem Srbije, in: S. Orlović (Ed.) *Partije i izbori u Srbiji. 20 Godina*, pp. 11–70 (Beograd, Serbia: Friedrich Ebert Stiftung).

Ost, D. (2007) Social forces and the post-communist transition: Why labor turns right, in: D. Lane (Ed.) *The Transformation of State Socialism: System Change, Capitalism or Something Else?*, pp. 77–91 (Basingstoke, UK: Palgrave Macmillan).

Pavlović, D. (2006) Socijalna cena tranzicije, *Sociološki pregled*, XXXX(2), pp. 263–281.

Petritsch, W. (2014) Bosnians Are Hungry in Three Languages. Available at http://www.balkaninsight.com/en/article/bosnians-are-hungry-in-three-languages (accessed 19 March 2014).

Sachs, J. (2012) What I Did in Russia. Available at http://jeffsachs.org/2012/03/what-i-did-in-russia/ (accessed 4 June 2013).

THE EUROPEANISATION OF CITIZENSHIP GOVERNANCE

Schubert, K., Hegelich, S. & Bazant, U. (Eds) (2009) *The Handbook of European Welfare Systems* (London: Routledge).

Shaw, J. & Štiks, I. (2013) Introduction: Citizenship in the new states of South Eastern Europe, in J. Shaw & I. Štiks (Eds) *Citizenship after Yugoslavia*, pp. 1–14 (Oxford, UK: Routledge).

Slavujević, Z. (2003) Razvrstavanje biračkog tela i relevantnih stranaka Srbije na osi "Levica-Desnica", in: J. Komšić, D. Pantić & Z. Slavujević (Eds) *Osnovne linije partijskih podela i mogući pravci političkog pregrupisavanja u Srbiji*, pp. 129–162 (Beograd, Serbia: Friedrich Ebert Stiftung).

Spoerri, M. (2010) Crossing the line: Partisan party assistance in post-Miločević Serbia, *Democratization*, 17(6), pp. 1108–1131.

Stambolieva, M. (2011) Conclusion: The post-Yugoslav welfare states – from legacies to actor shaped transformations, in: M. Stambolieva & S. Dehnert (Eds) *Welfare States in Transition – 20 Years after the Yugoslav Welfare Model*, pp. 345–363 (Sofia, Bulgaria: Friedrich-Ebert-Stiftung).

Stambolieva, M. (2012, 12–13 October) Kosovo – from state of welfare emergency to welfare state? in: *Economic Development and Political Transition in Kosovo* (Prishtina: American University in Kosovo).

Stambolieva, M. (2013) Welfare and democratization – comparing Croatia, Serbia and Macedonia, *Social Policy & Administration*, 47(2), pp. 142–160.

Stanojević, M. & Klarić, M. (2013) The impact of socio-economic shocks on social dialogue in Slovenia, *Transfer: European Review of Labour and Research*, 19(2), pp. 217–226.

Stojiljković, Z. (2010) Sindikati i zaposleni u raljama tranzicije i krize, in: FES, CSSD & CeSID (Eds) *Kako građani Srbije vide tranziciju: istraživanje javnog mnenja tranzicije*, pp. 149–164 (Beograd, Serbia: Friedrich Ebert Stiftung).

Stubbs, P. & Zrinščak, S. (2009) Croatian social policy: The legacies of war, state-building and late Europeanization, *Social Policy and Administration*, 43(2), pp. 121–135.

Stubbs, P. & Zrinščak, S. (2015) Citizenship and social welfare in Croatia: Clientelism and the limits of 'Europeanisation', *European Politics and Society,* 16(3), pp. 395–410.

Tavits, M. & Letki, N. (2009) When left is right: Party ideology and policy in post-Communist Europe, *American Political Science Review*, 103(4), pp. 555–569.

UATUC (2010) *UATUC Info No. 11 May/Jun 2010* (Zagreb: Union of Autonomous Trade Unions of Croatia).

Uvalic, M. (2010) *Serbia's Transition: Towards a Better Future* (Basingstoke, UK: Palgrave Macmillan).

Vidović, D. & Pauković, D. (2011) Welfare state in transition: Political transformations. The case of Croatia, in: M. Stambolieva & S. Dehnert (Eds) *Welfare States in Transition – 20 Years after the Yugoslav Welfare Model*, pp. 92–114 (Sofia, Bulgaria: Friedrich-Ebert-Stiftung).

Vlada Crne Gore (2013) *Nacionalni Plan Razvoja 2013–2016 "CRNA GORA 2016" Prvi nacrt* (Podgorica, Montenegro: Vlada Crne Gore).

Vuković, D. & Perišić, N. (2011) Opportunities and challenges of social security transition in Montenegro, in: M. Stambolieva and S. Dehnert (Eds) *Welfare States in Transition – 20 Years after the Yugoslav Welfare Model*, pp. 165–201 (Sofia, Bulgaria: Friedrich-Ebert-Stiftung).

Whyman, P. B., Baimbridge, M. & Mullen, A. (2012) *The Political Economy of the European Social Model* (London: Routledge).

World Bank (2002) *FYR Macedonia: Public Expenditure and Institutional Review*, Report No. 23349-MK (Washington, DC: World Bank).

Zakošek, N. (2008) Democratization, state-building and war: The cases of Serbia and Croatia, *Democratization*, 15(3), pp. 588–610.

Citizenship and Social Welfare in Croatia: Clientelism and the Limits of 'Europeanisation'

PAUL STUBBS* & SINIŠA ZRINŠČAK**

*The Institute of Economics, Croatia
**Faculty of Law, University of Zagreb, Croatia

ABSTRACT   *This article addresses clientelism as a complex structure impacting on social welfare in the context of transition, war, new nation-state building and authoritarian populist political settlements. The paper explores the development of clientelistic welfare in Croatia through an examination of captured and categorical distributional effects, the dominance of nationality over territorial-based citizenship claims, and the politicisation of the nature and scale of governance. The privileging of the rights of war veterans and of those of Croatian ethnicity particularly from neighbouring Bosnia-Herzegovina constitute dominant clientelistic practices largely resistant to change. The capacity of the European Union (EU) accession process to counter clientelistic aspects of welfare has proved to be extremely limited. Although the accession process impacted on and reconfigured economic, political and social arrangements, this was not a radical 'break' with the social and political circumstances, particularly in the 1990s, which had produced and consolidated these clientelistic welfare arrangements. Indeed, after the gaining of EU membership on 1 July 2013, with the translation of EU-led austerity politics, ideas of social citizenship may be unravelling once more in Croatia.*

Introduction

This paper explores the governance and lived realities of citizenship and social welfare in the Republic of Croatia. It suggests that some important aspects of welfare entitlements, particularly in connection with citizenship, cannot be adequately understand and described without invoking the concept of clientelism. Although taking different forms in different historical conjunctures, clientelistic forms of capture, defined here as consisting of distorted modes of governance, exclusivist definitions of citizenship and an asymmetric redistribution of resources, continue to structure social welfare in Croatia. Clientelism, then, represents a strong structural force in politics, the economy and social policy, encompassing far more than a 'mindset' (Stambolieva, 2015). Clientelism may be explicit, when particular political elites trade directly favours for votes, or it can be institutional or hegemonic, defining an informal political common sense. Furthermore, the article argues that not only because of slow and late Europeanisation in Croatia compared to other Central and Eastern Europe countries, but also because of the very nature of the Europeanisation process, the capacity of accession to restrain the clientelistic aspects of welfare was extremely limited. Although the accession process impacted on and reconfigured economic, political and social arrangements, this was not a radical 'break' with the social and political circumstances, particularly in the 1990s, which had produced and consolidated these clientelistic welfare arrangements. Indeed, after the gaining of European Union (EU) membership on 1 July 2013, with the translation of EU-led austerity politics, ideas of social citizenship may be unravelling once more.

The paper begins by sketching the relationship between governance, citizenship and social welfare at diverse scales before addressing the issue of clientelism in general and in its post-communist and Southern European variants. This is then followed by an overview of the changing contours of both citizenship and social welfare in Croatia and the extent to which they have been affected by clientelism and other forms of exclusivity, notably ethnicised nationalism. A tentative final section outlines the prospects for changes in these arrangements in the context of the current economic and financial crisis and, in addition, the prospects for change in the light of EU membership.

Beyond Regime Theory

Here, what are often seen in the literature as unitary citizenship and welfare 'regimes' are treated as much more fluid, dynamic and fragmented 'assemblages', 'ensembles of heterogeneous elements' (Collier & Ong, 2005, p. 5) which should not be reified as 'final or stable states' (Marcus & Saka, 2006, p. 106). Processes of 'Europeanisation' are, therefore, also much more complex and multidimensional than is often discussed. A great deal of the 'Europeanisation' literature remains focused on the extent of 'catch-up' or 'convergence' towards a single model of European citizenship or welfare. In Radaelli's terms, Europeanisation refers to:

> processes of (a) construction (b) diffusion and (c) institutionalisation of formal and informal rules, procedures, policy paradigms, styles, 'ways of doing things' and shared beliefs and norms which are first defined and consolidated in the making of EU decisions and then incorporated in the logic of domestic discourse, identities, political structures and public policies. (Radaelli, 2003, p. 30)

This framing, in our view, limits the space to address contradictions, contestations and 'the play of contingency' (Hall, 2007). Both citizenship and welfare are mobile assemblages rather than hermetically bounded forms, so that their multiple articulations across diverse scales is better understood in terms of a variable geometry of constellations of forces and flows, sometimes coming together within 'perverse confluences' (Dagnino, 2007) deriving from two or more different, even antagonistic, sources or political projects.

Europeanisation, as Lendvai reminds us, is as much about 'constructing subjectivities and identities' (Lendvai, 2007, p. 27) as it is about policies. It is also about 'translation' and 're-domaining' as new policy sectors are created, old ones transformed and new mergers of different policy areas are created (Clarke et al., 2015). Ideas of 'European citizenship' and a 'European social model' encompass, therefore, a range of understandings that are constantly being reconfigured, reframed and recoupled, as well as disputed and

THE EUROPEANISATION OF CITIZENSHIP GOVERNANCE

contested. Crucially, in addition, some Europeanisation literature assumes a unidirectional and all-powerful impact of Europeanisation in which the changing of laws produces equivalent changes in lived practices, forgetting the translation work undertaken by a wide range of actors, including administrators and bureaucrats, advocacy NGOs and networks, and those on the receiving end of policy changes. In this context, there is a need to study Europeanisation together with other forces, including globalisation (Kostovicova & Bojičić-Dželilović, 2006), to trace carefully changes which occur in the process of EU accession and membership. It is not insignificant that Croatia joined the EU at a time when the relationship between the economic and social dimensions of the EU is being restructured as a reaction to the deep economic and financial crisis, culminating in a new core and periphery within the EU and the imposition of new kinds of disciplinary austerity politics. A 'European social model' which was already 'fuzzy' (Stambolieva, 2015) underpinned by the rather 'soft' conditionalities of the 'Open Method of Co-ordination' is now largely subordinated to neo-liberal economic logics although the impacts of these logics take different forms in different places.

Marshall's view of 'citizenship' as a linear, sequential, progression from civic/legal, through political to social citizenship (Marshall, 1950), also needs reworking. Outside of the particular British context which he, arguably, misreads, it is not merely that, elsewhere, the process is slower, more uneven and chaotic but, rather, as Garcia (1994) argues regarding Southern Europe, and we would assert regarding post-socialist societies, it is 'completely different'. Understanding that 'forms of citizenship are situated in historical contexts, political projects and cultural formations' (Clarke et al., 2014, p. 12) draws attention to the 'work' needed to make or re-make citizenship. Citizenship, then, is located inside, and not prior to, the social relations which constitute it. These can be seen as both 'vertical', the relation between states (and state-like actors) and individuals ascribed as citizens or non-citizens and, crucially, also horizontally, in terms of the relationships between individuals and groups themselves. These processes are, also, always embedded in transnational and translocal processes, often ignored within a dominant 'methodological nationalism' and within an equally flawed and flattening 'methodological Europeanisation'.

Citizenship, then, is fluid, contested and 'enacted' from below (Isin, 2008, p. 16), sometimes in ways which do not fit with *de jure* or de facto assigned statuses. As Sassen noted, 'citizenship results in part from the practices of those who are excluded by it' (Sassen, 2005, p. 84) so that, in a way, it is defined 'at its margins' (Clarke et al., 2014) or through its paradoxes and exceptions. The 'work' needed to naturalise the concept, and see it as equivalent to, variously, the nation, the state, ethnicity, culture and the like, is crucial to particular political projects, including those which were part of the wars of the Yugoslav succession and the creation of new nation-states in the post-Yugoslav space (see Stambolieva, 2015). Citizenship requires the repetition of rituals and norms within the 'habits of the everyday' (Isin, 2008, p. 17). The rescalings of citizenship which occurred, and are still occurring, in an emergent post-Yugoslav space, were multiple, complex and contested, causing a further questioning of radical breaks and a simple equivalence between legal status and lived practices.

Marshall, not unlike welfare regime theorists, is in danger of extrapolating social welfare from the power relations which both produce it and are produced by it, into a more or less constant set of goods and services. Again, a focus on the nation-state level can miss both the transnational dimensions of social welfare and the impact of transnational actors

THE EUROPEANISATION OF CITIZENSHIP GOVERNANCE

(cf. Deacon et al., 1997). How resources are allocated between different groups, including varieties of defined 'non-citizens' is, also, of immense importance. Social citizenship needs to be set 'within a context in which the policies and discursive practices attached to the provision of social rights (may be) ... exclusionary and/or differentiated along lines of class, race, gender, ability and sexuality' (Williams, 1995, p. 145). Regime-based theories, then, are unable to address the multidirectional restructurings of social welfare and, moreover, the diverse ways in which welfare was 'lived' before, during and after the wars of the Yugoslav succession, by different groups holding different status positions in different spaces. The 'co-constitution of multiple spatial scales and the multiscalarity of economic transformation and institutional restructuring' (Lendvai, 2013) also questions the appropriateness of linear models.

Rethinking Clientelism

The concept of clientelistic capture draws attention to the dynamic and active role of political agency in shaping particular assemblages of welfare and citizenship which both include and exclude, enabling us to move beyond rather abstract notions of 'modernisation' and 'Europeanisation' to describe processes of change over time and the complex ways in which these changes are lived, accepted and resisted. Expanding on earlier arguments regarding the 'captured' nature of social policy in the context of war, an authoritarian nationalist and populist state-building, and a 'delayed Europeanisation' (Stubbs & Zrinščak, 2009), our understanding of clientelism in terms of governance, citizenship and redistributional practices allows for a reconceptualisation of the nature of Croatia's multiple transitions.

Mainstream political science treats 'clientelism' as a kind of 'patronage', to refer to 'the trade of votes or other kinds of partisan support in exchange for public decisions with divisible benefits' (Piattoni, 2001, p. 4) or as 'the distribution of selective benefits to individuals or clearly defined groups in exchange for political support' (Hopkin, 2006, p. 2). It can also be understood as 'a problem-solving mechanism mediated through personalised political relationships and re-signified through symbolic promises' (Iraola & Gruneberg, 2008, p. 3). Most of the literature underlines 'exchange' as a key element in clientelism, usually between politicians and their clients (Weitz-Shapiro, 2009), or as a particular mode of exchange between electoral constituencies and politicians (Kitschelt & Wilkinson, 2007, p. 7). Clientelism may be compatible with formal political competition provided there are elements of elite capture of the state, public administration, electoral rules and processes, the judiciary, and/or the mass media (Grzymala-Busse, 2008).

Our understanding of clientelism refers to a broad set of hegemonic political practices and strategies marked by particularistic modes of governance, exclusivist definitions of citizenship, and asymmetrical distribution and redistribution of resources. Hence, rather than the development of ever more complex typologies of varieties of clientelism, or even 'clientelistic regimes', it is more productive to trace the main dimensions in practice in particular contexts and settings. In Croatia, the conjunction of clientelism and 'authoritarian populism' in the context of new nation-state building reworks notions of who are the key political actors, what are their political projects and above all, breaks down hard and fast distinctions between top-down and bottom-up social processes.

The ways in which the capture of institutions, services, jobs and resources by certain groups is traded for political advantage and for the benefit of a ruling group, albeit

THE EUROPEANISATION OF CITIZENSHIP GOVERNANCE

within formally democratic frameworks marked by the rule of law, is particularly interesting here (Roniger, 2004). The uneven allocation of citizenship which confers particular rights on some while denying those rights to others is, we would suggest, a key feature of clientelism in the context of emerging new nation-states, especially in the aftermath of ethnicised conflicts. While 'fair' distribution is, of course, a cornerstone of modern welfare states, clientelistic patterns of redistribution refer to the capturing of resources and distorted spending on certain categories or groups in, direct or indirect, exchange for votes.

Elements of clientelism have been said to be central to the Southern European welfare model or type (Ferrera, 1996, 2000), in which the family is important, both ideologically and as a welfare provider, in the context of strong religious influence and a legacy of authoritarian regimes, leading to a rather rudimentary welfare state. The model is said to be marked by the persistence of 'institutional particularism' in which 'patronage machines' distribute cash subsidies and perform particularistic manipulations of sections of the welfare state:

> It is certainly true that some form of institutional particularism characterises all developed systems of social protection. But when particularistic ties or networks play a prominent and in some cases determinant role in granting access to important benefits and services, when they even display some form of formal institutionalisation (as was the case in Italy in the sector of invalidity benefits or in Spain in the sector of unemployment benefits for the agricultural unemployed during the 1980s), then particularistic norms and clientelistic circuits start to make a difference in systemic terms. (Ferrera, 2000, p. 170)

Gal (2010), adding Cyprus, Israel, Malta and Turkey to Spain, Portugal, Italy and Greece as an 'extended family' of 'Mediterranean welfare states', suggests that late industrialisation, segmented labour markets, a legacy of authoritarian or colonial rule, and clientelistic bureaucracies, tended to result in rather limited and particularistic forms of social protection. He suggests that the forms of clientelism vary, ranging from the provision of jobs in welfare bureaucracies and the distribution of resources based on political affiliation to the development of practices and legislation favouring groups which are identified with one political party.

Croatia, in our view, exhibits many of these characteristics, together with some aspects of post-communist transition which are neither fully 'authoritarian' nor fully 'democratic'. Cook (2010) has tended to suggest that social welfare and its reform in post-communist countries in Eastern Europe and the former Soviet Union, with the exception of some of the poorer, more rural parts of some countries, which she terms 'neo-patrimonial', cannot be framed in terms of the concept of 'political clientelism'. Nevertheless, the forms of political patronage and corruption which she points to, in which elites play 'fiscal games', social welfare providers become 'brokers for themselves', and services are subjected to 'spontaneous privatisation' and 'shadow commercialisation', can be subsumed under a broad definition of clientelism. Indeed, the fact that 'interest representation' is more likely to be present in the clientelistic Russian Federation than in either 'democratic' Poland or 'authoritarian' Kazakhstan (Cook, 2007), tends to reinforce the salience of the trading of particularistic welfare benefits for political support. The importance of informality in post-communist welfare arrangements can be seen both in terms of the structural capacity of the state to redistribute and in terms of the role of informal local brokers to ensure that basic needs are met. The familiar idea that, in both communist and post-communist societies, the majority of the population have little trust in institutions per se, and tend to resort to connections in terms of people they trust who work in these institutions, is also relevant in terms of the study of clientelism and social welfare.

In Latin America, as in parts of Southern Europe and the post-communist world, survival strategies can become embedded in clientelistic networks which exist as a kind of substitute for, or parallel to, a formal welfare state (Ley, 2011). The role of non-state actors, the increasing use of social funds, as well as innovative and, often, 'pilot' programmes in the provision of welfare is, also, relevant in this context since they often rely on key pro-moters at national and, more importantly, sub-national levels (Penfold-Becerra, 2006; Iraola & Gruenberg, 2008; Weitz-Shapiro, 2009). Much of the literature points to hybrid forms of clientelism somewhere between 'direct' and 'institutional' clientelism in which political actors direct programmes to particular areas or groups in return for electoral support.

A Political Economy of Clientelism and Citizenship in Croatia

Aspects of clientelistic capture can be traced back to the period when Croatia was a part of the communist Yugoslavia, particularly in the context of the political, economic and social crisis in 1980s, reinforcing a view that historical legacies matter (see Stambolieva, 2015). The Croatian sociologist Županov (2002) referred to this period as 'political capitalism', when managers of state-owned companies freed assets primarily through their links with local and national elites who, more or less, behaved as 'oligarchs'. Nevertheless, it was the particular economic, political and social circumstances of the 1990s which shaped sig-nificantly clientelistic social relations. In war and post-war conditions, democracy was con-solidated slowly and in the context an 'authoritarian mode of rule' (Dolenec, 2013, p. 143) and the dominance of one political party, The Croatian Democratic Community (HDZ), in power throughout this period (Kasapović, 2001, p. 21). HDZ, originally more of a network of networks than a formal political party, forged in the quest for statehood and state-build-ing and, ultimately, in the war to secure it, crafted a new political and economic elite, at the same time maintaining power through clientelistic relations with a large number of interest groups, providing access to public goods and other resources in return for political support forming 'a client-patron axis that helped transfer many features of wartime rule into sub-sequent years' (Dolenec, 2013, p. 142). Kasapović points both to the diversity of resources on offer: lavish subsidies from the state budget, privileged access to public sector jobs and diverse forms of privileged benefits, resources and rights; as well as to the diversity of groups supported: Croatian war veterans and the families of war victims, displaced Croats and Croatian refugees from Bosnia-Herzegovina, Vojvodina and Kosovo, and indeed Bosnian Croats more generally, former political prisoners of the Communist regime, and returning Croatian diaspora including former political emigrants (Kasapović, 2001, p. 22).

The wars of the Yugoslav succession played a crucial role, of course. The wars in Croatia and in Bosnia-Herzegovina had massive, albeit complex, implications for the maintenance of clientelistic relations and for a fundamental reworking of citizenship in the context of state-building. Crucially, significant parts of Croatia, the so-called *Republika Srspka Krajina*, captured in fighting between July and December 1991, remained outside of

THE EUROPEANISATION OF CITIZENSHIP GOVERNANCE

Croatian government control, representing an estimated 26 per cent of Croatian territory. Massive internal displacement, estimated at between 250,000 and 500,000, occurred in the last six months of 1991 (Stubbs, 1999, p. 21), followed by over three years of uncertainty, impasse and small-scale military actions. More significant military actions in May 1995 in Western Slavonia and in August 1995 in Dalmatia returned three of the four UN designated sectors to Croatian government control, resulting in a mass exodus of the mainly Serbian population, some 12,000 Serbs leaving in May 1995 and over 200,000 in August 1995 (Stubbs, 1999, p. 22). The Erdut Agreement in November 1995 led to the peaceful reintegration of the final part of occupied Croatian territory, Eastern Slavonia, including the symbolically important city of Vukovar, with a United National Transitional Authority handing over full control to the Croatian Government in January 1998. This sequencing is important since it means that during much of the 1990s, a period of 'ethnic engineering' (Koska, 2011), a significant part of Croatia's population had no connection with Croatian central authorities and no access to Croatian citizenship. Subsequently, a whole battery of laws, institutional arrangements and informal practices hindered the attainment of citizenship, the repossession of housing and the right to social security for those who remained and, even more so, those who left (Koska, 2011).

A second fluid aspect of an emerging citizenship assemblage concerns ethnic Croats from Bosnia-Herzegovina, all of whom had the right to obtain Croatian citizenship. During the war in Bosnia-Herzegovina, over 350,000 people, mostly but by no means all, ethnic Croats, left to Croatia, initially as refugees, many of whom claimed citizenship (Stubbs, 1999). Of course, there were strong linkages between the war in Croatia and the war in Bosnia-Herzegovina, both militarily and politically, with ethnicised nationalisms seeking, but ultimately failing, to construct a stable relationship between ethnicity and statehood (Oberschall, 2007). In addition, Croatia gave the right to ethnic Croats and their descendants, anywhere in the world, to apply for and acquire Croatian citizenship, without losing any other citizenship rights, reflecting the significant role of the wider diaspora in the quest for Croatian statehood and the strong linkages between HDZ and sections of the Croatian diaspora, including Bosnian Croats. Of course, this had a fundamental impact on Croatia's post-war relations with Bosnia-Herzegovina. The fact that most ethnic Croats in Bosnia-Herzegovina gained Croatian citizenship during the war even if they did not settle in Croatia is decisive in terms of subsequent political and social rights. In terms of political rights, Bosnian Croats with Croatian citizenship were, until very recently, doubly enfranchised, being able to vote as part of the Croatian diaspora on a reserved list for Parliament, and, if they had a registered address in Croatia, to vote as 'regular' Croatian citizens. Until recently amended, the electoral register in Croatia contained more registered voters, not including the diaspora, than the census count of the entire Croatian population.

In addition, political authoritarianism contributed to the development of an inherently 'undemocratic' form of capitalism, where close interpersonal relations were instrumental to garner rents and to limit competition, allocating public services, private property and the proceeds from privatisation, on the basis of these relationships even within a nominally functioning 'rule of law' (Ivanković & Šonje, 2011). The legacy of the 'organised robbery' (Baletić, 2003) of privatisation, the lack of transparency in the registration and allocation of private property, and close links between the dominant elite and key sections of the mass media, remain relevant in contemporary Croatia. The dominance of 'insider interests, extreme clientelism, non-market-based financial sector allocation, and a close link of the state and the government with entrepreneurs and the financial sector' (Bićanić, n.d., p. 1) is also still apparent. In short, what others have termed 'crony capitalism' (Bićanić & Franičević, 2000) may be more systemically embedded than was initially thought, taking new forms as new kinds of transnational capitalist arrangements are in place (Cvijanović & Redžepagić, 2011).

Although much has changed in the meantime, in particular with the process of consolidating democracy and the Europeanisation process throughout the 2000s, our argument is that clientelistic relations remained very much in place, albeit, often, in more subtle and less visible forms. In many ways, governments that were in power in the post-2000 period 'socialised high level corruption, state politicisation and continued abuses of public office' (Dolenec, 2013, p. 149). Both processes of democratisation and Europeanisation brought new regulations, more transparency, new procedures, but did not challenge in any systematic way the existing political and economic power relations. Processes of Europeanisation were not 'fictions' (Lendvai, 2015) or 'fake' (Noutcheva, 2007) but they confined compliance to a particular set of technical and political issues which, often, did not address the deep structures of clientelism. Indeed, in some ways, the EU accession criteria in the second half of 2000s actually added a new layer of clientelism within dominant politics. The translation of EU conditionalities regarding minority rights, for example, led to the creation of new forms of interest relations with some minority groups. The main political party representing the Serbian community in Croatia, the Independent Democratic Serbian Party (SDSS), was part of the coalition government from 2003 to 2011, succeeding in changing some discriminary laws which the EU accession process had focused on, but having little impact on de facto discrimination of Croatian Serbs in everyday life. In addition, the election of a Roma MP in 2007, supporting the then ruling coalition although not formally part of it, also coincided with significantly increased investments in some Roma settlements. In a budget revision in 2014, additional monies were allocated for minority projects, in part to secure the votes of minority Members of Parliament. In all three cases, it can be argued that subsidies for particular projects favoured by minority politicians have been as important, if not more important, than structural reforms which create changed conditions challenging discrimination against minorities.

Another important aspect of maintaining clientelistic relations is located in the territorial political structure of Croatia. Although a detailed exploration of this is beyond the scope of this paper, the very creation of counties (*županije*) was used by HDZ Governments in the 1990s to curb the power of urban centres, at that time very much centres of opposition. The counties still remain and, indeed, have played more important roles in the development of social welfare, despite evidence that their existence and powers are more of an obstacle than a driver of effective regional development. In addition, there has been the massive expansion of units of local self-government (be they towns or municipalities) to over 500, many of them lacking sustainability, but having an important role in distributing jobs and resources. Counties and municipalities, together with a battery of state-owned enterprises and new agencies, multiplied the sites of governance in Croatia and, crucially, the multiplication of informal power networks.

Finally, the conditions under which Croatia joined the EU, in the midst of a deep economic and financial crisis, limited the likelihood that membership, per se, would act as a force for change. The fact that new EU disciplinarities focus only on economic conditionalities and, in particular, the need for cuts under the excessive deficit procedure could not create the social preconditions necessary for any kind of radical break with inherited political and clientelistic practices. Indeed, as already visible in many European

THE EUROPEANISATION OF CITIZENSHIP GOVERNANCE

countries, this tended not only to slow down democratisation processes but also to accentuate conservative, semi-authoritarian and xenophobic tendencies, favouring distorted modes of governance, exclusivist definitions of citizenship and an asymmetric redistribution of resources. In the translation of austerity politics, the Croatian government's balancing of domestic pressures and pressures from the EU has tended to reinforce rather than erode clientelism.

Clientelism and Social Welfare in Croatia

There has been very little academic work which explicitly seeks to understand Croatian social policy in the context of clientelistic social relations. Most texts tend to adhere to the 'radical break' thesis in which the election of a new democratic Government in 2000 allowed for a slow Europeanisation of social policy in the last decade, expedited by the process of agreeing a Joint Memorandum on Social Inclusion with the European Commission (Stubbs & Zrinščak, 2010). At the same time, the discussion of the 'captured' nature of social policy and the consequent blockages of attempts at reform have not focused enough on specific political agency, nor on the legacies of war and post-war authoritarian nationalism from the 1990s (Stubbs & Zrinščak, 2009). In addition, there is a lack of qualitative, ethnographic, work on the lived reality of people's livelihood strategies and their encounters with state welfare agencies. Part of the problem is that, within a broad sectoral approach to social policy, there is little scope to address the influence of clientelism, not least in the context of a lack of available data. Still, and despite the absence of empirical analysis, there is sufficient evidence to argue that part of the Croatian social policy cannot be adequately understood outside of the framework of clientelistic relations. This concerns primarily benefits of veterans, disability pensions and the social rights of ethnic Croats in Bosnia and Herzegovina.

The main set of clientelistic relations in Croatian social welfare consequent upon the war, in terms of benefits for veterans of the war from the Croatian side, is not difficult to chart and identify. After the 1991–95 war Croatia developed a comprehensive system of rights and privileges for Croatians who saw active service in the army or as volunteers (termed Croatian 'defenders'), including those killed or disabled in the war and members of their families. Although comparisons are difficult, it does seem Croatia has one of the most comprehensive systems of protection of war veterans, with a significant package of largely passive benefits, as well as positive discrimination for their children (Dobrotić, 2008). The range of support includes personal and family invalidity benefits, pensions, some other cash benefits, additional health-care protection, as well as grants for restoration of destroyed houses, additional unemployment benefits, cheaper credit for business start-ups and additional rights in obtaining shares in privatised companies. The system is largely based on a passive, 'compensational', approach offering relatively high levels of cash assistance, and much less concerned with the social and economic re-integration of ex-combatants. Often, in fact, benefits can be maintained even if the recipient obtains work, thus maximising the 'peace dividend' to Croatian ex-combatants. In addition, it seems to be maintained by both main parties whenever in power. Thus, a report from the Croatian Pension Insurance fund, covering pensions paid in December 2012,[1] lists four kinds of pension and disability pension beneficiaries: (I) those with rights via pension insurance; (II) military, police and others; (III) war veterans from the Homeland War in the Croatian army HV and (IV) war veterans who served in the Bosnian Croat

67

THE EUROPEANISATION OF CITIZENSHIP GOVERNANCE

army HVO in Bosnia. It is clear that pension rights for those in category III are significantly higher than those for other groups. In total, there are 70,579 beneficiaries in Category III, including 58,424 recipients of invalidity benefits. The average pension is over €700 per month compared to only €320 for Category I recipients.

Related to Croatian war veterans' rights and benefits, the issue of disability pensions is also central to understanding the workings of clientelism in Croatian social policy. Croatia's rate of 12,000 beneficiaries of disability pension per 100,000 people is the highest in Europe (Bađun, 2011). In March 2011, a total of 328,018 disability pension beneficiaries included 138,962 whose rights, based on different categorisations used for former soldiers, derived from service in the 'Homeland War' between 1991 and 1995. Disability pension expenditures amounted to 2.7 per cent of GDP compared to an average of 2.1 per cent in the EU 27, whilst overall pension expenditures were only 7.6 per cent of GDP in 2005 compared to 11.1 per cent in the EU 27. Bađun (2011) has shown that disability pension beneficiaries are generally young (43 per cent are under 59 years of age), and on average enter the pension system when they are 52.6 years old. However, notwithstanding their earlier entrance into the pension system they receive pensions on average for only one year more than old-age pension beneficiaries, which indicates their rather poor health conditions. While this suggests that the general health status of the Croatian population, harsh work conditions and poor socio-economic conditions all contribute to the high rate, it is the combination of war events, particular legislative conditions and the prevalence of corruption which is of most interest here. Based on a medical assessment of the degree of impairment (or invalidity as it is still termed in the Croatian content), based on a notion of percentage of damage to organic functions, the level of impairment of the veterans who receive benefits is significantly lower than non-veteran recipients. While non-veterans who qualify for benefits are assessed as, on average, having a 70 per cent loss of function, some 80 per cent of veteran recipients are assessed at between 20 per cent and 40 per cent, including 37.2 per cent with 20 per cent loss of function. The most common diagnosis among war disability beneficiaries is post-traumatic stress syndrome. Although other beneficiaries have a longer working record and higher levels of disability, on average war disabled receive 2.5 times higher pension than civil disabled people. The most significant legislative changes occurred in 1999 and 2007, both election years, prompting significant increases in the numbers of beneficiaries on each occasion. In the context of high levels of corruption and informal or out-of-pocket payments in the health service, there is a widespread perception that payments to doctors help to account for the high numbers of beneficiaries but there is no clear evidence on this.

The combination of large numbers of beneficiaries, higher levels of benefits for veterans, pre-election changes of legislation which, in contrast to official rhetoric restricting rights, actually created new disability rights and possible corruption, all point to the influence of clientelism. Indeed, the lack of reform in terms of tighter control and monitoring, more transparent and accountable assessment procedures, and a unified register of persons with disabilities, all of which have been proposed in various policy papers but never implemented, despite proved impact in terms of lowering costs, provides further evidence here. It is worth noting that high levels of passive disability benefits for veterans rests alongside a severely underdeveloped system of support services for civil disabled and low levels of integration of children with disabilities into mainstream education.

Although it is more the mode of distribution than the type and level of expenditures which is indicative of clientelism (Weitz-Shapiro, 2009), public discourse and debate

THE EUROPEANISATION OF CITIZENSHIP GOVERNANCE

about the treatment of war veterans is highly instructive. Namely, there is a powerful argument, formulated and circulated mainly by international financial institutions and, indeed, strengthened, in the context of Croatia entering the EU's excessive deficit procedure, that Croatia is a high spender in terms of social protection, suggesting that this is more than it can afford. The World Bank, for example, claims that overall spending on social assistance is high by (rather vaguely defined) 'regional standards' at 3.61 per cent of GDP (World Bank, 2010). This figure includes what are usually termed 'categorical benefits', mainly spending on war veterans and their survivors, which accounted for 1.8 per cent of GDP in 2009. Spending on other social protection benefits was rather low, including child and family benefits for families (0.81 per cent), civilian disabled, (0.07 per cent), vulnerable children, adults and elderly (0.22 per cent), low-income households (0.27 per cent) and around 0.5 per cent of GDP as welfare spending by local governments. Comparative EU data (Eurostat, 2013) show Croatia spent 20.6 per cent of GDP on Social Protection in 2011 (similar to figures for 2009 and 2010). Among the EU members Croatia is the 18th ranked in terms of size of spending, with Bulgaria, Czech Republic, Estonia, Latvia, Lithuania, Luxemburg, Malta, Poland, Romania and Slovakia spending less. Spending in neighbouring Hungary (23.0 per cent) and Slovenia (25.0 per cent) is higher. Croatia is the most exceptional, however, when we come to look at the proportion of benefits spent on different social protection functions. 51.1 per cent of social protection expenditure (or 10.7 per cent of GDP) is spent on sickness/healthcare and disability, presumably distorted by veterans' disability benefits.

Any suggestions for reducing this raft of benefits have been fiercely rejected by veterans' associations and leading figures within all major parties, both nationally and locally. The discourse in favour of maintaining benefits is largely moralistic, in terms of the 'debt' to those who made it possible for all to live in a free, independent and prosperous Croatia. Politicians of all parties, but particularly the right, continue to frame politics in terms of the significance of the 'Homeland War' in achieving Croatian statehood and territorial integrity. Although there is no recent research on public perceptions, it is likely that the principle would receive broad support, bearing in mind that in a general low-trust society, both in institutions and people, war veterans' organisations are among those most highly trusted. In a sense, it is less the fact of the wide range of benefits and rights, or their efficiency or lack of it as a social protection tool, but, rather, the fact that such benefits are based on a clientelistic exchange between politicians and a particular organised group which is of interest here. On this and other matters, as noted above, war veterans' organisations act in public not only as interest organisations but as powerful networks exercising political agency on a wide range of political issues, often merging with those of key HDZ figures. It would be wrong to consider war veterans as a unified block: there are a range of veterans' voices across the political spectrum, but the political symbiosis between leading associations and the dominant political elite is clear and demonstrable. Even more, the political significance of veterans' affairs has been recognised by politicians from all parties and reflected in the fact that in every Government there has been a Ministry to address their interests and concerns. A Veterans' Register also exists, issued by the Ministry of Defence in 2005 and updated in 2008. The register was finally made public, amid numerous protests, in December 2012 and includes some 500,000 names, far in excess of the number who saw front-line service of any kind. Although the register is the basis of a set of privileges and rights for veterans and their families, it is still unclear if the fact of making it public will contribute to deconstruction of these clientelistic relations. Veterans' protests tend to be more radical when a centre-

THE EUROPEANISATION OF CITIZENSHIP GOVERNANCE

left government is in power, with an organised encampment outside the Ministry of Veterans' affairs in late 2014 a proactive attempt to cement veterans benefits within the Croatian Constitution and demanding the removal from office of those who they see as 'relativising' the suffering of Croatian war veterans with civilians or with those fighting on the other side.

The lack of data is particularly the case in terms of the issue of social rights claimed by ethnic Croats in Bosnia-Herzegovina but this issue is still highly instructive for understanding clientelistic relations. Of course, the extension of citizenship rights can be traced rather clearly, whereas the existence of a kind of transnational ethnicised social policy assemblage, in which the Croatian state's social policy is extended to those Croats living in Bosnia-Herzegovina, is harder to track in any meaningful way. In addition to these 'normalised' citizenship rights, there is also speculation that many holders of dual Croatian and Bosnian citizenship, whose primary residence is in Bosnia-Herzegovina, claim some specific social benefits in Croatia. The incentive to claim maternity and child benefits may be particularly acute since there is a significant difference between these benefits in Croatia, where they are linked as much to a rhetoric of demographic renewal as to an anti-poverty discourse, and Bosnia-Herzegovina where only a small number of regional government units (Cantons) have any such benefits and, usually, at rather low levels. The fact that claiming and receiving such benefits necessitates a Croatian address also suggests the importance of clientelistic relations and the role of local political party and other intermediary structures.

In addition, although the illegal siphoning of funds to a political–military complex of Bosnian Croats has ended, there remain elements of Croatian state support for both education and health services in the Croatian parts of the Federation of Bosnia-Herzegovina, aided by the fact that, under the Bosnian constitution as a part of the Dayton peace agreement, health and education services are the responsibility of Cantons so that each canton has a Ministry of Health responsible for primary and secondary health care and a Ministry of Education responsible for education services and the curriculum. Inevitably, then, risk-sharing and economies of scale in health care and education has brought Bosnian Croats into a wider transnational ethnicised system, although the extent of this is difficult to ascertain directly. With regard to education, the Government supports a University in Mostar. Sarajlić (2012, p. 15), using Ministry figures, suggests that in 2011, the Croatian Government allocated over €800,000 to support 159 different educational institutions in Bosnia-Herzegovina, mainly in Croat-majority areas but also to support Croatian minority projects and programmes.

In terms of health care, in addition to a state of the art hospital in the city of Mostar, Sarajlić (2012, p. 16) suggests that the 2011 budget allocated some €200,000 to support health centres and local NGOs, often linked to support for Bosnian Croat war veterans. In addition, some health care is provided to Croat citizens living in Bosnia-Herzegovina, particularly mothers giving birth to children in Croatian hospitals where facilities are better than where they reside. Underpinning all of these practices is, in fact, a Constitutional pledge to be concerned with those Croats living outside of the Republic of Croatia although recent, stricter, rules regarding residence, brought in to curb electoral abuses, may also have implications in terms of social welfare.

What is very clear is that the process of EU accession and, indeed, membership, has had little or no impact on clientelism in social welfare. In part, of course, this is because, as noted above, social policy is much more of a 'soft' than a 'hard' conditionality, in the context of most aspects of social policy retained as a nation-state responsibility, untouched

THE EUROPEANISATION OF CITIZENSHIP GOVERNANCE

by the negotiations around Chapter 19 of the *acquis* on social policy and employment. As noted above, the development of a Joint Inclusion Memorandum was important in changing some social policy practices although, within regular progress reports, this was more focused on the implications for governance and administration than on specific restructuring of social welfare. Crucially, issues of veterans and disability benefits, and issues of support to Bosnian Croats, were never raised as significant issues. In some ways, the new excessive deficit procedure as an EU member state reinforces a demand to curtail social spending in the name of fiscal consolidation and austerity. This continues, as we noted above, a long tradition of similar demands from the World Bank. However, again, most if not all of the clientelistic benefits remain outside of discussion reinforcing, instead, a discourse of high social benefits and widespread fraud which are focused on so-called undeserving beneficiaries.

Conclusions

Although more in-depth research is needed, the paper has shown that many aspects of contemporary social welfare in Croatia: the welfare rights of Croats in neighbouring Bosnia and Herzegovina, and the extent of rights enjoyed by war veterans, including those diagnosed as disabled, cannot be understood outside of the notion of clientelistic exchange, framed through suboptimal governance and exclusivist ideas of citizenship. Many of these aspects of Croatian social welfare have become woven into political 'common sense', so that no major political party dare question them, thus undercutting the political advantage to be gained by one political party, while ensuring that they remain core elements of Croatian social policy regardless of changes in Government.

In addition, clientelism in social welfare is multi-scalar, involving also regional and local exchange relations which have a degree of relative autonomy from central structures. In this context, and when the current deep and transnational economic and financial crisis is considered, there is little hope for EU membership to change significantly Croatian social policy. According to comparable data, Croatia had an at-risk-of-poverty level of 21.1 per cent in 2011 which is the fifth highest in the EU, after Bulgaria, Romania, Greece and Spain. The EU's main concern is, however, with Government debt so that the state budget has experienced significant cuts in recent years, affecting also the budget for social and health care, and although this was not communicated in public, cuts meant much less money for services. The reduction has been visible in lowering standards, less money for different categories of social care beneficiaries (disabled persons, victims of family violence and so on) and particularly in the health-care sector. The dominance of a fiscal austerity frame over a concern with the consolidation of democracy or the strengthening of social rights is a key element of contemporary post-accession Europeanisation. Though we do not have hard data and lack the full picture, we are witnessing the fragmentation of welfare arrangements, and a significant deterioration of welfare standards. There are also indicators that problems in offering services contribute to a 'strategy of looking for alternatives' which means a rising level of informal and private, quasi-marketised, solutions inside the public sector. This is also fertile soil for bribery, corruption and enhanced clientelism. The kind of welfare assemblage which will emerge from this in the future is hard to predict but any change will depend on rather more fundamental changes to practices of governance and broader socio-economic reforms. In this sense, any appeal for

THE EUROPEANISATION OF CITIZENSHIP GOVERNANCE

'justice-based distributive practices not only in the national, but also in a regional context' (Sarajlić, 2012, p. 22) appears unlikely to resonate, at least for the foreseeable future.

Disclosure Statement

No potential conflict of interest was reported by the authors.

Note

[1] http://www.mirovinsko.hr/UserDocsImages/publikacije/statisticke_informacije/2012/4/Statisticke_informacije HZMOa_4_2012_veljaca2013.pdf (accessed 22 May 2013), http://www.mirovinsko.hr/UserDocsImages/ publikacije/statisticke_informacije/2012/4/Statisticke_informacijeHZMOa_4_2012_veljaca2013.pdf (accessed 22 May 2013).

References

Bađun, M. (2011) Zašto Hrvatska ima mnogo korisnika invalidskih mirovina? (Why are there so many disability pensions beneficiaries in Croatia?), *Newsletter*, Institut za javne financije (Zagreb: Institute of Public Finance), 56.

Baletić, Z. (2003) A wrong conception of stabilisation, in: M. Meštrović (Ed.) *Globalization and Its Reflections on (in) Croatia*, pp. 275–299 (New York: Global Scholarly Publications).

Bićanić, I. (n.d.) The Economic Role of the State in Southeast European Economies in Transition, Paper for WiiW. Available at http://balkan-observatory.net/archive/bicanic.pdf (accessed 22 May 2013).

Bićanić, I. & Franičević, V. (2000) Dismantling crony capitalism: The case of Croatia, CERGE-EI Research Seminar Series 1999-2000. Prague. Conference report: Political clientelism, social policy, and the quality of democracy: Evidence from Latin America, lessons from other regions. Available at http://iis-db.stanford.edu/ evnts/6693/Quito_Conference_Report–Final.pdf (accessed 23 May 2013).

Clarke, J., Coll, K., Dagnino, E. & Neveu, C. (2014) *Disputing Citizenship* (Bristol, UK: Policy Press).

Clarke, J., Bainton, D., Lendvai, N. & Stubbs, P. (2015) *Making Policy Move: Towards a Politics of Translation and Assemblage* (Bristol, UK: Policy Press).

Collier, S. & Ong, A. (2005) Global assemblages, anthropological problems, in: A. Ong & S. Collier (Eds) *Global Assemblages: Technology, Politics, and Ethics as Anthropological Problems*, pp. 3–21 (Oxford: Blackwell).

Cook, L. (2007) Negotiating welfare in postcommunist states, *Comparative Politics*, 40(1), pp. 41–62.

Cook, L. (2010, November 5–6) Political clientelism and social policy: The postcommunist experience. Paper presented to NDRI conference Political clientelism, social policy and the quality of democracy, Quito.

Cvijanović, V. & Redžepagić, D. (2011) From political capitalism to clientelist capitalism? The case of Croatia, *Zbornik radova Ekonomskog fakulteta u Rijeci*, 29(2), pp. 355–372.

Dagnino, E. (2007) Citizenship: A perverse confluence, *Development in Practice*, 17(4/5), pp. 549–556.

Deacon, B., Hulse, M. & Stubbs, P. (1997) *Global Social Policy* (London: Sage).

Dobrotić, I. (2008) Sustav skrbi za branitelje iz Domovinskog rata (Social care system for defenders from the Homeland War), *Revija za socijalnu politiku*, 15(1), pp. 57–83.

Dolenec, D. (2013) *Democratic Institutions and Authoritarian Rule in Southeast Europe* (Colchester, UK: ECPR).

Eurostat (2013, 21 November) News release – social protection, 174/2013.

Ferrera, M. (1996) The "southern model" of welfare in social Europe, *Journal of European Social Policy*, 6(1), pp. 17–37.

Ferrera, M. (2000) Reconstructing the welfare state in Southern Europe, in: S. Kuhnle (Ed.) *The Survival of the European Welfare State*, pp. 166–181 (London: Routledge).

Gal, J. (2010) Is there an extended family of Mediterranean welfare states? *Journal of European Social Policy*, 20(4), pp. 283–300.

Garcia, S. (1994) Implications for a citizen's Europe and the Spanish experience, in: J. Llobera, V. Godard & C. Shore (Eds) *Anthropology of Europe*, pp. 255–275 (London: Berg Press).

Grzymala-Busse, A. (2008) Beyond clientelism: Incumbent state capture and state formation, *Comparative Political Studies*, 41(4–5), pp. 638–673.

Hall, S. (2007) Epilogue: Through the prism of an intellectual life, in: M. Brian (Ed.) *Culture, Politics, Race and Diaspora: The Thought of Stuart Hall*, pp. 269–291 (London: Lawrence and Wishart).

THE EUROPEANISATION OF CITIZENSHIP GOVERNANCE

Hopkin, J. (2006) Conceptualizing political clientelism: Political exchange and democratic theory. Paper for APSA annual meeting, Philadelphia.

Iraola, V. & G. Gruenberg (2008) Clientelism, poverty and gender: Cash conditional transfers in the loop. Paper for GTZ workshop on gender and corruption in development co-operation. Available at http://www.gtz.de/de/dokumente/gtz2008-en-workshop-paper-victoria-iraolaclientelism.pdf (accessed 22 May 2013).

Isin, E. (2008) Theorising acts of citizenship, in: E. Isin & G. Nielsen (Eds) *Acts of Citizenship*, pp. 15–43 (London: Palgrave Macmillan).

Ivanković, Ž. & V. Šonje (2011) *Nedemokratski kapitalizam i nova tranzicija* (Undemocratic Capitalism and the New Transition), ZEF – 1. zagrebački ekonomski forum 2011 (Zagreb: Friedrich Ebert Stiftung).

Kasapović, M. (2001) Demokratska konsolidacija i izborna politika u Hrvatskoj (Democratic consolidation and electoral politics in Croatia 1990–2000), in: M. Kasapović (Ed.) *Hrvatska politika 1990–2000* (Croatian Politics 1990–2000), pp. 15–40 (Zagreb: Fakultet političkih znanosti).

Kitschelt, H. & Wilkinson, S. I. (2007) Citizen-politician linkage: An introduction, in: H. Kitschelt & S. I. Wilkinson (Eds) *Patrons, Clients, and Policies*, pp. 1–49 (Cambridge: Cambridge University Press).

Koska, V. (2011) *The Evolution of the Croatian Citizenship Regime: From Independence to EU Integration*, University of Edinburgh CITSEE Working Paper 2011/15.

Kostovicova, D. & Bojičić-Dželilović, V. (2006) Europeanizing the Balkans: Rethinking the post-communist and post-conflict transition, *Ethnopolitics*, 5(3), pp. 223–241. doi:10.1080/17449050600911091

Lendvai, N. (2007) Europeanization of social policy? Prospects and challenges for South East Europe, in: B. Deacon & P. Stubbs (Eds) *Social Policy and International Interventions in South East Europe*, pp. 22–44 (Cheltenham, UK: Edward Elgar).

Lendvai, N. (2013) Permanent transitions: 'Variegated welfare capitalism' in post-communist Europe, unpublished manuscript.

Lendvai, N. (2015) Soft governance, policy fictions and translation zones, in: J. Clarke, D. Bainton, N. Lendvai & P. Stubbs (Eds) *Making Policy Move: Towards a Politics of Translation and Assemblage*, pp. 131–156 (Bristol: Policy Press).

Ley, S. (2011) Clientelism and formal welfare states: A relationship of substitution? Presented to workshop on democratic accountability states, Duke University. Available at http://duke.edu/~kkk4/2011_clientelism/Ley_4_3_Clientelism%20and%20Formal%20Welfare%20States.pdf (accessed 22 May 2013).

Marcus, G. & Saka, E. (2006) Assemblage, *Theory, Culture, Society*, 23(2/3), pp. 101–106. doi:10.1177/0263276406062573

Marshall, T. (1950) Citizenship and social class, reprinted in: J. Manzer & M. Sauder (Eds) (2009) *Inequality and Society*, pp. 148–154 (New York: W.W. Norton).

Noutcheva, G. (2007) *Fake, Partial and Imposed Compliance: The Limits of the EU's Normative Power in the Balkans*, CEPS Working Document No. 274.

Oberschall, T. (2007) *Conflict and Peace Building in Divided Societies: Responses to Ethnic Violence* (Abingdon, UK: Routledge).

Penfold-Becerra, M. (2006) Clientelism and Social Funds: Empirical Evidence from Chavez's "Misiones" Programs in Venezuela. Available at http://siteresources.worldbank.org/INTDECINEQ/Resources/1149208-1147789289867/IIIWB_Conference_Clientelism_and_Social_FundsREVISED.pdf (accessed 13 May 2013).

Piattoni, S. (2001) Clientelism in historical and comparative perspective, in: S. Piattoni (Ed.) *Clientelism, Interests and Democratic Representation*, pp. 1–30 (Cambridge, UK: Cambridge University Press).

Radaelli, C. (2003) The Europeanization of public policy, in: K. Featherstone & C. Radaelli (Eds) *The Politics of Europeanization*, pp. 27–56 (Oxford: Oxford University Press).

Roniger, L. (2004) Review article: Political clientelism, democracy and market economy, *Comparative Politics*, 36(3), pp. 353–375.

Sarajlić, E. (2012) *Citizenship and Social Justice in Croatia, Bosnia and Herzegovina and Serbia*, University of Edinburgh CITSEE 2012/24.

Sassen, S. (2005) The repositioning of citizenship and alienage: Emergent subjects and spaces for politics, *Globalizations*, 2(1), pp. 79–94. doi:10.1080/14747730500085114

Stambolieva, M. (2015) Welfare state change and social citizenship in the Post-Yugoslav states, *European Politics and Society*, 16(3), pp. 379–394.

Stubbs, P. (1999) *Displaced Promises: Forced Migration, Refuge and Return in Croatia and Bosnia* (Sweden: LPI).

Stubbs, P. & Zrinščak, S. (2009) Croatian social policy: The legacies of war, state-building and late Europeanisation, *Social Policy and Administration*, 43(2), pp. 121–135.

THE EUROPEANISATION OF CITIZENSHIP GOVERNANCE

Stubbs, P. & Zrinščak, S. (2010) Social protection and social inclusion from Lisbon to Europe 2020, in: V. Samardžija & H. Butkovic (Eds) *From Lisbon Strategy to Europe 2020*, pp. 164–181 (Zagreb: Institute for International Relations).

Weitz-Shapiro, R. (2009) Choosing clientelism: Political competition, poverty, and social welfare policy in Argentina. APSA 2009 Toronto meeting paper. Available at http://papers.ssrn.com/sol3/papers.cfm?abstract_id=1450238 (accessed 13 May 2013).

Williams, F. (1995) Race/ethnicity, gender and class in welfare states: A framework for comparative analysis, *Social Politics*, 2(2), pp. 127–159.

World Bank (2010) Croatia. The Social Impact of the Crisis and Building Resilience. Available at http://www.worldbank.hr/WBSITE/EXTERNAL/COUNTRIES/ECAEXT/CROATIAEXTN/0,,contentMDK:22631300~pagePK:141137~piPK:141127~theSitePK:301245,00.html (accessed 12 May 2013).

Županov, J. (2002) *Od komunističkog pakla do divljeg kapitalizma* (From Communist Hell to Wild Capitalism) (Zagreb: Sveučilišna naklada).

Citizenship and Education in the Post-Yugoslav States

NATAŠA PANTIĆ

School of Education, University of Edinburgh, UK

ABSTRACT   *This paper explores interactions between citizenship and education in six post-Yugoslav contexts. The aim is to map out policies shaping the intended young citizens' identities, which might differ from their lived experiences of citizenship. Focusing on the ethnocentric, multicultural, and civic dimensions of citizenship, the paper looks at how education governance structures and policies promote inclusive and exclusive citizenship by adopting and adapting international norms protecting group and individual rights. Universal and consociational education systems have been distinguished, with the ethnocentric and exclusive citizenship concepts reflected in the context-dependent status of different minorities, and in the language policies that perpetuate dominant ethnic groups. Inclusive elements have been recognised in the anti-discriminatory measures for inclusion of Roma students in mainstream education. Minority language instruction options reflect multicultural approaches to linguistic and cultural rights in education, although ethnocentric motives can be discerned behind their territorial implementation. Observance of the EU membership criteria and relevant norms are an important driving force for adopting social inclusion and minority rights in education-relevant legislation and policy documents. The study illustrates how the domestic consolidation and limited implementation of these norms created tensions between ensuring group rights in education and protection of individual human rights and non-discrimination.*

Introduction: Citizenship and Education

This paper examines the interactions between citizenship regimes and education governance structures and policies in six post-Yugoslav countries (Bosnia and Herzegovina, Croatia, Kosovo, Macedonia, Montenegro, and Serbia). Previous studies have identified the ethnocentric, multiethnic and civic dimensions of the citizenship regimes in these countries (Džankić, 2012; Koska, 2012; Krasniqi, 2012; Sarajlić, 2012; Shaw & Štiks, 2012; Spaskovska, 2012; Vasiljević, 2012) based on the most salient features of their constitutions and functioning. In almost all of the post-Yugoslav countries, these studies have found a practice of ethnic engineering, described as the intentional policy of governments and lawmakers to influence the ethnic composition of their population in favour of their dominant ethnic group, whether this practice is legally codified (as in the Serbian constitution defining Serbia as the state of Serbs and others) or pursued through various institutional and administrative practices set within or against the existing laws.

Education is one of the public spheres in which ethnic engineering can be a powerful tool for favouritism of ethnic core groups and the exclusion of others, since political socialisation of citizens is one of its core functions (Gutmann, 1987). Who belongs to the state, nation or homeland is often implied in ideologies, narratives and beliefs that can be officially or unofficially endorsed through education policies and practices. Some of the mechanisms through which inclusive and exclusive concepts of citizenship can be promoted include curricula and the use of languages in schools (Steiner-Khamsi et al., 2002), which shape the institutional arrangements for students' experiences within education structures.

Central to the exercise of full membership in a society are citizens' rights and duties. EU membership criteria and observance of the relevant international norms are an important driving force for adopting social inclusion and anti-discrimination principles. In their education-related legislation and policies, all post-Yugoslav countries have incorporated provisions protecting rights *to* and *in* education. The countries are signatories to a number of European and other international instruments[1] that protect individual rights, as well as grant various group rights, such as cultural and linguistic minority rights. For example, the UN Convention on the Rights of the Child grants individuals the right to equal access to compulsory and free primary education, free access to secondary education and higher education accessible to all (Art. 28).[2] The key instrument protecting minority rights is the Framework Convention for the Protection of National Minorities (FCNM), which covers education on culture, language, history and the religion of minorities (Art. 12–14).

Some studies from the region identified overemphasis of group over individual rights (Pantić et al., 2011; Krasniqi, 2012; Sarajlić, 2012; Spaskovska, 2012). Other studies from the Central and Eastern European countries (Agarin & Brosig, 2009) point to the tensions between upholding ethnic and linguistic minority rights, and developing inclusive education systems while respecting diversity. This paper examines how the ethnocentric, multicultural and civic dimensions of citizenship operate in education governance structures and policies. In particular, it explores the ways in which these structures and policies encourage inclusive and exclusive concepts of citizenship, officially or otherwise, and the ways in which relevant 'European norms' are consolidated locally, for example, whether groups are favoured over individuals in their entitlements to education rights.

A qualitative comparative methodology is used looking for cross-cutting themes that can be illustrated by all or some of the country cases. The data are collected through analysis and close textual interpretation (Merriam, 1998) of education policy documents, while informal interviews with the members from academia, governmental and non-governmental sectors were used to check the accuracy of these interpretations. All data have been collected between January and June 2012. The analysis involved an interpretative approach to determining meaning, salience and connections (Ritchie & Spencer, 1994) and identifying 'themes' by looking at the logics of particular country contexts as part of a wider regional context (Scheppele, 2004).

Interactions Between Citizenship Regimes and Education

The interactions between citizenship regimes and education are analysed applying three sets of interpretative frameworks that distinguish between three dimensions of citizenship:

THE EUROPEANISATION OF CITIZENSHIP GOVERNANCE

(1) collective and individual identities;
(2) ethnocentric, multicultural, and civic interactions between citizenship and education; and
(3) inclusive and exclusive concepts of citizenship

Collective and Individual Identities

According to Joppke (2003, 2007), citizenship is essentially membership in a polity to which *rights* and *identities* are connected. The rights dimension of citizenship includes social rights, protection from discrimination and multicultural recognition. Anti-discrimination measures attempt to remove ethnicity or race as a marker of individual and group differentiation, whereas recognition seeks to perpetuate such differentiation (Joppke, 2007). Citizenship as identity refers to individuals' acting and conceiving of themselves as members of a collective, or the normative conceptions of such acting and conceiving propagated by the state. Thus, citizenship as identity has two possible meanings – the official views propagated by the state and the actual views held by ordinary people, which can differ (Joppke, 2007).

One of the aims of education is to prepare citizens for civic participation and interaction with the state by developing their individual and collective identities (Gutmann, 1987; Spiecker & Steutel, 1995; Bieber, 2007; Čorkalo Biruški & Ajduković, 2008). Education for citizenship can also be seen at the policy or social, and at the individual level (Steiner-Khamsi et al., 2002). At the social level, education is often seen as political socialisation – typically understood to include processes by which states transmit political values and modes of behaviour to citizens (Gutmann, 1987). At the individual level, education is a process by which collective identifications are given private and personal meanings (Steiner-Khamsi et al., 2002). These processes are mutually formative and interdependent as will be discussed later.

This study focuses on the interaction between citizenship regimes and the *policy level* of education for citizenship promoted by the state. It looks at the ways in which education governance structures and policies shape the intended space and dominant discourses within which citizens internalise their identities, views, and experiences of citizenship. However, individuals acquire knowledge and internalise values only partly through what is present at the broader, societal level (see Hromadžić, 2015). Although the individual level is not the focus of this study, this point will be illustrated with other studies on the attitudes of students, parents, and teachers.

Ethnocentric, Multicultural and Civic Interactions Between Citizenship and Education

Ethnocentric, multicultural, and civic dimensions of citizenship are defined drawing on Gutmann's (1987) theories of 'a family state', ' a state of families' and 'a state of individuals', which are subsequently sought in the assumed (desired) relations between the collective and the individual in post-Yugoslav education systems and policies.

Ethnocentric Education for Ethnocentric Citizenship in 'a Family State'

The defining feature of 'the family state' (Gutmann, 1987, p. 23) is that it claims exclusive educational authority as the means of establishing a constitutive relation between individuals and the social good based on knowledge. The family state seeks to create a level of unity and like-mindedness among its citizens (that can be expected only in families, and perhaps not even there) based on its status as the political parent of its citizens. In this perspective, the purpose of education is to cultivate such unity among its citizens by defining and transmitting educationally worthwhile knowledge.

Ethnocentric citizenship regimes seek to affirm an ethnic majority as the dominant conception of nationhood in a given country, which according to Joppke (2003, 2007) has little in common with the legal form of citizenship. In an ethnocentric version of the family state, ethnic belonging comes forth as the defining feature of citizens' identity aligned with the idea of collective (ethnic) good. The purpose of education for the ethnocentric concept of citizenship would, then, be to prepare citizens to think of themselves within the framework of their ethnicity under which their individual ideas of a good life are to be subsumed. Some of the methods for building the ethnocentric nation state through education include establishing a state language and promoting a unified, homogenised historical narrative (Bieber, 2007) by controlling the sources of knowledge considered valid by the education authorities.

Multicultural Education for Multicultural Citizenship in 'a State of Families'

The family state's claim of an exclusive authority over education might never be questioned in a society whose members already agree about what is good and educationally worthwhile. In multicultural societies, such claims are bound to constrain the choices among different ways of life and educational purposes, in a manner that is not always compatible with parents' cultural views. Radically opposed to the family state is 'the state of families', which places authority exclusively in the hands of parents to predispose their children, through education, to choose a way of life consistent with their familial heritage based on their cultural rights (Gutmann, 1987, p. 28).

Multicultural citizenship regimes adopt a conception of minority cultures that grants certain collective rights to such minorities, although no single formula can be applied to all groups (Kymlicka, 1995). This entitlement has been challenged on the grounds that cultural community is a dynamic concept – centuries of contact will have had effects on the groups as they now exist (Tomasi, 1995; Čorkalo Biruški & Ajduković, 2008). Multiple identities and combining group and other identities are the norm in modern societies (Osler & Starkey, 2001). According to Tomasi (1995), each individual has a dynamic cultural membership equally. Thus it cannot generate special rights. The provision of basic education is also an individual right, so we need to distinguish between the instantiation of the principle of universal and free basic education for every child, and the granting of special, group rights to students of different cultural groups.

Multicultural education emphasises the need to preserve the specific cultures of minority groups, for example, through linguistically and culturally sensitive curricula. To avoid the 'free-rider' problem and assure all children the freedom to choose in the future, the state of families limits parental supremacy by requiring schools to teach mutual respect (Gutmann, 1987) and intercultural dialogue (Čorkalo Biruški & Ajduković, 2008).

Civic Education for Civic Citizenship in 'a State of Individuals'

In the civic understanding, citizenship is a territorial construct connected to the states' obligations to individuals based on international law (e.g. protection of human rights and non-

THE EUROPEANISATION OF CITIZENSHIP GOVERNANCE

discrimination), and a decoupling of the state from nation-building (Joppke, 2003). As in the family of states, in a civil society many loyalties and affiliations are tolerated or encouraged (including family, cultural and religious denominations), but cultural difference appears through individual rather than through group rights (Joppke, 2007). In 'the state of individuals' (Gutmann, 1987, p. 33) a desired educational authority is the one that maximizes future choices without prejudicing children towards any conceptions of a good life. This conception of education adopts Rawls' view of citizenship in a constitutional democracy, which regards its citizens as free and equal (Spiecker & Steutel, 1995). Two layers of citizens' identity can be distinguished: a political identity based on the rights and duties of sustaining fair social cooperation over time, and citizens' 'deeper aims and commitments' – their non-institutional, moral identity (Rawls, 1993, p. 30). Citizens must adjust and reconcile these two aspects of their identity in order to affirm the values of justice and see them embodied in political institutions. The role of education is to help children become cooperating members of society, ready to 'propose fair terms of cooperation it is reasonable to expect others to endorse', and be 'willing to abide by these terms provided others can be relied on to do likewise' (Rawls, 1993, p. 81).

Inclusive and Exclusive Concepts of Citizenship

Among the drivers of educational reforms in the region are EU's agendas for social inclusion and regional reconciliation through education as part of the Thessaloniki agenda promoting regional peace, stability and prosperity. The European Commission (2004) defines social inclusion as a process that provides people exposed to the risk of poverty and social exclusion with the opportunity and means for full participation in economic, social and cultural life of the society in which they live. There is a distinction to be made between peaceful coexistence of differences in society ensuring the welfare of all its members, and the capacity of a society to minimise disparities and avoid polarisation, referred to as social cohesion (McGinn, 2008), which involves harmonious intercommunity relations and trust (Green et al., 2003) that can be affected through socialisation, civic participation and cross-cultural understanding, for example, by exposing children to the ways of life that are different from those of their parents, through intercultural contact and interaction, learning with and about others and learning the different languages of fellow citizens.

The extent to which inclusive or exclusive concepts of citizenship are encouraged in education policies is recognised in how they promote human rights and shared values, make positive references to cultural diversity, and the ways they conceptualise minorities. Exclusion is reflected in discrimination against groups or individuals (e.g. by ethnicity, mother tongue, social class, religion, etc.), preventing full participation, intolerance, and support of *us* and *them* attitudes (Osler & Starkey, 2001, p. 292). The inclusive or exclusive concepts of citizenship are greatly dependent on the contexts. The same phenomenon can be interpreted as inclusive and exclusive as will be seen in the contexts under study.

Citizenship and Education Governance in Post-Yugoslav States

In line with Gutmann's (1987) suggestion that the central political question of how a society shapes its future citizens through education needs to look at the ways authority over educational institutions is allocated, this inquiry focuses on the education governance

THE EUROPEANISATION OF CITIZENSHIP GOVERNANCE

structures. Specifically, it looks at the ways individuals are incorporated in educational systems, universally or consociationally (Tomasi, 1995, p. 581), the ways minorities are defined and provided for at different levels, and the way education perpetuates the dominance of particular ethnic groups at different levels, in particular through language policies.

Universal and Consociational Education Systems

Some of the ways in which post-Yugoslav citizenship regimes operate in education relate to the ways these countries define their minorities (e.g. as 'nationalities', 'communities' and '(constitutive) peoples'). These definitions relate to the arrangements for (minority) rights *to* and *in* education. While the six states grant universal access to primary and secondary education, in some countries this right is de facto exercised consociationally by some 'minorities'.[3] For example, in their constitutions Croatia and Serbia define themselves as countries of the Croat and Serb majority, respectively, and of 'national minorities' who are granted certain group (linguistic and cultural) rights within one centrally governed system of education. Montenegro's civic constitution (although it does not define the country's majority) also grants all 'members of minorities' a right to public education in their language with one central curriculum sensitive to minority cultures and their histories (Art. 79).

In contrast, examples of the consociationally exercised right to education are found in Bosnia and Herzegovina, with special arrangements for a linguistically and culturally sensitive education of the three 'constitutive peoples', who are also de facto minorities in parts of the country, along with other minorities. In Kosovo, members of the Serb 'community' are educated in a parallel system managed by the Serbian Ministry of Education. In Macedonia, the Albanian 'community' exercises the right to education in a separate system of schools and classes in the Albanian language.

Context-Dependent Status of Different Minorities

Granting of the cultural rights to 'minorities' in the region is an example of the adaptability of systems, or the governing elites, to act in compliance with the international norms while adapting these norms to advance their local agendas. Commentators of minority policies in post-communist countries sometimes argue that in general the policies shifted from those of assimilation aimed at the desired socialist homogeneity, to a greater concern for the protection of human and minority rights as a more appropriate arrangement in multicultural contexts (Angelovska & Skenderi, 2009; Nikolić, 2009). At the same time such policies have been criticised for reinforcing the ethnic divides and distance among school children, and sometimes leading to segregation due to the misinterpretation of the rights of communities (MESRM, 2009; Swimelar, 2013).

A variety of arrangements for the education of different minorities can be found in the region, ranging from the noted cases of separate education systems for some minorities (or 'communities' and 'peoples') to those reducing minority identities to folk dances (Bieber, 2007). Different treatments of different 'minorities' in education can be linked to the post-conflict contexts, and to the history of minority protection and relations with kin states.

Examples of fragmented, divided and politicised systems and institutions include post-war Bosnia and Herzegovina, ethnically divided Macedonia and Kosovo, and post-conflict

THE EUROPEANISATION OF CITIZENSHIP GOVERNANCE

areas within countries, such as the area of Vukovar in Croatia. Bosnia and Herzegovina has the most fragmented education system with 13 education ministries in the 2 entities, the 10 Federation cantons, and the Brčko district. The right to a culturally and linguistically sensitive curriculum is mostly practised through mono-ethnic schooling of the constituent peoples. The most notorious examples are those of segregated schooling of Bosniak and Croat children in 'two schools under one roof' in which teachers and students of the two groups are physically separated, use different curricula, and sometimes also 'linguistically' arranged shifts, different entrances, different staff rooms, and even different break times.[4] The way such divided spaces are used for creating and transcending boundaries between the two ethnic groups is illustrated in the next paper of this special issue. In Macedonia's linguistic (ethnic) separation of schools and classes, Albanian students are reported to be most isolated, while students from non-Albanian ethnic communities attend schools in the Macedonian language (UNICEF, 2009). In Kosovo's heavily politicised education system, non-Albanian communities are caught in a crossfire between the Albanian majority and the Serb community which does not recognise the Kosovo authorities (Bieber, 2007).

Segregated schooling for some minorities does not always imply that students are disadvantaged. In some cases, linguistically separate education for some minorities can mean that pupils enjoy an advantage in terms of support from and mobility towards kin states for post-school opportunities. These cases link to the history of some nationalities (*narodnosti* in Yugoslavia) that enjoyed substantial autonomy and minority rights in education. For example, Italian schools in Istria have more favourable student–teacher ratios than an average number of students per class in Croatia overall, and are better equipped thanks to financial support from Italy (Pantić et al., 2011). The Hungarian minority in Serbia inherited high levels of autonomy with entitlement to education in their language from primary through to university education, especially in Vojvodina where minority protection is generally reported to be higher than in Serbia proper, with National Councils representing minorities more systematically consulted in education matters (Bieber, 2007; OSCE, 2008).

Specific treatment is evident in all countries of the Roma minority, for whom being a minority often coincides with a low socio-economic condition. The segregation and exclusion of sometimes extremely impoverished Roma children is reported across the region (Bieber, 2007). Dropout rates due to poverty are significantly higher among Roma, often educated in schools and classes for children with special needs (Bieber, 2007, p. 63).

In the recent reforms of their education systems, all countries have introduced affirmative measures to target inclusion and desegregation of Roma, often supporting anti-discriminatory practices rather than promoting recognition of the cultural and linguistic rights of the Roma minority, which does not neatly link to a culture or language (Agarin & Brosig, 2009). All six countries joined the Decade of Roma Inclusion (2005–15) and developed action plans to improve access and bring Roma children into regular education through the introduction of Roma assistants in schools, providing free textbooks and scholarships, and expanding preschool attendance (Pantić et al., 2011). Sometimes these measures removed barriers for access to education of Roma children, for example, by allowing enrolment without the proof of parents' residence in the new legislation in Serbia (Parliamentary Assembly of Republic of Serbia, 2009). Sometimes measures targeting Roma students have contributed to building anti-discriminatory educational practices more generally, for example, through use of handbooks supporting anti-discriminatory school cultures (Pantić et al., 2011).

THE EUROPEANISATION OF CITIZENSHIP GOVERNANCE

In a study of the integration of Roma in Macedonia, Nikolić (2009, pp. 286–287) remarked that the majority of ethnic Macedonians 'do not perceive Roma as intimidating or threatening when put in the context of the persistent tensions with the much larger and politically stronger Albanian minority'. This might explain why it is politically less controversial to embrace policies aimed at including the Roma than other, post-conflict minorities. Where examples of nascent conciliatory practices have been reported, they resulted from efforts of conscientious teachers and school principals, in spite of, rather than in response to education policies (Pantić et al., 2011).

The Use of Education to Perpetuate the Dominance of Particular Ethnic Groups

All the six countries use education in their ethnocentric nation-building projects, but the loci of ethnic engineering varies from the national level (Croatia, Montenegro, and Serbia) to varying levels of decentralised education governance (Bosnia and Herzegovina, Kosovo, and Macedonia).

In the states with one dominant constitutive majority, the ethnic, cultural, and linguistic interests of the 'state-bearing' group are embedded in the design of policies and institutions. For example, in Croatia and Serbia, the constitutions establish the state language and script, and policies promote a homogenised narrative most obviously through the national curricula. The central management of these education systems allows high levels of control over educationally 'valid' knowledge by the education authorities at the national level. Thus, young citizens learn almost exclusively about the majority group's narrative, history, culture, and religion, while minorities usually seek to secure their group's linguistic and cultural rights in education. Their levels of success and involvement of the bodies representing a given minority in curricular design vary, depending on the group's integrity, stability, political clout, and relations with kin states.

While education reforms in all the six countries included strategies for the transfer of some authorities in education to the school level, in the consociational systems, the powers were also transferred to the lower levels of education authorities such as entities and cantons in Bosnia and Herzegovina, and municipalities in Macedonia and Kosovo. Proponents of group rights recognise decentralisation and autonomy for local authorities in education as a positive force allowing groups to practice and protect their cultural identity, language, and religion (Kymlicka, 1995). However, in these post-conflict contexts, the decentralisation of educational authority has often meant greater power for local nationalists and less involvement by school staff, parents, and students. In some cases, as in Bosnia and Herzegovina, pressure and/or manipulation from administrators and authorities have resulted in parents themselves pushing for educational segregation (Swimelar, 2013), which illustrates the interdependent and formative relations between the intended and internalised identities.

Multicultural states' constitutions and legislation often provide that lower level authorities shall respect certain nationally set standards while using their local powers. The Kosovo constitution obliges municipalities to respect the constitution and the applicable legislation in the areas of their own competencies including those in education (Art. 124). In Macedonia, the so-called Badinter majority applies for laws that concern the use of languages and education. The Assembly adopts decisions by the majority of votes that is constituted from the present members, provided that the majority of votes comes from MPs who are members of communities that are not a majority in the state (Angelovska & Skenderi, 2009). However, at the local level, dominant groups – be they majority or

THE EUROPEANISATION OF CITIZENSHIP GOVERNANCE

minority – are reported to often make decisions with little consultation with others (Bieber, 2007). In these contexts, decentralisation brings both opportunities for multicultural recognition and risks of discrimination against other groups or individuals due to doubtful local capacities, or simply due to local authorities not using their legal mandates to deal with daily school issues. For example, in Macedonia, school boards of mixed composition are reported to have had very little involvement in dealing with issues related to interethnic communication under their legal mandate (UNICEF, 2009). Intercultural solutions in day-to-day interactions between individuals with various cultural, ethnic, and linguistic backgrounds remain a challenging task for schools in some places. In Kosovo, numerous attempts made by local and international bodies to develop educational cooperation between Serb and Albanian communities have failed, despite the report of 'general openness to discussion of all issues by school principals and teachers' (Rexhaj et al., 2010, p. 35).

Citizenship and Language Policies

Language policies are among the most frequently employed mechanisms for promoting inclusive and/or exclusive concepts of citizenship in education. Legislation in the region provides a number of language instruction options. In most cases, the six states have opted for the promotion and recognition principles (designating certain selected languages as 'official' and according a series of rights to speakers of those languages), incorporated in constitutions, legislation, and other statutory and policy documents. For example, the Kosovo constitution stipulates that members of communities have the right, individually or in community, to receive public education at all levels in one of the official languages, and to use their language and alphabet freely in private and in public (Art. 59).

The six countries provide different models for the implementation of linguistic rights in education. For instance, Serbian legislation (Parliamentary Assembly of Republic of Serbia, 2009) affirms the practice of education of minorities in their first language in all subjects, and only in exceptional cases bilingually or in the Serbian language. In Croatia, the *Constitutional Act on the Rights of National Minorities* (Hrvatski Sabor, 2002) grants national minorities the right to education in their first language and script in preschool, primary, and secondary education. Minorities exercise this right through one of three models: model A foresees schooling in the national minority language and four hours of Croatian a week; model B envisages bilingual teaching, with the social sciences and humanities taught in the minority language and natural sciences taught in the Croatian language, again with four hours of Croatian a week; and model C enables nurturing of the mother tongue and minority culture through five hours per week of instruction in the given minority language (Batarelo-Kokić et al., 2010).

The choices of some 'linguistic minorities' clearly link to post-conflict contexts. For example, in the area of Vukovar in Croatia – where the Serb minority opted for model A (education in their own language) – Croat and Serb students were separated in different schools or shifts until September 2007, despite the five-year limit for this arrangement established by the *Erdut Agreement* in 1995. In Macedonia, any community constituting 20 per cent or more of the population of a municipality has the right to education in their mother tongue at all levels, pursuant to the *Ohrid Framework Agreement* that sets an agenda for increased participation in public life, primarily by ethnic Albanians. The Constitution of Bosnia and Herzegovina and especially the *Interim Agreement on*

THE EUROPEANISATION OF CITIZENSHIP GOVERNANCE

Satisfying Special Needs and Rights to Returnee Children (2002) guarantee special rights in education to the members of any of the three constituent peoples forming a minority in areas that are predominantly populated by the members of another constituent people (Kafedžić et al., 2010, p. 32).

In these contexts, separate education for accommodating linguistic rights is based on the territoriality principle meaning that the availability of options depends on their geographical region (Kymlicka & Patten, 2003). In actual fact such linguistically separated education is also based on an ethnic ground in these post-conflict societies. Many of the claims to group rights are politically motivated, and may be less about the practicality of language use and communication, and more about the symbolic nature of language as a key to one's history and identity (Swimelar, 2013). This might explain the prevalence of the recognition principle over the norm-and-accommodation approach where the key priority is to enable communication between public institutions and citizens or residents with limited proficiency in the language in public use, so that the latter can access the rights to which they are entitled (Kymlicka & Patten, 2003). Montenegro is an interesting case in this regard, with the recognition principle built into the Constitution, yet with the norm-and-accommodation principle applied in the implementation of linguistic rights. The Constitution stipulates the official use of Serbian, Bosnian, Albanian, and Croatian languages along with Montenegrin (Art. 13). In practice, education in their own language is provided only for the Albanian minority for whom communication would not be possible in Montenegrin due to the degree of linguistic difference, and not for the other official languages commonly referred to as 'the mother tongue' (VRCG, 2005; Bieber, 2007; Milić et al., 2010).[5]

Language is in some cases both a real and a politicised question. The degree of linguistic difference between languages has implications for possible intercultural cooperation between segregated schools and classes. For example, given the willingness on the part of school staff and a given local community, such cooperation is easily practicable, for example, for Bosniak and Croat students in Bosnia and Herzegovina or between Croat and Serb students in schools in Vukovar (Croatia), while intercultural cooperation between Albanian and Serb schools in Kosovo would require the mutual learning of languages.

Availability of Minority Language Education

Discrepancies are noticeable between learning the minority languages by the majorities and vice versa. For example, Macedonia introduced the learning of the Macedonian language for non-Macedonian students from grade 1, while the introduction of local languages for Macedonian students is withheld (UNICEF, 2009). Learning a minority language is often challenging, especially if it is not the language of an economically or culturally attractive kin state or a foreign language with greater allure, like English (Bieber, 2007).

The option of education in the first language is usually provided, pending on a threshold number of students, favouring territoriality over the universal principle, and group over individual rights. All six countries (except Croatia) have established a requirement for a minimum number of students for establishing specific classes or schools for a minority (lower than normally stipulated for educational institutions). For example, in Serbia education in a minority language is granted for a minimum of 15 students or upon a request and with approval by the Minister for fewer than 15 pupils. Sometimes, the legislation is

THE EUROPEANISATION OF CITIZENSHIP GOVERNANCE

not precise about threshold numbers, like in Kosovo, although the application of a threshold of 15 in practice has been reported (Bieber, 2007, p. 52).

According to Bieber (2007), imprecise definitions of numbers sometimes contribute to poor implementation of rights to education in minority languages. For example, Bosnia's *Framework Law on Primary and Secondary Education* (Parliamentary Assembly of Bosnia and Herzegovina, 2003) provides that 'The language and culture of any major minority living in Bosnia and Herzegovina shall be respected and shall fit into schools to the largest extent viable, in line with the Framework Convention on Protection of Rights of Ethnic Minorities' (Art. 8). The provision is then integrated in various forms into the entity and cantonal legislation. For example, in *Tuzla Canton Law on Minorities* (Tuzla Kanton Assembly, 2009) different thresholds apply for different modes of provision: one-third of a total number of pupils in a school for instruction in the mother tongue, and one-fifth of a total number of pupils in a school for additional classes of the minority language, literature, history, geography, and culture, if this is requested by the majority of their parents (Art. 8). *Republika Srpska* had a threshold of 20 pupils that it abolished in 2004 upon the FCNM Advisory Committee's criticism that it was too high. Subsequently, local authorities are obliged to organise additional classes in a minority language, history, and culture regardless of student numbers (Bieber, 2007).

In reality most schools function under a mono-ethnic curriculum given that most geographical units are themselves mono-ethnic, with minority student numbers usually too small for entitlement for curriculum in their language, or to form their own school. Thus, in most parts of Sarajevo where Bosniaks are the majority, the schools use the Bosniak curriculum, while in Banja Luka, *Republika Srpska*, students learn from the Serb curriculum. In some cases, if a teacher can be found and if there are enough students, separate classes for the group of 'national subjects' is created. It is also common that many Bosnian Serb parents living in Sarajevo send their children across the inter-entity boundary to *Republika Srpska* so that they can attend a school following the curriculum in Serbian, even if the quality of education is lower and the distance greater, and even if children have to walk considerable distances along main roads (Swimelar, 2013).

The numerical threshold provisions inevitably limit the geographical scope of the right to education in a minority language – an Albanian speaker in Macedonia might be able to learn Albanian in Tetovo, but not in Štip (Bieber, 2007, p. 16). These provisions also contribute to differences in the actual exercise of the right to education in one's own language by different minorities, notably withdrawal of such a right to less numerous or less vocal ones. Sometimes, the right to culturally and linguistically sensitive curriculum is denied on the pretext of 'technical limits' and lack of resources (teachers, textbooks, and financing). Shortages of minority teachers are often due to their being trained abroad in kin states (Bieber, 2007, p. 68), or for other context-specific reasons. For example, the guarantee in the *Use of Languages in Kosovo Act* (2002) protecting the right of minorities to be educated in their own languages is implemented for Turkish, Bosnian, and part of Gorani community (who attend schools in the Bosnian language), while Serbs and part of Gorani who attend schools in the Serbian language follow curricula from Serbia. Serbia offers full education in Hungarian, but only limited courses in Romani. In Macedonia, Albanian, Turkish, Macedonian, and Serbian languages are available as languages of instruction, while Roma, Bosniaks, and Vlachs are offered optional subjects in their languages. The right to education is most often denied to the Roma minority whose members are as a rule educated in the language of the majority in the place where they reside. Thus, in Croatia, Roma attend classes in the Croatian language; in Kosovo, Roma who live in a predominantly Albanian environment attend school in Albanian, while Roma who live in Serbian enclaves attend Serbian language schools (Bieber, 2007).

In summary, although the language policies in the six states are broadly consistent with multicultural views of the need to grant cultural and linguistic group rights in education, there is only limited promotion of the mutual respect and interethnic contact, and limited individual choice of the language of instruction by both majorities and minorities.

Education Governance, Policies, and Citizens' Identities – Tales of Two Cities

In post-war Balkan geographies, the claims of collective linguistic rights potentially lead to exclusion and work at cross purposes against universal human rights, civic ideals, non-discrimination, and inclusion (Swimelar, 2013). Language is a significant stumbling block to the promotion of inclusive concepts of citizenship, often used for maintaining separation and exclusion, as can be illustrated by the Mostar Gymnasium case. On the other hand, the fully integrated school system in Brčko (Moore, 2013) suggests that the issue might not be insurmountable.

The international community initiated the integration of the Mostar Gymnasium (attended by Bosniak and Croat students), while the Croat political community claimed its cultural, and especially its linguistic rights (Hromadžić, 2008). The school has been administratively unified, but preserved separate curricula and the ethnic segregation characteristic of the 'two schools under one roof'. Hromadžić's study (2008) shows how this kind of concurrently shared and separated schooling shapes students' experiences and generates distrust among the young citizens in post-conflict Bosnia and Herzegovina.

In contrast, the integration of schools in the Brčko district has been cited as an example of a concerted effort of the international community, education authorities, professionals, and communities to overcome the divides along ethnic lines (OSCE, 2007). In 2001, the Brčko Supervisor[6] imposed the district level *Law on Education* and a newly developed curriculum. The law set a platform for integrated education by stipulating that students of the three ethnicities receive instruction in their own languages in the same classroom, and use the Latin and Cyrillic alphabets on equal terms in curricular and extracurricular activities. The law also stipulated that the ethnic composition of teachers should reflect that of the students in a school. A comprehensive public awareness campaign was run parallel to policy measures obliging teachers to use all three languages when teaching, and to sign a Code of Conduct accepting the reform principles. Such policies were accompanied by incentives[7] and an offer of short-term (annual and biannual) contracts to teachers in Brčko with a view towards ensuring sustained commitment to the reform principles. In the 2001/2002 school year, children of the three ethnicities started to go to the primary schools together with some separate classes for the 'national subjects'. Integrated schooling of the secondary students was achieved gradually over four years and a public opinion poll conducted in 2004 showed that parents in Brčko were more in favour of integrated schooling than parents in Bosnia and Herzegovina on average (OSCE, 2007).

The cases of Mostar and Brčko illustrate how citizens' views and attitudes are at least to some extent shaped by the institutional arrangements and policies. A well-known 'contact thesis' put forth by Allport (1954), and noted by scholars in the region (Čorkalo Biruški & Ajduković, 2008; Swimelar, 2013), points to the importance of interpersonal contact for reducing prejudice and building tolerance. Ordinary citizens, including children and

THE EUROPEANISATION OF CITIZENSHIP GOVERNANCE

young people, seem to be aware of the importance of interethnic contact in education. A survey in Macedonia showed that the majority of citizens felt that education, alongside Macedonia's membership of the EU, is the most significant factor for improving interethnic relations in their municipality (Angelovska & Skenderi, 2009). In a study of the perceptions of the role of education in reconciliation (Magill et al., 2009), young respondents from Bosnia and Herzegovina tended to emphasise the need for contact between schools with pupils of different ethnicities. A subsequent study of the attitudes of parents, teachers, and students towards separate education of Croats and Serbs in the Vukovar area showed more positive attitudes towards integration in 2007 than in 2001, although all groups, except the teachers of the curriculum in Croatian, were still mostly in favour of separate education (Čorkalo Biruški & Ajduković, 2008).

Influences of 'Europeanisation'?

It is difficult to say to what extent the governance structures and policy choices have been influenced by the countries' aspirations for EU membership, given the dynamic nature of the process and wide range of potential effects (Grabbe, 2001). Some influence of the observance of the 'European norms' can be discerned in the promotion of human and minority rights in the institutional solutions and of social inclusion in the education policy documents, both with a distinctly local take.

In the absence of an *acquis* on education per se, EU has little leeway in influencing the reforms of the education systems. The most tangible effect of EU's conditionality has been identified in the area of minority rights promotion. For example, Petričušić (2008) argues that in Croatia the policy towards minorities has been unquestionably due to the European integration process, as the issue of minority rights has been given particular attention in the screening of the *acquis* by the Commission that requested passing of a comprehensive action plan for the implementation of *the Constitutional Law on the Rights of National Minorities*, in order to proceed with the negotiations. However, Stubbs and Zrinščak (2015) point in the paper of this special issue that changing of the discriminatory laws in the EU accession process had little impact on de facto discrimination of Croatian Serbs. Similarly, different treatment of different minorities presented in this paper suggests that this compliance might be instrumental and symbolic, rather than a principled commitment to the promotion of the cultural and linguistic rights of the minorities.

The question of any EU influence needs to be considered distinguishing between formal change, for example, of legal rules, and the behavioural change through their implementation, application, and enforcement (Sedelmeier, 2006). Education is one of the areas where there is an apparent gap between the values adopted in the legislation and policies and their implementation (Pantić et al., 2011). Promotion of human rights and social inclusion, and the protection of minority rights are seen as essential for progress towards integration in the EU. Significant majority of the populations see their future within the EU, with the integration process reported to have had a catalytic effect on the consolidation of strategic planning under a more systematic approach (see, e.g. UNDP & ORI, 2007). An appeal to 'Europe' is commonplace in policy documents and education reform strategies, but the EU has no specific test of institutional change or compliance with its requirements (Grabbe, 2001). In this situation, it is not unusual that adjustments are patchy and selective especially in policy areas with limited concrete EU demands, or that the domestic actors use

EU requirements to justify institutional and policy choices in line with their own priorities (Grabbe, 2001; Sedelmeier, 2006).

The main mechanism for influencing policy transfer in education, if any, seems to be provided by social learning (Börzel & Risse, 2003) with actors motivated by internalised values and norms, rather than bargaining about the conditions and rewards (Schimmelfennig & Sedelmeier, 2004; Sedelmeier, 2006). The EU's main mechanisms for effecting change in the area of education is benchmarking and monitoring, and technical assistance involving intensive interactions between domestic officials and experts with EU counterparts. EU agencies and other international organisations together with the growing civil sector have been essential in the promotion of minority rights in the region, but also reported to have contributed to minority integration not always being valued for its intrinsic worth (e.g. as positively affecting institutional performance) but as representing, rather, a symbolic engagement to comply with international demands (Agarin & Brosig, 2009).

Conclusions

The study reported in this paper offered the following insights into the themes of the analysis of the education system governance structures and policies in the post-Yugoslav countries.

Strong primacy of group over individual rights is evident in the minorities' entitlements to education in their own language with most of the countries having adopted the principles of promotion and recognition of linguistic rights, and favouring territorial over universal principle in the implementation of these rights, by providing education in the first language depending on threshold numbers and students. In the post-conflict contexts, this has created problematic multicultural solutions that led to minimal intercultural contact and prevalence of static concepts of diversity and essentialised (ethnic) groups. The problem with homogenising groups for policy purposes – even where there is a degree of interaction between the groups – is that interactions take place between individuals who classify each other predominantly in terms of belonging to specific ethnic or cultural communities.

Ethnocentric and multicultural elements of citizenship regimes can be identified in the education system governance structures and education policies, while the ethnocentric ones prevail in the ways policies are implemented. Multicultural policy options are most obvious in the recognition of the right to linguistically and culturally sensitive curricula, although ethnocentric motives can be discerned behind their territorial implementation, and in the varied arrangements for some minorities, communities, and peoples in the systems of education. On the one hand, classes and schools separate pupils linguistically even where there is an almost complete mutual understanding, as in Bosnia and Herzegovina, and Croatia. On the other hand, there is little evidence of a genuine intention to ensure bilingual education where language does represent a real barrier for building intercommunity trust, as in Kosovo and Macedonia. This leads to a conclusion that the promotion of multicultural language policies might be more of a symbolic value than about genuine concern for citizens' cultural recognition and communication.

The 'linguistic' policies are often used to support the development of different ethnic identities, while examples of anti-discriminatory policies are rare. Attempts to make education more inclusive can be recognised in the measures to increase access and prevent segregation of Roma minority in all countries. Exclusive conceptions of citizenship are reflected in the separate ethnic narratives promoted in separately governed systems and

THE EUROPEANISATION OF CITIZENSHIP GOVERNANCE

the messages students might be getting from hidden curricular practices preventing intercultural contact. Paradoxically, these practices are sometimes legitimised by the multicultural policies promoting linguistic and cultural rights in education – an example of coexistence of the inclusive and exclusive conceptions of citizenship in education policies.

The observance of 'European norms' is mainly seen in areas of minority rights and declared social inclusion policies, while their application in practice is limited to the use of different languages in education, with poor understanding of mutual respect and acceptance of differences. In the absence of systematic monitoring of protection of individual human rights and non-discrimination practices, the EU requirements seem to be used to justify institutional and policy choices in line with the domestic nation-building priorities. The upholding of rights to a culturally sensitive curriculum and schooling in the mother tongue has sometimes inadvertently led to segregated education.

In summary, the interactions between citizenship and education policies in the post-Yugoslav states can be characterised as the rise of *ethnocentric*, on the pretext of ensuring *multicultural* education of young citizens in line with the European ideals of respecting cultural and linguistic diversity. The cases of Mostar and Brčko illustrate how, for better and worse, the governance structures and policies might contribute to the shaping of citizens' identities, and how this might be mediated by schooling environments and teachers. Hromadžić (in this special issue illustrates how ethnic governance of the Mostar Gymnasium could be at least partly disrupted if not completely transformed through teachers' actions, just as Brčko students and teachers might embrace nationalistic narratives despite the policies aimed at integration. Moreover, the same teachers might resist and embrace such narratives at different times.

Post-Yugoslav societies, like others, are stratified by different interrelated layers of diversity, for example, living conditions in urban and rural environments, social and family cultures, religious and secular views, gender, and so on. Which particular dimensions of diversity come to the forefront in public debate and policy agendas is guided by the political concerns of the moment. The post-conflict education debates have been dominated by the issues of linguistic and cultural rights. However, many of the concerns about the quality of education, such as pupils' functional knowledge and employability, are shared by all parents. The increasing presence of these substantive issues in education debates and media might shift the foci of public pressure and the priorities of education authorities.

Disclosure Statement

No potential conflict of interest was reported by the author.

Notes

[1] These include the European Convention on Human Rights (1950); the UNESCO Convention against Discrimination in Education (1960); the UN Convention on the Rights of the Child (1989); the Council of Europe Framework Convention for the Protection of National Minorities (1995); the revised European Social Charter (1995); and the European Charter for Regional or Minority Languages (1992).

[2] The study covers primary and secondary education which is granted as free and universally accessible in these countries. Primary education is also legally compulsory, while secondary is compulsory only in Macedonia.

[3] It is sometimes suggested that there is no majority ethnic group in the region as a whole and that all groups should be regarded as minorities in some sense (OECD, 2003).

THE EUROPEANISATION OF CITIZENSHIP GOVERNANCE

[4] Recently, the first court decision ruled that the segregation in 'two schools under one roof' is a violation of the Law against discrimination in Bosnia and Herzegovina.

[5] Recently, heated debates over the name of this common language produced a composite name for the school subject called *Montenegrin-Serbian, Bosnian and Croatian Language and Literature.*

[6] A supervisory body established by the Brčko Arbitration Tribunal and administered by a Deputee High Representative for Brčko.

[7] At the time teachers' salaries in Brčko were twice the average teacher salary elsewhere in Bosnia and Herzegovina.

References

Agarin, T. & Brosig, M. (Eds) (2009) *Minority Integration in Central and Eastern Europe: Between Ethnic Diversity and Equality* (Amsterdam: Rodopi).

Allport, G. W. (1954) *The Nature of Prejudice* (Cambridge: Perseus Books).

Angelovska, E. & Skenderi, S. (2009) *Analysis of the Interethnic Relations in Republic of Macedonia* (Skopje, Macedonia: Zaednički vrednosti).

Batarelo-Kokić, I., Vukelić, A. & Ljubić, M. (2010) *Mapping Policies and Practices for the Preparation of Teachers for Inclusive Education in Contexts of Social and Cultural Diversity.* Croatia Country Report (Turin, Italy: European Training Foundation). Available at http://www.etf.europa.eu/webatt.nsf/0/C12578310056925BC125772E002BD5AB/$file/NOTE85SBD6.pdf (accessed 15 March 2012).

Bieber, F. (Ed.) (2007) *Guide to Minorities and Education: Foundation of Stable Relations in the Region* (Brussels: Civic Initiatives and the King Baudouin Foundation).

Börzel, T. & Risse, T. (2003) Conceptualising the domestic impact of Europe, in: K. Featherstone & C. M. Radaelli (Eds) *The Politics of Europeanization*, pp. 57–83 (Oxford: Oxford University Press).

Čorkalo Biruški, D. & Ajduković, D. (2008) Stavovi učenika, roditelja i nastavnika prema školovanju: što se promijenilo tijekom šest godina u Vukovaru? [Attitudes of students, parents and teachers towards schooling: what has changed in the course of six years in Vukovar?], *Migracijske i etničke teme*, 24(3), pp. 189–216.

Džankić, J. (2012) Understanding montenegrin citizenship, *Citizenship Studies*, 16(3–4), pp. 337–351.

European Commission. (2004) *Joint Report on Social Inclusion* (Luxembourg: Office for Official Publications of the European Communities). Available at http://ec.europa.eu/employment_social/social_inclusion/docs/final_joint_inclusion_report_2003_en.pdf (accessed 15 March 2012).

Grabbe, H. (2001) How does Europeanization affect CEE governance? Conditionality, diffusion and diversity, *Journal of European Public Policy*, 8(6), pp. 1013–1031.

Green, A., Preston, J. & Sabates, R. (2003) Education, equality and social cohesion: A distributional approach, *Compare*, 33(4), pp. 453–470.

Gutmann, A. (1987) *Democratic Education* (Princeton, NJ: Princeton University Press).

Hromadžić, A. (2008) Discourses of integration and practices of reunification at the Mostar gymnasium, Bosnia and Herzegovina, *Comparative Education Review*, 52(4), pp. 541–563.

Hromadžić, A. (2015) Dissatisfied citizens: Ethnonational governance, teachers' strike and professional solidarity in Mostar, Bosnia–Herzegovina, *European Politics and Society*. doi:10.1080/23745118.2015.1061803

Hrvatski Sabor. (2002) Ustavni zakon o pravima nacionalnih manjina. *Službeni list Republike Hrvatske*, br. 155/02 [The Constitutional Act on the Rights of National Minorities. *Official Gazette of the Republic of Croatia*, no. 155/02].

Joppke, C. (2003) Citizenship between de- and re-ethnicization (I), *European Journal of Sociology*, XLIV(3), pp. 429–458.

Joppke, C. (2007) Transformation of citizenship: status, rights, identity, *Citizenship Studies*, 11(1), pp. 37–48.

Kafedžić, L., Džemidžić-Kristiansen, S. & Pribišev-Beleslin, T. (2010) *Mapping Policies and Practices for the Preparation of Teachers for Inclusive Education in Contexts of Social and Cultural Diversity.* Bosnia and Herzegovina Country Report (Turin, Italy: European Training Foundation). Available at http://www.etf.europa.eu/webatt.nsf/0/C12578310056925BC125772E002B2093/$file/NOTE85SB89.pdf (accessed 15 March 2012).

Koska, V. (2012) Framing the citizenship regime within the complex triadic nexuses: The case study of Croatia, *Citizenship Studies*, 16(3–4), pp. 397–411.

Krasniqi, G. (2012) Overlapping jurisdictions, disputed territory, unsettled state: The perplexing case of citizenship in Kosovo, *Citizenship Studies*, 16(3–4), pp. 353–366.

THE EUROPEANISATION OF CITIZENSHIP GOVERNANCE

Kymlicka, W. (1995) *Multicultural Citizenship: A Liberal Theory of Minority Rights* (Oxford: Oxford University Press).

Kymlicka, W. & Patten, A. (2003) Introduction: Language rights and political theory, in: W. Kymlicka & A. Patten (Eds) *Language Rights and Political Theory*, pp. 1–51 (Oxford: Oxford University Press).

Magill, C., Smith, A. & Hamber, B. (2009) *The Role of Education in Reconciliation: The Perspectives of Children and Young People in Bosnia and Herzegovina and Northern Ireland* (Londonderry, UK: University of Ulster).

McGinn, N. F. (2008) Education policies to promote social cohesion, in: W. K. Cummings & J. H. Williams (Eds) *Policy-making for Education Reform in Developing Countries: Policy Options and Strategies*, pp. 277–308 (Plymouth, UK: Rowman and Littlefield).

Merriam, S. B. (1998) *Qualitative Research and Case Study Applications in Education* (San Francisco, CA: Jossey-Bass).

MESRM (Ministry of Education and Science of the Republic of Macedonia) (2009) *Steps Towards Integrated Education in the Education System of the Republic of Macedonia* (Skopje, Macedonia: MESRM).

Milić, T., Marić, A., Bošković, V. & Šćepović, V. (2010) *Mapping Policies and Practices for the Preparation of Teachers for Inclusive Education in Contexts of Social and Cultural Diversity*. Montenegro Country Report (Turin, Italy: European Training Foundation). Available at http://www.etf.europa.eu/webatt.nsf/0/C12578310056925BC125772E002C7903/$file/NOTE85SBHH.pdf (accessed 15 March 2012).

Moore, A. (2013) *Peacebuilding in Practice: Local Experience in Two Bosnian Towns* (Ithaca, NY: Cornell University Press).

Nikolić, S. (2009) Empowerment as a two-way process: The role of Romani NGOs in the integration of Macedonian society, in: T. Agarin & M. Brosig (Eds) *Minority Integration in Central and Eastern Europe: Between Ethnic Diversity and Equality*, pp. 279–304 (Amsterdam: Rodopi).

OECD (Organisation for Economic Cooperation and Development). (2003) *Reviews of National Policies for Education: South Eastern Europe* (Paris: OECD).

OSCE (Organisation for Security and Cooperation in Europe). (2007) *Lessons from Education Reform in Brčko*. A report prepared by OSCE Mission to Bosnia and Herzegovina.

OSCE (Organisation for Security and Cooperation in Europe). (2008) *Ethnic Minorities in Serbia: An Overview* (Belgrade, Serbia: OSCE Mission to Serbia).

Osler, A. & Starkey, H. (2001) Citizenship education and national identities in France and England: Inclusive or exclusive?, *Oxford Review of Education*, 27(2), pp. 287–305.

Pantić, N., Closs, A. & Ivošević, V. (2011) *Teachers for the Future: Teacher Development for Inclusive Education in the Western Balkans* (Turin, Italy: European Training Foundation). Available at http://www.etf.europa.eu/webatt.nsf/0/9E076CFB736A59AFC125788F0033258C/$file/Teachers%20for%20the%20future_web.pdf (accessed 15 March 2012).

Parliamentary Assembly of Bosnia and Herzegovina. (2003) Okvirni zakon o osnovnom i srednjem obrazovanju. *Službeni glasnik BiH*, br. 18/03 [Framework Law on Primary and Secondary Education, *Official Gazette of BiH*, no. 18/03].

Parliamentary Assembly of Republic of Serbia. (2009) ZOSOV (Zakon o osnovama sistema obrazovanja i vaspi-tanja). *Službeni glasnik Republike Srbije*, br. 72/ 09 [Law on the fundamentals of the education system. *Official Gazette of the Republic of Serbia*, no. 72/2009].

Petričušić, A. (2008) European integration process in Croatia: Powerful tool for minority rights improvement, in: E. Lantschner, J. Marko & A. Petričušić (Eds) *European Integration and Its Effects on Minority Protection in the South East European Countries*, pp. 167–187 (Baden-Baden, Germany: Nomos).

Rawls, J. (1993) *Political Liberalism* (New York: Columbia University Press).

Rexhaj, X., Mula, M. & Hima, A. (2010) *Mapping Policies and Practices for the Preparation of Teachers for Inclusive Education in Contexts of Social and Cultural Diversity*. Kosovo (under UNSCR 1244) Country Report (Turin, Italy: European Training Foundation). Available at http://www.etf.europa.eu/webatt.nsf/0/C12578310056925BC125772E002C487E/$file/NOTE85SBG9.pdf (accessed 15 March 2012).

Ritchie, J. & Spencer, L. (1994) Qualitative data analysis for applied policy research, in: A. Bryman & R. Burgess (Eds) *Analyzing Qualitative Data*, pp. 173–194 (London: Routledge).

Sarajlić, E. (2012) Conceptualising citizenship regime(s) in post-Dayton Bosnia and Herzegovina, *Citizenship Studies*, 16(3–4), pp. 367–381.

Scheppele, K. L. (2004) Constitutional ethnography: An introduction, *Law and Society Review*, 38, pp. 399–406.

Schimmelfennig, F. & Sedelmeier, U. (2004) Governance by conditionality: EU rule transfer to the candidate countries of Central and Eastern Europe, *Journal of European Public Policy*, 11(4), pp. 661–679.

THE EUROPEANISATION OF CITIZENSHIP GOVERNANCE

Sedelmeier, U. (2006) Europeanisation in new member and candidate states, *Living Reviews in European Governance (LREG)*, 1(3). Available at http://ideas.repec.org/a/erp/lregxx/p0003.html (accessed 17 May 2013).

Shaw, J. & Štiks, I. (2012) Citizenship in the new states of South Eastern Europe, *Citizenship Studies*, 16(3–4), pp. 309–321.

Spaskovska, L. (2012) The fractured 'we' and the ethno-national 'I': The Macedonian citizenship framework, *Citizenship Studies*, 16(3–4), pp. 383–396.

Spiecker, B. & Steutel, J. (1995) Political liberalism, civic education and the Dutch government, *Journal of Moral Education*, 24(4), pp. 383–394.

Steiner-Khamsi, G., Torney-Purta, J. & Schwille, J. (Eds) (2002) *New Paradigms and Recurring Paradoxes in Education for Citizenship: An International Comparison* (Amsterdam: Elsevier Science Press).

Stubbs, P. & Zrinščak, S. (2015) Citizenship and social welfare in Croatia: Clientelism and the limits of 'Europeanisation', *European Politics and Society*. doi:10.1080/23745118.2015.1061798

Swimelar, S. (2013) Education in post-war Bosnia: The nexus of societal security, identity and nationalism, *Ethnopolitics*, 12(2), pp. 161–182.

Tomasi, J. (1995) Kymlicka, liberalism, and respect for cultural minorities, *Ethics*, 105, pp. 580–603.

Tuzla Kanton Assembly. (2009) Zakon o manjinama Tuzlanskog Kantona. *Službeni glasnik TK*, br. 14/09 [Tuzla Canton Law on Minorities. *Official Gazette of Tuzla Canton*, no. 14/09].

UNDP (United Nations Development Programme) and ORI (Oxford Research International). (2007) *The Silent Majority Speaks: Snapshots of Today and Visions of the Future of Bosnia and Herzegovina* (Sarajevo, Bosnia and Herzegovina: UNDP).

UNICEF. (2009) *Study on Multiculturalism and Inter-ethnic Relations in Education* (Skopje, Macedonia, UNICEF Country Office).

Vasiljević, J. (2012) Imagining and managing the nation: Tracing citizenship policies in Serbia, *Citizenship Studies*, 16(3–4), pp. 323–336.

VRCG. (2005) *Strateški plan reforme obrazovanja za period 2005.-2009. Godine* [Strategic plan of education reform for period 2005.-2009]. (Podgorica, Montenegro: Government of Montenegro).

Dissatisfied Citizens: Ethnonational Governance, Teachers' Strike and Professional Solidarity in Mostar, Bosnia–Herzegovina

AZRA HROMADŽIĆ

Department of Anthropology, Syracuse University, USA

ABSTRACT *This ethnographic and anthropological study documents the contours of professional solidarity among teachers in postwar and postsocialist Bosnia–Herzegovina. The article illustrates how ethnically divided Croat and Bosniak teachers at the first 'reunified' school in postwar Bosnia and Herzegovina – the famed Mostar Gymnasium – came together to strike together, and to voice their profession-shaped citizen demands. These teachers frequently referred to themselves as* nezadovoljni građani *or dissatisfied citizens, stressing the generational, moral and economic aspects of their predicament. The combined feelings of citizen-dissatisfaction, loss of social status and being left out of administrative procedures – which enable access to rightful entitlements – led to the formation of a teachers' protest group across the lines of ethnic citizenship. These joint actions generated a shift in the teachers' political subjectivities, however provisional, and they probed the horizon of ethnic politics in postwar and postsocialist Bosnia.*

Introduction

The terrain of citizenship in Bosnia–-Herzegovina[1] has been saturated by ethnonational (di)visions: both domestic and international elites in the country have been using and supporting the war-produced policies, ideologies and systems of governance that favor ethnic autonomy and national segregation (see Pantić, 2015). As a result of these (di)visions, since the beginning of the Bosnian war (1992–95), the terrain of citizenship has been reduced to an ethnonational script. This narrow, ethnonational understanding of citizenship is possibly most visible in the domain of 'educational governance structures and policies' (Pantić, this volume) since it is here that the structures and ideologies of ethnic inclusion and exclusion (Pantić, 2015) powerfully converge. For example, the main international and local policies and projects focusing on education often reproduce, legitimize and

THE EUROPEANISATION OF CITIZENSHIP GOVERNANCE

reinsert the importance of ethnicity as the organizing principle of Bosnian society, regardless of their mission to overcome ethnocentric forces within education (see Pantić, 2015; also see Hromadžić, 2015).

In this article I show that lived citizenship in Bosnia–Herzegovina cannot be exhausted by the spectrum of ethnonationalism. Rather, by focusing on a highly symbolic 'revelatory incident' (Fernandez, 1986, p. xi) – the teachers' strike in the divided Herzegovinian city of Mostar – in this article I highlight the socioeconomic, moral and generational dimensions of professional solidarity as a site of citizenship. During the strike, the ethnically divided teachers came together as *nezadovoljni građani* or dissatisfied citizens to request 'equal rights', which, in this instance, referred to the increase in the teachers' base pay. These teachers' actions cannot be simply glorified as a form of cross-ethnic solidarity or as an expression of professional teachers' ethic, however, nor dismissed as supportive of an ethnonational regime, since these practices are never monologic, oppressive or liberatory. Rather, these performances of coming together and striking together illuminate the blurred distinctions between the state and citizens, the professional and personal, and the hegemonic and sincere.

It is therefore most productive to think of this professional solidarity and the citizen subjectivities it generated in terms of citizens' 'weak power' (Fiske, 1993). This form of power, though socially feebler than the dominant, 'strong, top-down, "imperializing"' (Fiske, 1993, p. 11) ethnonational power is far from unproductive; rather it is a 'localizing form of power' (Fiske, 1993, p. 11) used by 'ordinary' people to control their immediate social conditions. The notion of weak power thus acknowledges the possibility of transformative potential of citizen-practices, but locates this transgressive potentiality within larger, dominant and oppressive social structures; in this case the script of the ethnonational order of things.

This article is thus structured around two domains of citizen-solidarity in contemporary Bosnia–Herzegovina: ethnonational and professional. In order to understand these converging yet separate modalities of citizenship, I situate them in their historical and sociocultural contexts. I therefore preface the discussion of ethnicization of lives, spaces and actions at the Mostar Gymnasium and beyond with a discussion of (post)war Mostar; I show how political orientations and social belonging stem out of the war-produced spatial governmentality and cultural incommensurability that favor ethnic solidarity. Similarly, I introduce the discussion of professional solidarity and teachers' strike with a concise portrayal of the history of education and teaching profession in the former Yugoslavia. To the war and Mostar, however, I turn first.

Coordinates of Ethnonational Belonging: Zooming into (Post)war Mostar[2]

After the declarations of independence by Slovenia and Croatia from Yugoslavia in the early 1990s, Bosnia–Herzegovina found itself in a position where it had to choose between independence (supported by the majority of Bosnian Muslims and Croats) and remaining in the Yugoslav federation (supported by the majority of Serbs). In February 1992, a referendum for independence from Yugoslavia took place, which was boycotted by Bosnian Serbs. Regardless of the boycott, Bosnia–Herzegovina became an independent state on 6 April 1992. On the same day that Bosnia–Herzegovina was officially recognized, Serbian paramilitary units and the Yugoslav People's Army (Jugoslovenska Narodna Armija (JNA)) attacked Bosnia–Herzegovina's capital, Sarajevo, and started the war in

THE EUROPEANISATION OF CITIZENSHIP GOVERNANCE

Bosnia–Herzegovina.[3] The army of the self-proclaimed Republika Srpska within Bosnia–Herzegovina, with the help of men and weapons from Serbia, succeeded in conquering close to 70 per cent of the country's territory by the end of 1993. It also perpetrated some of the most brutal acts of violence exercised against the non-Serb populations, which involved mass killings, rape and torture.

After more than three years of failed negotiations, bloody conflict, over 100,000 deaths, and the displacement of 1.5 million people as refugees, on 14 December 1995, the Dayton Peace Agreement – brokered by the USA – brought an end to the Bosnian war and inserted the consociational model of democracy in Bosnia–Herzegovina. While claiming to have reconciliation, democracy and ethnic pluralism as its objectives, in the eyes of its critics the agreement inscribed in law the ethnic partitioning of Bosnian Serbs, Bosnian Croats and Bosniaks (Bosnian Muslims[4]) (Chandler, 1999). This internationally designed and implemented agreement divided Bosnia–Herzegovina into two entities: the Federation of Bosnia–Herzegovina (FBiH), with a 51 per cent share of the territory and inhabited by mostly Bosniaks and Bosnian Croats, and the Republika Srpska, with 49 per cent of the territory and populated almost exclusively by Bosnian Serbs. Further, the agreement separated the FBiH into ten cantons, with little intermixing between the ethnic groups.[5] I call the nexus between people and territory 'spatial governmentality' – ideological, political and social mechanism of governance that relies on spatial segregation and disciplining of ethnically conceived peoples in Bosnia–Herzegovina.[6] When married with the ideology of 'incommensurable cultural identities' *rooted in local nationalisms* (Sarajlić, 2011, p. 63; see also Gagnon, n.d., Stolcke, 1995), which also framed the international actors' vision of Bosnian–Herzegovinian people and territories, spatial governmentality naturalized and legitimized the war-produced ethnicization of Bosnia–Herzegovina.

The collapse of Yugoslavia and Bosnia–Herzegovina was particularly destructive in Mostar, which has often been described as a microcosm of the Bosnian state. With over 100,000 inhabitants, it is the largest city in Herzegovina. During the Yugoslav period, Mostar was a symbol of ethnic coexistence in Yugoslavia. However, its history of heterogeneity and intermarriage ended in 1992, when Mostar became the scene of one of the bloodiest conflicts of the war. First, the Serb-dominated JNA attacked Mostar from the eastern hills of the city, driving the inhabitants to the western part of town in search of protection and encouraging most Serbs to leave the town (Vetters, 2007). After initially defending the city against JNA forces jointly, fighting then broke out between the Croats and the Bosniaks leading to a complete division of the town into a Croat-dominated western part and a Bosniak-dominated eastern side (Vetters, 2007). When Croatian nationalists destroyed the sixteenth-century Old Bridge in November 1993, this punctuated the physical and symbolic segregation of the two communities. Even after the opening of the new 'Old Bridge' on 23 July 2004 – an event framed by the international diplomats and Bosniak political leadership as a symbol of hope for Bosnia–Herzegovina's reconciliation – the people of Mostar remain divided.

The international actors in charge of the postwar governance, peace-building and state-making efforts made the integration of schools in Bosnia–Herzegovina a crucial element of their reconstruction efforts. This is understandable, since education in Bosnia–Herzegovina has been segregated along ethnic lines since the beginning of the war and schools have been imagined as primary sites in which ideas about (ethno)national loyalties are disseminated and attachments to national states are formed. I conducted nine months of ethnographic research in the first reintegrated school in Bosnia–Herzegovina, the Mostar Gymnasium, which has become one of the most important symbols of the internationally directed peace-building and state-making efforts in Bosnia–Herzegovina.[7]

Mostar Gymnasium

Among the first schools to be integrated in Bosnia–Herzegovina was the famed *Stara Gimnazija* (Old Gymnasium), as people in Mostar refer to the school. After several years of heated negotiations, demonstrations and the investment of large sums of money in reconstruction, the school was reunited on an administrative level in February 2004.[8] The school's reunification was celebrated by the Organization for Security and Cooperation in Europe (OSCE) – the main international body in charge of reunification – and some local politicians as the most powerful symbol of the city's reunification. However, the school's integration has to be viewed in the context of pervasive ethnic segregation, as the vice-principal was quick to point to me:

> They [international and local politicians and the general public] expect a lot from us, and we are doing our best ... but let's be realistic! How much can we achieve when everything below us [elementary schools, neighborhoods ...] and everything above us [FBiH, Bosnia-Herzegovina] remains totally divided!

Still, much hope and attention was focused on the school when in September 2004, for the first time since 1991, Bosniak and Croat students began learning in the same building (OSCE, 2005, p. 5).

The two schools became one administratively unified school but with separate instruction in all subjects.[9] In practice, this means that reunification has maintained separate national curricula for the students of the two ethnic groups, thus preserving ethnic segregation through unification.[10] Therefore, the school became a powerful metaphor for the internationally conceptualized state as a whole, where ethnically conceived populations were brought together to work and learn, while retaining deep structural divisions visible in separate curricula, divided spaces of learning, working and being. As a result, the processes of reunification, which embodied the notions of spatial governmentality and cultural incommensurability, continuously challenged and reinserted ethnic divisions which have been shaping the 'Bosnian way of life' under the regime of peace.

Cartography of Ethnic Governance and Ethnicization of Everyday Life[11]

The process of integration of the Mostar Gymnasium clearly displayed the international and local governance of the country that posits the state as an ethnic problem requiring a particular spatial solution. This ethnicization of territories and citizenship has been sometimes couched in the language of European integration, as the following comment by the then OSCE Education Director, Claude Kieffer, clearly illustrates: 'without integration [of schools] you will never become part of Europe' (Keiffer quoted in Farrell, 2001, p. 17). In this way, ironically, the integration policies often exacerbated and cemented the problem they allegedly tried to alleviate – the perpetual ethnicization of politics and everyday life, as I explain below. Furthermore, this comment also reveals the belief in the responsibility and the power of education to transform undemocratic (Bosnian) citizens into European citizens.

THE EUROPEANISATION OF CITIZENSHIP GOVERNANCE

From the very first day of my fieldwork in Mostar I was overwhelmed by the ethnic conceptualization of the 'integrated' school's geography. The precision of ethnic symmetry in the geography of the school is ubiquitous. For instance, the Croat classrooms are marked with the Roman (grade) numbers and lowercase English-alphabet letters (e.g., I-a, II-b, III-c, IV-a) to mark a specific class of a specific grade. Meanwhile, the Federal curriculum (predominantly Bosniak) classrooms are marked with Arabic numbers and with Roman (grade) numbers (e.g., I-2, II-3, IV-2). So, if one is to say III-1 or II-a, everyone at the school would know if the person was referring to Croat or Bosniak students and to which curricula. There are plaques with class numbers on the doorway of each classroom. During the short breaks between classes, students typically stand in ethnically homogenous groups in the hallway in front of their classroom, while gazing at the students of the different group standing in front of their classrooms, at safe distance. In order to avoid total segregation, however, the OSCE and the management of the school decided to alternate Croat and Federal classrooms, so the classroom sequence is Croat–Federal–Croat–Federal–Croat, and so on. This process of spatial governmentality at the school reduces potentially dynamic social life to conceptions of homogenous ethnic territories, thereby reducing complexity and contingency.

The only time the sequence of spatial governmentality broke down is in the case of the general-purpose rooms, such as the library, the computer lab, the student council room, the student duty room and the teachers' room. In the joined teachers' room, teachers had to learn to accommodate ethnic differences in order to achieve practical, professional goals (Bekerman, 2012). But even within these spaces, the ethnic distribution was often preserved. For example, the teachers' room is located at the center of the second floor. It is a clean, nicely lit room, decorated with several tall, green plants. On one side, the room borders with the administration and the principal's offices, and on the other side with the vice-principal's office. In the room itself, there is a large, wooden table, with 20–25 plain chairs placed around the table. From the first day on, the teachers 'naturally' divided up around the table: the Federal curriculum teachers sat on the left side of the table, and the Croat teachers sat on the right side of the table, thus *performing* ethnicity within the ethnicized geography of the school. The only Bosniak teacher who taught in the Croat curriculum at the time frequently sat in between the two groups. This teacher often tried to initiate dialogue between the two sides. This performance of (trans) ethnicity here does not presuppose artificiality; 'it is not "put on" or antithetical to "reality"' (Taylor, 1997, p. 185); rather, it highlights the productive and uneven gap between lived, organic ethnonationality and the rigidity of ethnonational script/cartography/ideology.[12]

Everyday life is thus not a map and the forms of ethnonationalism that exist on the ground are not mere replicas of authoritative discourse of the nationalist parties and (international) governance[13] (see Kurtović, 2011; Hromadžić, 2015). For example, some teachers who taught only a few classes at the school were not immediately aware of ethnic segregation and they 'made a mistake' by sitting at the wrong side of the table, as one teacher explained: 'At the beginning, I sat on the wrong side. Who cares? Everyone at the other side of the table gave me looks. Because, you know, there are two sides of the table.' The tension between the two sides of the table was easily felt, and was manifested as whispering and short exchanges in low voices among the teachers on the one side of the table, but rarely across the divide. More recently, several more experienced teachers who used to teach together before the war have started to exchange words over the invisible wall in the middle of the table. In addition, several younger teachers, who despised the division, intentionally sat on the 'wrong' side of the table thus consciously challenging the ethnonational governance and cartography. The words of exchange across the divided table were uttered in an artificially loud voice, indexing something unnatural and daring about the act of communication. Regardless of these 'small' signs of progress, the tension was present and easily perceptible in the teachers' room, as Nadja explains:

> We will never mix in the teachers' room. *Why?* Because there is a habit in the people! Since the first day when we sat down [separately], we kept that habit. And it continues like that today – we sit on one side, and they [Croat teachers] sit on the other.

The class books – the large notebooks for each class in school with the names of students and their grades – were also divided based on the curriculum. The Croat ones were black and they were horizontally positioned on a small table next to the door of the teachers' room (so that teachers could grab them on the way to class), while the Federal ones were dark red and vertically positioned on a narrow shelf next to the table. This ordering of books and bodies along the contours of ethnic ideology of identity shaped, conveyed and confined the emotions and expressions of ethnic identity (Gilbert, 2008), visible in everyday discourses; even though the ethnic categories were not often mentioned in everyday speech at the school, the terms designating difference were frequently used, such as 'they' and 'us' (Čorkalo et al., 2005, p. 155). These conversations consistently included kin-like discursive formations such as 'our children/their children' and spatial indexicals that inserted ethnic bipolarity, such as 'our side/their side' .These linguistic utterances were sometimes followed by 'self-corrections' – some teachers, realizing the tension between integration and segregation in their speech, amended themselves by saying 'you know what I mean, they are all our kids, but I only interact with the ones in our curriculum so I call them "ours". But they are all our kids, of course'.

These articulations of ethnically conceived integration both challenge and subscribe to ethnic orientation, governance and citizenship. They reveal the ideological limitations and index its possible 'wrongness', especially discernible in the comment: 'but they are all our kids, of course'. At the same time, these comments reinsert the power of nationalist sentiments and linguistics orientations (such as 'our children/their children') at the level of an ethnic group, based on the ideology of an imagined horizontal relationship, loyalty, attachment and trust. These feelings and articulations of ethnic belonging where deepened during teachers' meetings which were mostly separated according to the curriculum, and where many articulations of internal embarrassment (about *our* students performing worse than those from the other curriculum, or about some teacher–parent incident that had to be minimized so that *they* would not think that *they* are more 'civilized', or …) and/or pride (that *our* kids did better at this competition, or that *our* curriculum was more progressive, or …) provided additional viscosity to cultural intimacy, thus solidifying ethnic identifications through intimate feelings of pride and embarrassment (Herzfeld, 2005). These feelings of fuzzy familiarity that acting ethnicity generated were powerfully congealed by the precision and overwhelming nature of ethnic spatiality and governmentality at the school, making instances of cross-ethnic solidarity during the strike all the more salient, visible and symbolic.

In addition to having to navigate the simultaneously divided and united space of work, many teachers realized that ethnic identities and identifications could not embrace the entire repertoire of the self at work – the shared experiences of social devaluation and

THE EUROPEANISATION OF CITIZENSHIP GOVERNANCE

economic struggle illuminated similarities between ethnically divided teachers. These similarities in teachers' subjectivities have their own, socialism-produced history, to which we now turn.

Economies and Poetics of Teaching: Then and Now

School used to be at the center of moral instruction and social upbringing during the time of Yugoslav socialism. While teachers never made fortune by instruction, their salary allowed for an economically decent and socially respectable life. The lack of economic capital was balanced with a great amount of cultural capital, since teachers were seen as the main engine for educating new socialist (wo)men. During the time of massive socialist growth and modernization in the 1950s and 1960s, teachers had an especially strong influence on their students; while many of the students' families were constrained by traditional, religious and conservative value systems that they frequently and secretly attempted to transmit to their children, the teachers' role was to 'liberate' youth from the limitations of tradition and family, and to educate them in a way suitable for the modern age of state socialism. Therefore, the role of teachers was of great importance for the socialist regime which charged teachers/education with the project to limit and contain the sources of traditionalism, religious practice, ethnonationalism and other related forms that the regime named as 'backward' or threatening to its socialist ideology.

The massive transformation of education in the early years of socialism demonstrates the ideology of educational policy to create a certain educated socialist person. It also points at socialism's great investment in schooling, and related authority of teachers, who were generally better educated than the rest of population. This started to change during the 1970s and the 1980s, as the illiteracy rate was decreasing rapidly and the population was becoming more educated in multiple fields. However, the symbolic and cultural capital of teachers remained relatively high.

This teacher positionality, however, changed drastically during recent times of 'war and peace' in the Balkans, which brought monumental political and social upheavals leading to paralyzing transformations, exaggerated social injustices, amplifying forms of conspicuous corruption and an increasing sense of disillusionment, political withdrawal and 'hibernation' in the general population (Hromadžić, 2014). The uncomfortable marriage between capitalism and undemocratic postwar democracy generated the crumbling of socialist services, and a strong desire for a fast road to material success, which often excluded traditional education. As a result, schooling became the site of 'semi-abandonment', enormous critique and an arena where greater frustrations about the absence of 'the system' were articulated via processes of massive cheating, purchasing of exams/diplomas and devaluation of types of knowledge that was difficult to transfer into immediate economic capital. Teachers were therefore dislocated from the center of the socialist project to the margins of the postwar (undemocratic) democracy. The investments in public education also shrank quickly, and when coupled by tremendously complicated bureaucracy, fragmented education infrastructure (Pantić, this issue), inadequate facilities, dramatic reduction in teachers' salaries and the low spirits in the profession, it became exceptionally morale-sapping (Farrell, 2001, p. 18). The rapid transformation and shrinking of economic status and declining social and cultural capital, decreased some teachers' eagerness to put their energy into educating youth, as Saša[14] explains:

THE EUROPEANISATION OF CITIZENSHIP GOVERNANCE

> … [F]or example, when I came to work here [immediately after the war] I was full of élan and enthusiasm, and that caused me some problems because students went home and said to their parents that they want to study history at college, because I taught history then. But now, I am just like the old teachers, I became the same.

The respect and authority of the teaching profession was additionally diminished, I was told, by the infiltration of prolific corruption and connections, so that even those teachers who wanted to stay 'clean' had no choice at times but to give in under heavy social pressure. This created a great amount of frustration, dissatisfaction and feeling of helplessness in the face of larger transformations, which were experienced as endemic to modernity, democracy and capitalism. The tension between teachers and students' parents, many of whom were perceived by teachers at the Mostar Gymnasium as new, 'immoral' elites, was constantly articulated within and outside the classroom space. The following note from the field captures one of those moments when the tension between economic and cultural capital was powerfully explicated by a geography teacher at the school.

In her lecture on Mostar landscape, the teacher introduced the rise of a new type of *novo-pečene elite*, literally 'newly baked elites' and their dangerous, kitschy and huge homes:

> … due to the type of soil on which the homes in the Strana neighborhood [where many new elites construct their homes] in Mostar are built, if there is an earthquake or a big flood, all those houses with their big fake lions [one of the main symbols of kitsch and 'bad' taste] are going to start sliding and they will push *narod* (common folk) into the Neretva [river].[15]

The teacher emphasized that the new elites who quickly and illicitly gained fortune overnight are lacking in cultural capital and she labeled them as 'uneducated and uncultured'. Their 'lack of culture' was visible in the absence of knowledge about the poor quality of Mostar's soil. In other words, in order to behave 'properly' one would need to 'know' Mostar – the type of knowledge only available to those with deep roots in *gradska sredina* ('urban environment'). These new, rural elites, who did not have deep roots in *gradska sredina* that generates cosmopolitan awareness and disposition, became, for this teacher, the source of the overall cultural decline, dangerous for the social, moral and even physical safety of (urban) Mostarians. The teacher suggested that the new elites 'simply' *ne znaju kako imati* (do not know how to have money) and that they are *nezasiti* (insatiable). Their greediness is explained as a consequence of their fast and questionable accumulation of money during and after the war, their upbringing and their habitus, which is described as raw, rural and *prost* (vulgar). These open critiques of those who were economically successful but culturally 'unequipped' were often dismissed by students and their parents as unpolished expressions of teachers' economic frustrations, their mal-adjustment to the new times, and teachers' inability to accept their declining status and fading authority.

What is more, various parents blamed teachers and crumbling education for the increasing 'withdrawal' of youth from school. They accused teachers of being unable to make schooling useful and interesting to young people coming of age in a postwar society. On the other hand, numerous teachers explained their inability to deal with youth in the language of 'the clash of generations'; the teachers described students' parents as 'impossible', disinterested in informing themselves about the work and behavior of their children,

THE EUROPEANISATION OF CITIZENSHIP GOVERNANCE

as Zemka complained: 'They [parents] do not want to deal with them at home, they do not know what to do with them, so they just send them to school, to us to raise them.' Some teachers, such as a well-experienced Suad, explained this disorientation and disinterest of parents as being an effect of the war:

> Parents are that generation ... that generation is specific since it found itself in the parental role during the war. And that was chaos ... as a result, these parents are not fully developed as persons, and I think that they simply do not know how to educate their children, or maybe it is better to say that they do not know how to find the right way to prepare that child to be a responsible adult in this chaotic world ... where to start from, which things to follow? These parents are lost, and they need help as well. But no one wants to admit that. What is lost, I think, is parents' vision of their children as persons, not just as a student who will get a piece of paper, but a person with developed moral components. That is important but it is not important to them. *What is important to them you ask?* Well, only the goal, not the effort to reach that goal.

Suad's comments illustrate how the grammar of generation is being used to articulate differences in upbringing, morality and life style; numerous teachers were linking the lack of students' respect toward their teachers to the declining family values and problematic home upbringing, disclosing deeper societal – including economic, cultural and generational – ruptures. The following teacher, Damir, went even further in these evaluations, while uncovering the intricate relationship between the war-produced generational identifications and divides, and contemporary economic and cultural capital:

> What you can see the most in the kids is the lack of fear. Honestly, I am not for a relationship based on fear. But kids misuse that lack of fear. You cannot do anything to them. [But] when I hear other professors saying that kids are impossible, I do not agree. Come on, kids are always the same, they are born *tabula rasa*, the real problem are *the parents*. They made their kids this way. They let them do anything; they do not discipline them at all. When I went to school, I got 20 cents per day because that is how much a bread role cost. Why would I need more? These kids however, they have anything they want. I know of parents who applied for loans just to afford new cell phones for their kids. Kids do not have to try hard for anything, including school, because they know they will get everything anyhow ... but they [parents] are probably emotional about the fact that these kids lived their early years during the war. Maybe they are just happy that their kids are alive ... But what I hate the most is that when you come to class you have to look at the name book and see whose kids are there, who their parents are. I promised to myself that I will never give better grades to someone because he is from a certain family, but recently I had a case when G. (one of school's employees) came up to me and said: 'Come on, he is the son of that and that guy, and he [the father] hopes his child can get a C in your subject.' But this student is illiterate and tomorrow he will get into the university and professors there will ask: 'where are these kids coming from?' Now I have one mother whose daughter I moved, because of bad behavior, from one seat to another, and she [mother] is ready to push it to the end just to have her child returned to the front desk. I was very firm about sticking to my actions, but the two people in our

management took me aside and said, 'Do not cause trouble for all of us.' And I let her (the student) come back to her seat. And I lost my authority in the classroom. And I felt terrible. Terrible. ... That same mother comes occasionally to inform herself about her child, and if her child has a bad grade in some subject, she makes threats. *What kinds of threats?* Well, she says how she will pay someone to beat that professor or she threatens to push them down the staircase. And I listen to her as she threatens us, and I think, 'Are we, the teachers, *always* the problem? Really?' These parents do not see themselves or their children realistically.

These teachers encapsulate multiple changes and upheavals in postwar society – the larger context of generational raptures deepened by the war; social injustice, corruption, alleged deterioration of moral standards, related loss of 'the system'; ethnicization of people and territory; and wasting away of bodies and souls. In the following excerpt from an interview I conducted with Vera, a teacher at *Stara Gimnazija,* the discontent, disorientation, despair and a deep sense of postsocialist social disillusionment became especially visible:

> Vera: Well, the mentality of a student has changed. The experience of schooling changed. The school lost its authoritative position [in the society]. School is not at the center of life anymore, it is marginal.
>
> Azra: What is the center today?
>
> Vera: Well I do not know. I could not ... When I think about their [youth's] way of life, I see in them some emptiness, terrible emptiness. Something would have to replace the role of school or school would have to become different ... in my students before, I recognized some interest, a sense of inquiry, preoccupation with some larger problems, through which I saw that process of maturing, how they develop, piece by piece, into complete persons ... but, now I see some passivity, some indifference which I do not understand, because we all suffered some traumas, and none of us are the same as we were before the war. They simply lost school as a value. [For them] School is a necessary evil, not a goal. Something definitely has to change ... I am thinking about moral values, human values, simply some *system* which respects progress, work, and knowledge. That is lost. A great problem is the corruption of the society, that mentality in which everything can be exchanged and bought. And students see that.

Vera, Saša and Damir captured beautifully the profound ideological and social changes that have been shaping everyday lives of 'ordinary' Bosnians, by pointing at the collapse of the 'system' – during the Yugoslav times, they indicated, there was a (moral) 'system' of values, rules and practices that was available, enforced, lived and embodied.[16] The war and the end of socialism all but destroyed this order, creating massive social, economic and moral raptures which resulted in what felt like an existential crisis, forcing good people, including teachers, to behave unethically (Greenberg, 2011, p. 89). Teachers' moving reflections on the purpose of education and the teaching profession revealed the loss of balance in the shifting social fields and disrupted value systems which obstructed communication between the main stakeholders: teachers, parents and students. Teachers also pointed at larger social injustices, especially conspicuous, open and even celebrated corruption, for debasing the youth so that they started to think that today 'everything

THE EUROPEANISATION OF CITIZENSHIP GOVERNANCE

can be bought', thus absorbing an ideology that material wealth is sympathetic to moral wealth (Pilkington, 2002, p. 125).

Several months after I left Stara Gimnazija I received an email from a school employee who informed me that Vera was a victim of a violent attack. A student whom she failed twice on the final exam tried to strangle her. While many people I talked to about this incident said that the student's behavior was unacceptable, others blamed the teacher, saying:

> what can one say about this? We all expected this behavior of the student, because Vera's communication with them is dying out. I hoped that she would learn something from this incident, but nothing has changed, she still makes mistakes in her work with students, for example she forgets what she said to them, she is not consistent in her work, she has no fixed criteria or expectations, and many other things.

Being caught between several levels of what they experienced as deep injustices – including the loss of status, low salaries, physical threats and continuous complaints of the students – teachers from both curricula, regardless of their ethnically defined and spatially produced citizenship, shared the same burden of confronting the larger society 'without the system'. The effects of these multiple tensions, expectations, disillusionments and frustrations, that teachers as dissatisfied and devalued postwar (ethnically divided) and postsocialist (economically diminished and socially displaced) citizens faced in everyday life, became especially visible during the teachers' strike in February 2006.

Striking Together: Coordinates of Professional Intimacy

Soon after I returned to Mostar from winter vacation in 2006, a turbulent wave of activities shook up the school. In early February the new teachers' strike became the most frequently discussed issue at the school and beyond; when ethnically divided 'Croat' and 'Bosniak' teachers came together to support teachers elsewhere in the country, and to request better salaries, respect and dignity, they had to carefully navigate the dominant, ethnonational domain of citizen-intimacy.

Media wrote and reported extensively on the question of the approaching strike. Teachers' strikes became a regular phenomenon in postwar Bosnia–Herzegovina; this time the main reason for the strike was the request of the elementary and secondary schools teachers' unions to receive an equal base salary with those employed in the city and cantonal administration. The government met with the representatives of the teachers' unions, and after numerous talks, made no progress.

On a crisp but sunny day in early February, I came to the teachers' room to learn that teachers in the neighboring Croat-dominated West Herzegovina Canton had already been on strike for 20 days. On this day, Stara Gimnazija and other schools in west Mostar decided to start a solidarity strike to support the teachers form the neighboring canton. This at first applied only to the teachers in the Croat Curriculum, again asserting the contours of ethnicity and ethnically conceived selves at work. The solidarity strike meant that teachers in this curriculum would not teach the last class period but would let the kids loose. If, however, the aforementioned teachers unions' requests were not to be met by the cantonal government, the general strike was to begin on 13 February.

Some days before the strike, in a popular political show on Federal television, the head of the High School Teachers' Union for the Croat Curriculum announced the

103

THE EUROPEANISATION OF CITIZENSHIP GOVERNANCE

13 February date and he said that on that day teachers would start peaceful demonstrations on the streets:

> 'You see how far we have to go. Teachers' have to go out on the streets, but that is our reality. It will be embarrassing to go back to the classrooms after this is over, to sit with students, but the state of education is such that we are forced to do this. And those government officials who sit in their nice armchairs threatened us. L. [the president of the cantonal government] said that he will fire all 1,200 high school teachers in the canton, and that he will bring Ukrainians to teach.' He smiled and concluded: 'I suggest to him that it would be better if he would bring the Ukrainian women' [alluding to the sexual trade of women].

The next day I spoke about this comment to several teachers who felt disturbed by the interview, as Iva explained: 'Did you see that? I really think that we have good reasons to go on strike. But look who is leading me: *Prostak* (Vulgar man)! How can I follow him when he is so sexist, so primitive?'

When I entered the teachers' room on 11 February, I stepped into an unusually active, loud and heated discussion among the teachers. Damir explained to me that they were discussing the certainty of the approaching strike, and that the Federal Curriculum teachers were to join the teachers in the Croat Curriculum and strike together. During the loud exchange, I learned about many grievances that the teachers in both curricula shared: that the gap between teachers' and cleaning women's salaries was the narrowest in history, for example. I was given details about the teachers' request to increase their base salary by 30 per cent. The fury about economic inequalities brought the ethnically divided teachers' together into a heated discussion, narrowing the gap between the two ethnically divided sides of the large table. Literary everyone, including the ethnographer, was talking at the same time, discussing the possibilities of acting together. Teachers' bodies gravitated toward the center of the room, as they were physically leaning over the table, toward the center of it, as if temporarily disregarding the imperceptible yet potent walls of ethnicity. And yet, the contours of ethnic divisions permeated the newly found professional viscosity of bodies and life projects: there were two teachers' unions, for example, the union of the teachers employed in the Croat Curriculum and the union of the Federal Curriculum teachers, showing once again, the intertwined yet inharmonious relationship between professional and ethnic solidarity. In this situation they closely cooperated through the language of professional ethic and economic struggle, minimizing the prevalence of the ethnic order of things, as the head of the Elementary Schools Teachers' Union, Omer Spaho explained:

> Our common problems unite the unions. We really have a huge support of all unions in the canton. We also have their signatures of support, as well as the signatures of the teachers who are not in the union, but who also want, just like us, to live normal lives. The support comes from all workers, therefore the whole canton is like one man, and that is the proof of our success. I do not know when the unions that work according to the Croat Curriculum and the ones that work according to the Federal Curriculum will be united. We are in a totally identical situation, especially now, and these problems we have in common will make us even more united, and soon we will all be

THE EUROPEANISATION OF CITIZENSHIP GOVERNANCE

like one. We are, I stress, very united even now, and many things we solve jointly. (*Nova Sloboda*, 2006, br. 26, pp. 10–11)

As if echoing Spaho's words, on the windy day of the strike, more than a few hundred teachers and students from both sides of town/curriculum came together in front of the Cantonal Ministry on Mostar's west side. Even though the new sense of commonality developed among the teachers of the two unions and by extension the two ethnic groups, it also created tensions since the strike embodied conflicting forms of maneuvering and political hopes. The complexity of these interactions became visible when some teachers started to see the strike and the unions as spectacles of nationalist politics, as Irma explains:

> I am very upset that I went to protest in front of the government building. I feel manipulated … someone calls me there to protest in the name of teachers' cause, and then they talk to me about the church and religion. How can it be? How can I follow someone who tells me that nation is the same as religion? And that someone tells me at the end 'let's all observe the minute of silence for the death of government.' Imagine! I do not want anyone's death. We were all very well manipulated by someone who wanted this for their political gains … the elections are approaching, and they are using this. These people to lead me? Never! I finished at the emergency room last night, I was freezing out there for four hours, and I got so upset with everything. At the end I had to take some *tablete za smirenje* (tranquilizers).

This example demonstrates the bodily effects of the tension between professional solidarity and ethnonational citizenship. In this tense yet fluid space of social poetics, different categories of belonging were negotiated to temporarily include or exclude ethnic others. This fluidity was shaped by contingent economic, political and historic momentum, and it pointed at the tension between simultaneously convergent (professional, social and economic) and a dispersive (ethnonational) conception of collective intimacy and citizen-agency. Furthermore, these tensions were often articulated through the non-linguistic register of the somatic – it was Irma's body that became the diagnostic of the pulls between different forms of belonging, political engagement and acting; many people experienced the strike as an intertwined issue of 'health and wealth' (Jašarević, 2011) manifested in the visits to the emergency room, in bodies frozen by the weather and paralyzed by political maneuvering, and in open consumption and circulation of tranquilizers to 'calm the nerves' during the strike.

Even though they were on strike, teachers were still obligated to come to school and teach if there were any students present. Students' were asking teachers what to do; if they should come to school or not, and many of them joined their teachers at strike. Teachers developed their own, idiosyncratic ways of explaining the purposes and goals of the strike to their students, many of whom felt ambivalent about the teachers' requests, their parents' incompatible interpretations of the events, and their own desires and horizons of hope and expectation. The management of the school, which sided with the government, sent the message that for as long as there is one student in class, teachers still have to teach and that all students should attend classes. Some teachers, irritated by these orders, disobeyed the rule and said to students to leave the classroom. In order to prevent the management from intimidating the teachers, Zvonimir, the head of the Croat High School Teachers

THE EUROPEANISATION OF CITIZENSHIP GOVERNANCE

Union and a teacher at the school, came to school early one Wednesday, and allegedly started threatening the students he saw at the school that they would fail his class if they did not leave the school. Many students stopped coming to school after this incident, which was sharply criticized by the government and the media who accused the professor and the unions for using 'children as weapons'. Many teachers agreed with Zvonimir that the government, via management of the school, tried to manipulate the teachers and the public opinion, but they also disagreed with the way in which Zvonimir handled this issue. They remained publically silent, in a state of limbo, aware of the precariousness of the situation, even though they relentlessly complained to each other about Zvonimir and his, as one teacher put it, 'sexist, aggressive and nationalist' ways.

The opposing messages of the management of the school on the one side and the teachers on the other confused the students and their parents at first. Some students continued to come to school regularly while others, who said that they wanted to support the teachers, stopped coming and spent most of their school time at nearby coffee shops. The head of the Student Council told me that the Council met to discuss the situation, and 'all we could conclude was that we cannot say anything because we are too confused'.

The chaos continued as the gap between the teachers' unions and the government widened, and since the government accused and constantly repeated that the unions were using 'children as weapons'. The media also criticized the behavior of the few teachers who allegedly threatened students with bad grades if they attended classes. Meanwhile, the teachers' room became a micro world of society in its full complexity. Confusion trickled into this space, where teachers' started to frequently speak in louder voices, continuously complaining about being misused by everyone: by their own unions and by the government that threatened them, while securing 17 times higher salaries for themselves (teacher's comment). These multiple discourses and contradictory expectations thus reflected the teachers' unique professional ethic as well as identifications with the hegemony; the hegemony stressed the profession's service over personal gain. This hegemony in turn exploited the teachers since 'one of the distinctions of a profession is that it means to its followers service and enthusiasm rather than income' (Bekerman, 2012, p. 553).

This was the polygonal background against which parents and the general public accused teachers of not being 'true' to their profession and for using 'children as weapons'. As the antagonism between the government and the teachers grew, teachers nick-named Jago Musa, then the Cantonal Minister of Education, 'Mussolini'. Teachers also complained, in the language of hegemony (sacrifice, enthusiasm and love), that media was the government's ally since it took a stance against them: 'They all forget that no one cares more about these kids then we do! That [love for children] is why we became teachers in the first place!'

This chaotic situation also confused and angered students' parents. At first, parents were inactive. A month into the strike, after realizing the seriousness of the situation, parents decided to act as mediators between the government and the unions. As a result, the parents associations of six schools in Mostar got together and requested that the government and the unions sit down together and find a solution. They also admitted that partial responsibility rested on the Parents Associations because they did not address the problem in time. Parents stressed that they did not support either side but they urged both sides to find a compromise.

THE EUROPEANISATION OF CITIZENSHIP GOVERNANCE

While the official position of parents was admirable in its balanced rhetoric and self-critique, the opinions I collected in private were less balanced. I visited one student at home during the strike and her mother told me that she supported the government in this case: 'I understand that it is hard to be a teacher today, but it is hard for everyone in this country, and did you know that those teachers have higher salaries than some doctors?' she concluded.[17] Parents found themselves in a puzzling situation because many supported teachers' requests for better and more regular salaries, but they were worried about their children's prospects and they expected the teachers to act according to the altruistic ideology of a teaching profession. At the end, the second issue prevailed, as one parent explained:

> I support teachers in their quest for better and regular salaries. But children have to be protected, and they should not suffer because of someone's problems. We have to separate these two situations, because that is like a doctor going on strike when his patient is dying in the hospital.

While this parent reproduced the ideology of the teaching profession as selfless, other-invested and sacrificial, other parents were much more aggressive when articulating similar stances, and they often criticized teachers for their inability to see the whole picture, as Goran explains:

> I support the teachers, of course, but I do not support their means. They use my kids to get what they want. It cannot be that my child does not go to school for a month because of someone's request for the salary increase. In this kind of broken system, in this kind of divided society, teachers cannot behave as if they are outside of that society. What I mean is that you cannot compare their situation with the situation of the miners who are sitting in the mines, hungry, because they did not receive 25 salaries. My child should not suffer because of somebody's increase in the basic salary! Teachers really crossed the line.

Some teachers responded to these critiques by saying that the children of teachers also needed to eat, thus emphasizing the dire economic situation that their families had to endure. Regardless of these cries, the complexity of events and emotional states, including internal conflicts, aggressive actions and increasing despair, shifted parents' and public's opinion against the teachers and their chosen methods in meeting their request for better economic compensation, cultural capital and social status. The strike ended with teachers giving in to these growing pressures and returning to the classroom without having the majority of their needs met. Many teachers blamed the larger social tensions and forms of politicking for the strike's overall failure. And yet, many teachers at the Mostar Gymnasium remarked that the strike did bring about a fundamental change in their way of thinking about the politics of possibility and horizons of hope in an ethnically divided school/ state. This shift in the perception of the self, the other and the society was a form of 'weak power' (Fiske, 1993) that stays invisible under the larger structures of social organization, economic inequality and forms of cultural intimacy in a 'deeply divided society'. This weak power was still transformative, not of larger structures but of teachers' subjectivities since these dissatisfied citizens emerged from striking together as political subjects with a new layer and understanding of the nature, terrain and possibilities of professional solidarity across ethnic difference in an ethnically divided country.

Conclusion

The Teachers' strike in Mostar illuminated the complicated terrain of lived citizenship in postwar Bosnia–Herzegovina. The international and local political actors have been reproducing, in their policies and practices – including the reunification of the Mostar Gymnasium – a narrow script of ethnically managed groups and territories. At the same time, difficult economic circumstances and experiences of inequality motivated teachers at the Mostar Gymnasium and beyond to organize across ethnic lines in order to take collective action, thus engaging in a political struggle to articulate their citizen demands based on a shared economic predicament.

The teachers' feelings of being left out of administrative procedures – which enabled access to rightful entitlements – led to the formation of a teachers' protest group. Regardless of their deeply divided city and opposing ideologies, teachers – dissatisfied citizens – were protesting together, insisting on their right to be treated as equal citizens. On their path to professional citizen-affirmation, they continually negotiated a shifting terrain of practices, actions and identifications, and offered the possibility of imagining new horizons of solidarity and hope. These actions partially disrupted but never fully transformed the ethnonational order of things.

In this case, the expression of professional solidarity manifested itself in people coming together around issues of being citizen-teachers in a deeply transformed postwar and postsocialist country where being a teacher lost much of its former socialist prestige. This coming together was only seemingly unsuccessful, that is to say, disordered and incomplete, and 'weak' in the face of powerful spatial governmentality and cultural incommensurability. This diagnostic event was neither a powerful weapon of the weak, nor a hegemonic tool of ethnic nationalism. Rather, it emerged at intersections and through dialogue and renegotiation of prevalent forms of (ethnic) citizen subjectivities. In this way, the striking together was not separable from the history of socialism and ethnonationalism within which it materialized, to which it eventually returned, and with which it stayed intimately entwined. And yet, teachers' coming together and striking together offered a space for deepening citizen sensibility and democratic possibility, even if imperfect and provisional.

Acknowledgements

I am especially grateful to Larisa Kurtović for her intellectual contribution and to Heather M. Riddle for her help with editing. I also thank two anonymous reviewers for their encouraging, challenging and helpful comments.

Disclosure statement

No potential conflict of interest was reported by the author.

Funding

The research and writing of this article have been supported by a number of grants and fellowships received from the Social Science Research Council International Dissertation Field Research Fellowship; the United States Institute of Peace, the American Council of Learned Societies; the American Association of the University Women; the Spencer Foundation; Penfield; and the Josephine De Karman Fellowship.

THE EUROPEANISATION OF CITIZENSHIP GOVERNANCE

Notes

[1] In this article I mostly use Bosnia–Herzegovina when referring to the state. Where stylistically more appropriate, however, I use the shorter construction, Bosnia.

[2] Parts of this section, slightly modified, have been published in Hromadžić (2015), Introduction and Chapter I.

[3] Most people accept the beginning of the siege of Sarajevo, which started on 6 April 1992, as a start of the Bosnian war. Others, however, suggest that the beginning moment was the JNA's attack, in November 1991, on the Croatian village Ravno in eastern Herzegovina.

[4] At the congress of Muslim intellectuals in 1993 the terms Bosniak or Bosniac (*Bošnjak*) officially replaced the term Muslim.

[5] The ten cantons in FBiH fall into three groups: five in which Bosniaks are the majority population, three Croatian-majority cantons and two 'mixed' cantons.

[6] Here I expand on Merry's (2001) notion of spatial governmentality which she understands as gendered mechanisms of spatial segregation, discipline and punishment found in postmodern cities.

[7] The Mostar Gymnasium is the first of the 54 'two schools under one roof' which has been reunified. 'Two schools under one roof' refers to those schools in FB&H where Croat and Bosniak students are ethnically segregated while attending the same school building.

[8] Administrative unification includes the following:

> appointment of one school director; appointment of one, multiethnic school board; registration of the school as one legal body with a single school name; establishment of joint administrative personnel; development of a joint budget; and participation of school directors and teachers in joint planning activities for the new school year. (OSCE, 2005, p. 20)

[9] The computer science classes were fully integrated after I left the field, however. As a consequence, for the first time since the beginning of the war, Bosniak and Croat students jointly attended classes (Principal of the Gymnasium. E-mail to the author. 20 February 2008).

[10] The Croat curriculum emphasizes the Croat language, history and geography. The Federal curriculum focuses on the history of Bosnia–Herzegovina, primarily Bosniak authors, Bosniak-dominated history and Bosnian language.

[11] Parts of this section, slightly modified, have been published in Hromadžić (2015), Chapter II.

[12] I am grateful to Larisa Kurtović for this comment.

[13] See note 12.

[14] The names (and sometimes gender) of informants have been changed to protect their privacy.

[15] This paragraph has been published in Hromadžić (2015, p. 170).

[16] This semi-static image of unspoiled and irrecoverable past is crucial for the representations of 'a larger universe of system and balance' (Herzfeld, 2005, p.104). Herzfeld calls this phenomena 'structural nostalgia' which he defines as a 'collective representation of an edenic order – a time before time – in which the balanced perfection of social relations has not yet suffered decay that affects everything human' (Herzfeld, 2005, p. 104).

[17] This statement does not reflect reality – doctors are, in general, significantly better paid than teachers in the country.

References

Bekerman, Z. (2012) Teachers' 'contact' at the integrated bilingual schools in Israel, *Policy Futures in Education*, 10(5), pp. 552–562.

Chandler, D. (1999) *Bosnia: Faking Democracy after Dayton* (London: Pluto Press).

Čorkalo, D., Ajduković, D., Weinstein, H. M., Stover, E., Đipa, D. & Biro, M. (2005) Neighbors again? Intercommunity relations after ethnic cleansing, in: E. Stover & H. M. Weinstein (Eds) *My Neighbor, My Enemy: Justice and Community in the Aftermath of Mass Atrocity,* pp. 143–161 (Cambridge: Cambridge University Press).

Farrell, S. (2001) *An Investigation into the Experimental School Strategy in the Promotion of School Improvement and of Social Sohesion through Education, in Bosnia and Herzegovina* (Northern Ireland, University of Ulster: Master Thesis).

THE EUROPEANISATION OF CITIZENSHIP GOVERNANCE

Fernandez, J. W. (1986) *Persuasions and Performances: The Play of Tropes in Culture* (Bloomington: Indiana University Press).

Fiske, J. (1993) *Power Plays, Power Works* (London and New York: Verso).

Gagnon, Jr. V. P. (n.d.) *Liberal Multiculturalism and Post-Dayton Bosnia: Solution or Problem?* (Ithaca, NY: Cornell, Unpublished paper).

Gilbert, A. (2008) *Foreign Authority and the Politics of Impartiality in Postwar Bosnia Herzegovina* (Chicago, IL: University of Chicago, Ph.D. Dissertation).

Greenberg, J. (2011) On the road to normal: Negotiating agency and state sovereignty in postsocialist Serbia, *American Anthropologist*, 113(1), pp. 88–100.

Herzfeld, M. (2005) *Cultural Intimacy: Social Poetics in the Nation-State*, 2nd ed. (New York: Routledge).

Hromadžić, A. (2014) Only when the spider web becomes too heavy: Youth, unemployment and the social life of waiting in postwar and postsocialist Bosnia-Herzegovina, *The Journal of Social Policy*, 11, pp. 45–87.

Hromadžić, A. (2015) *Citizens of an Empty Nation: Youth and State-Making in Postwar Bosnia and Herzegovina* (Philadelphia: University of Pennsylvania Press).

Jašarević, L. (n.d.) *On the Queen's Couch, By the Wizard's Grave: Healing Surfaces and Political Dispositions in Postsocialist Bosnia* (Chicago, IL: University of Chicago Press, Unpublished article).

Kurtović, L. (2011) What is a nationalist? Some thoughts on the question from Bosnia-Herzegovina, *Anthropology of Eastern Europe Review*, 29(2), pp. 242–253.

Merry, S. E. (2001) Spatial governmentality and the new social order: Controlling gender violence through law, *American Anthropologist*, 103(1), pp. 16–29.

Nova Sloboda. (2006) Omer Spaho: "Prosvjetari u dilemi-štrajka (ne)će biti" [Omer Spaho: "Educators in a dilemma – strike will (not) be"], 10 February, 26(10), pp. 11.

OSCE (Office for Security and Cooperation in Europe) (2005) *Gymnasium Mostar, Mostar's 'Other Landmark': Reconstruction and Revitalization Efforts* (Mostar, Unpublished Report).

Pantić, Nataša. (2015) Citizenship and education in the post-Yugoslav states. *European Politics and Society*, 16 (3), pp. 411–428.

Pilkington, H. (2002) *Looking West: Cultural Globalization and Russian Youth Culture* (University Park: Pennsylvania State University Press).

Sarajlić, E. (2011) The Convenient Consociation: Bosnia and Herzegovina, Ethnopolitics and the EU. In F. Cheneval & S. Ramel (Eds) *From Peace to Shared Political Identities: Exploring Pathways in Contemporary Bosnia-Herzegovina.* Special issue, Transitions, 51(1–2), pp. 61–80.

Stolcke, V. (1995) Talking culture: New boundaries, new rhetorics of exclusion in Europe, *Current Anthropology*, 36(1), pp. 1–24.

Taylor, D. (1997) *Disappearing Acts: Spectacles of Gender and Nationalism in Argentina's 'Dirty war'* (Durham, NC: Duke University Press).

Vetters, L. (2007) The power of administrative categories: Emerging notions of citizenship in the divided city of Mostar, *Ethnopolitics*, 6(2), pp. 187–209.

Conclusion

Citizenship and the Practice of Governance in South-East Europe

ANDREW GEDDES

Department of Politics, University of Sheffield, UK

ABSTRACT *The key objective of this Conclusion is to highlight the broader conceptual, empirical and methodological contributions of this edited volume. Reflecting on the paired articles, the conclusion explores the implications of the collection on the interplay between the modes of governance that constitute citizenship regimes and their effects on 'lived citizenship' that characterise individuals' experiences of this governance.*

Introduction

It is a pleasure to have the opportunity to reflect upon and offer some concluding thoughts on the fascinating collection of articles brought together in this special issue. The articles demonstrate not only the skills and insight of the authors, but also reflect and further enhance the wider contributions made by the *The Europeanisation of Citizenship in the Successor States of the Former Yugoslavia* (CITSEE) project.

More specifically, the task assigned for this conclusion is to reflect on the broader contributions made by this collection, which has conceptual, empirical and methodological dimensions. By first drawing out some of the conclusions from the articles, or to be more precise, the paired articles, it is then possible to think about the advances that are made and about their contribution to the wider research field. It is suggested, in particular, that this could mean reflecting on the meaning of governance itself, the adaptive (or perhaps maladaptive) behaviour of governance systems and the quotidian practices of governance that play a key role in constituting citizenship. Indeed a focus on practices is central to this collection and that becomes particularly evident in those contributions that address the issue of 'lived citizenship', which directs attention not only to modes or strategies of governance but also to practices and experience of governance and their effects.

One other immediate and introductory point that foregrounds this discussion concerns the wider relevance of these articles. They all contain fine-grained analysis and mobilise an enormous amount of fresh material, but all can be seen to speak to much wider debates in contemporary European politics and also find some echoes outside south east

THE EUROPEANISATION OF CITIZENSHIP GOVERNANCE

Europe. To take just two examples, whether it be the interplay between visa policy and securitisation explored in Kacarska's contribution or the persistence and effects of clientelistic forms of politics in Croatia assessed by Stubbs and Zrinščak there are clear points of alignment with developments in other parts of Europe. While all the articles demonstrate sensitivity to context, they all also make points that go beyond the intricacies of the particular case studies that are being assessed to speak to wider conceptual and empirical debates. Not least, the meaning and practice of citizenship play key roles in domestic politics, relations with neighbouring states and actual or potential integration within the EU. The specific cases in this collection all highlight more general issues and for this – and other reasons – make important contributions to their respective research fields.

In terms of their organisation, these concluding remarks look first at the contributions made by the papers, which means thinking in particular about the range of social and political factors that shape lived citizenship in South East Europe. The next section then explores in more detail some of the implications of these papers for understandings of governance and also makes links between the governance, adaptation and practice. A final section then considers the wider implications of this special issue for future research.

Contributions of the Articles

Clearly, a key contribution offered by this special issue is to shed new light on the governance of citizenship practices that goes beyond an understanding of citizenship as a formal, legal status to also explore processes of citizenship. While the word 'laboratory' is inadequate, too cold and too clinical to capture the complexities and specificities of developments in Bosnia and Herzegovina, Croatia, Kosovo, Macedonia, Montenegro and Serbia, they all do provide fascinating tests of terms and concepts that resonate in debates about the development, consolidation and transformation of the state in south east Europe and more widely. These are necessarily entangled with the meaning and effects of European integration on citizenship and practices of governance, as well as a wider set of influences that emanate from other European and international norms and standards.

The articles also engage with another important theme in the contemporary analysis of the European Union (EU), which is the Union's so-called 'transformative power'. By assessing the range of external and internal influences on social and political change in South-East Europe, the articles provide interesting insight into this idea of the EU as exercising transformative power. This includes both the nature and characteristic features of this power – its normativity – as well as the mediation of this power in the context of social and political processes within the five countries.

Looming large in many of the articles is the centrality of ethno-national identities to citizenship policies and the key role, as Džankić et al. note in the Introduction, of citizenship as a pragmatic and symbolic representation of what the state is intended to be. While EU membership necessarily involves the striking of a 'sovereignty bargain' with some ceding or pooling of authority seen as bringing wider benefits, or a 'capacity bargain', such elite level 'bargains' have effects that work their way into the day to day practices of lived citizenship (Mattli, 1999; Geddes & Taylor, 2013).

The articles draw from a broad understanding of citizenship and extend their focus beyond the EU's influence to explore the resonance of a wider range of European and international standards on the meaning and practice of citizenship in South-East Europe. While

THE EUROPEANISATION OF CITIZENSHIP GOVERNANCE

not necessarily a new insight, the special issue demonstrates that Europeanisation should not be seen as unidirectional. In fact, and again in line with other work on the EU's effects, we see descriptors such as 'contested' added to the word 'Europeanisation' as well as a range of other factors both internal and external that can affect social and political change and interact with EU effects. It is not entirely surprising, as we do see in these articles, to see 'adaptation with national colours' to EU requirements, as this is already a key finding of the Europeanisation literature (Green-Cowles et al., 2001). But what we also see – and something that is evident more generally across the EU – is the increased contestation of European integration. For example, the articles by Stambolieva and by Stubbs and Zrinščak are framed by the effects of the economic crisis on social citizenship and welfare in Croatia, which unavoidably forms part of the context within which the effects of European integration will be mediated in domestic politics, as well as also influencing the standards and practices associated with adaptation to these EU requirements.

The pairing of the papers also helps to clarify the variation in EU effects. Džankić and Kacarska analyse regulatory issues of extradition, migration and mobility where the EU's impact is direct, strong and transformative with implications not only for state identity and citizen's rights but also for domestic adaptation to these requirements. Džankić's identification of four characteristics of Europeanisation is particularly helpful in specifying the meaning that the EU and its requirements can acquire as a shaper of governing practices. The four characteristics of Europeanisation that Džankić identifies are: initial stabilisation; tensions around sovereignty; the multivalent nature of external influences linked both to the EU influences and to other European and international norms and standards; and, finally, the scope for learning and adaptation and local variations. In short, these four characteristics capture the relationship and potential tensions between external influences and social and political processes within the five countries. This is a point reinforced by Kacarska's analysis that focuses, in particular, on the multivalency of Europeanisation as well as domestic processes of learning and adaptation. This means looking in close detail at the EU's effects at national level and how certain actors may be empowered and others weakened. Kacarska shows an effect of Europeanisation of visa policy has been the empowering of security actors and the establishment of 'securitised' governance practices that run counter to a rights-based discourse. Also highlighted are more informal processes of information sharing and knowledge exchange that, while informal, are clearly an important component of the transmission of ideas and practices within the EU.

The focus then shifts to articles that explore distributive questions of 'who gets what' through analyses that explore welfare, social rights and social citizenship. Again, the richness of the analysis and quality of the empirical contribution is very high. These are also areas where EU effects are less direct as the meaning and organisation of welfare and social rights will reflect established legacies as well as the effects of state transformation. This is not to say that external influences are irrelevant; clearly the EU plays a role as too do the effects of the post-2008 financial crisis, but as Stambolieva shows, the EUs effects are 'uneven'. Stambolieva provides a fine-grained assessment of the specificities of social citizenship as a status and a process in Bosnia-Herzegovina, Croatia, Kosovo, Macedonia, Montenegro and Serbia and its relationship to the institutions of the welfare state. She highlights the role played by clientelistic forms of politics, which is a point then taken forward by Stubbs and Zrinščak in their detailed assessment of Croatia within which clientelistic forms of politics and associated exchanges are seen as demonstrating the limits to Europeanisation and a rather gloomy prognosis about the future of social citizenship in Croatia.

THE EUROPEANISATION OF CITIZENSHIP GOVERNANCE

Stubbs and Zrinščak also offer interesting insight into governance, or more particularly into one of the descriptors that is frequently added to the word in EU studies: 'multi-level governance'. At its most basic, multi-level governance implies a conceptual broadening and widening of analysis of political authority and power to take into account the involvement of a wider range of public and private actors within the domestic polity plus the involvement of sub-national and, importantly, supranational actors at EU level in policy shaping and making (Taylor et al., 2013). Stubbs and Zrinščak move beyond a description of the Croatian political system as 'multi-level' – which in some senses is a statement of the obvious – to look much more closely at the captured and categorical distribution effects that arise as a result of clientelistic politics. Connecting thinking back to the first set of paired papers, there is also a link between the analyses of extradition and free movement offered by Džankić and Kacarska as those of welfare and social citizenship provided by Strambolieva and by Stubbs and Zrinščak. All draw our attention to the ways in which practices of governance play a key role in the construction of citizenship both as a status and process in South-East Europe. They also highlight the importance of exploring the adaptive – or maladaptive – features of governance systems. These points about governance, adaptation and practice are picked up again in the section that follows this.

The final two paired articles further enhance the level of insight as the focus shifts to education. Pantić looks at the interplay between education and citizenship to highlight once again the importance of practices of governance when specifying the key role played by governance structures in shaping social and political space and associated discourses of inclusion, exclusion, belonging and entitlement. Pantić also identifies the adaptability of both political systems and governing elites in adopting international norms to advance their own agendas and suggests that compliance with EU requirements might be instrumental or symbolic rather then representative of deeper transformation. The final paper by Hromadžić provides an ethnographic and anthropological perspective on the strike by Croat and Bosniak teachers at the Mostar Gymnasium as a way to articulate their 'profession-shaped citizen-demands'. Hromadžić moves beyond ethno-national understandings and associated 'governmentalities' of 'lived citizenship' to identify professional solidarity as a site of citizenship. Through her assessment of the localisation of power Hromadžić also shows that, even though such power may be weaker, it does have potentially transformative effects rooted in shared experiences and the living of citizenship previous shaped by the 'ethnonational order of things'. While markedly different from the top-down analysis of the EU's transformative power that was evident in other articles, it is possible to identify the importance of practices of governance in both the construction and meaning of citizenship in South-East Europe.

Governance, Adaptation and Practices

The articles all contribute directly and insightfully to the special issue's core purpose, which is to adopt a broad understanding of the policies that regulate the distribution of rights and thus to understand more about the governance of citizenship. All the papers have interesting and important things to say about citizenship, rights, the meaning of governance, the adaptive behaviour of governance systems as well as about the meaning and effects of practices. This final section now seeks to draw out some points about all three of these terms – governance, adaptation and practice – and to think through some of their implications.

THE EUROPEANISATION OF CITIZENSHIP GOVERNANCE

The term governance casts quite a long shadow over the articles in this collection whether it be modes or strategies of governance or the effects of governance understood as illustrative of governmentalities. There is not space here for a comprehensive overview of the meaning of governance. Instead, it might be more helpful to make two points. First, it does seem more common that analyses focus on the descriptor to be added to the term whether it be 'good', 'bad', 'multi-level' or 'sub-optimal'. The term governance also alludes to transformations of the state with a wider range of public and private actors involved in social and political decision-making and a re-scaling of these decision-making processes marked by a greater involvement by sub-national and supranational actors. Yet, this focus on the supposed changes induced or linked to new or multi-level modes of governance does not help with the meaning of the term itself. The articles in this collection can, in fact, help move towards a more refined understanding of the meaning of governance as a strategy, a process and a practice. The Introduction to the special points to the importance of a broad understanding of the policies and issues that relate to the governance of citizenship while each of the articles does attempt to conceptualise underlying social systems and their adaptive capacities. On this basis it can then be argued that there is a common understanding of the term governance that runs through this collection, which is to see it as involving both the conceptual representation of social systems and the empirical analysis of the capacity of these systems to change or to adapt (Pierre, 2000). This understanding privileges no particular site or location of governance and involves assessments that look both at the European, national and local levels, as well as the interactions between them. The result is that processes of systemic adaptation and change play out across a range of levels and involve very different actors, varying types of power relationship while also having markedly diverse effects. However, the common point that remains across all of the articles is an attempt to conceptualise the underlying dynamics of social systems in each of the five countries and in a variety of policy fields (extradition, visas, social rights, welfare and education) and then to understand more about adaptation, adaptability or perhaps even maladaptation, which may also be another way of thinking about the potential and limits of Europeanisation and governance strategies and practices whether they be 'effective' or 'sub-optimal'.

The sectoral variation that we see through the paired articles highlights the capacity of states to adapt, but also that, as Weiss (1998, p. 4) has observed, states are not uniformly effective in what they undertake, which means that any discussion of capacity must account for sectoral variations. Weiss' insights into what she calls the 'cataltyic state' resonate with some of the findings emerging from this special issue. The catalytic potential of a state is associated with the depth and the breadth of links between the state and other actors. To understand the catalytic potential of states, Weiss uses the term 'political crystallization' to explore the ways in which constellations of actors and resources can coalesce into policy networks. This can, for example, provide further insight into what Kacarska sees as both the formal and informal modes of governance linked to visa policy with important implications for citizens' rights because of the particular crystallisations that occur in the field of migration and mobility. These crystallisations also help to bring into the analysis the forms and types of social and political power that might be associated with these constellations and crystallisations. For example, drawing from Mann's work on the sources of state power can allow assessment of how particular crystallisations can promote 'infrastructural power', which can be understood as a state's capacity to penetrate civil society (Mann, 1984). The articles in this collection move beyond and enhance a discussion of

THE EUROPEANISATION OF CITIZENSHIP GOVERNANCE

infrastructural power as nationally bound by accounting for the multivalent nature of external influences from the EU and other European and international standards and the effects that these can have on the boundaries of inclusion and exclusion, resource mobilisations and governed interdependence within a catalytic state. As well as the capacity of a state to act as a catalyst, of course.

Focusing on adaptation means drawing from work on the capacity of social systems to respond to internal and external pressures. While the focus for much work on adaptation is on the effect on ecosystem services of environmental or climate change, there are also clear parallels to the analyses contained within the articles in this special issue many of which do make reference to adaptation and adaptability. It is, therefore, helpful to try to draw out the meaning of adaptation and to think about the effects of adaptive behaviour. This is particularly relevant to this special issue because one of its core purposes is to explore the effects of the EU on the governance of citizenship practices or, put another way, the adaptive requirements of the EU *acquis*. Adaptation can be understood as referring to decision-making processes, sets of actions, and associated capacities to deal with future changes to systems (Nelson et al., 2007). A system may be 'resilient' if the effects of change can be absorbed while the same controls on function and structure are maintained while it can be understood as 'vulnerable' to the extent that it is susceptible to and is unable to cope with adverse effects (Adger, 2006; Nelson et al., 2007). There can also be 'maladaptation', which refers to the ways in which adaptation actions that might arise as a result of pressure to accord with EU requirements can also have the effect of increasing the vulnerability of other groups and sectors or, in transboundary issue areas, to rebound negatively on other states (Barnett & O'Neill, 2010). Returning to a point made in the previous section, any discussion of adaptation, vulnerability, resilience and maladaptation requires attention to sectoral variation because of the different constellation and crystallisations that can occur. It also requires close attention to the ideological content of adaptive requirements because these will have powerful effects on the ways in which policy networks are constituted, the empowerment of certain actors and the weakening of others. In turn, these translate into an assessment of how, why and with what effects the boundaries of citizenship have adapted to the changes that they have experienced, as well as the effects of these adaptations.

This then leads to a third theme that is central to the contributions in this special issue, which is the *practice* of governance. Whether the focus is on extradition, visas, social citizenship, welfare or education, there is an attention not only to modes of governance but also how these translate into practices and what these mean for citizenship. The so-called practice turn in international relations highlights the importance of practice understood as the socially recognised competence of practitioners whether these be interior ministry officials or teachers asserting their professional status. The focus for this special issue on both the construction and meaning of citizenship in south east Europe resonates with the insight provided by Adler and Pouliot (2011, p. 3) when they wrote that: 'most political dynamics come to rest on the fixation of meanings – a hard work in which practices play a prominent role'. The practice of governance necessarily amounts to more than simply 'behaviour' or 'action' because it involves 'the patterned nature of deeds in socially organized contexts' (Adler & Pouliot, 2011, p. 3). These socially organised contexts can also be understood as 'communities of practice' that can emerge in a wide variety of social settings but necessarily involve groups of people that interact frequently to create the social fabric of learning. This resonates with Džankić's focus on learning as one of

THE EUROPEANISATION OF CITIZENSHIP GOVERNANCE

the four characteristics of Europeanisation. In each of the areas that are covered by the articles in this special issue we can see evidence of practice understood as a social process based on a shared sense of joint enterprise, mutual engagement and a shared repertoire of resources (Wenger, 2010, p. 229). This says more about the practice of governance and less about its normative content, but the wider point is that the practice of governance is necessarily a social endeavour and plays a key role in the production of meaning about citizenship as both a status and a process.

Implications for Future Research

This final section briefly reflects on the implications of this special issue for its research fields as well as for future research and centres on three observations. First, the articles offer a significant development in the understanding of the governance of citizenship practices in South-East Europe. The empirical material and conceptual insight that is brought to bear is an important contribution to knowledge, which is further strengthened by the coherence of the collection and its attention to a set of key questions and issues that centre on the relationships between governance and citizenship. The broad understanding of citizenship also facilitates new insight into the ways in which boundaries of inclusion and exclusion can be redefined within governance systems from the local to the EU level and what this mean for social and political relations in each of the five countries. Given the broad understanding of citizenship that is used, there is clearly scope for others to follow the path established by this special issue either through exploration of others areas of citizenship policy or to drill down deeper into the particular cases.

Second, the contributions also speak to broader debates. While context is clearly important, the papers offer insight into various debates about the role, purposes and future of the nation state in Europe. While local specificities obviously play a key role and should not be downplayed, we can also extract from the articles in this collection some more general points about issues such as Europeanisation and the idea of Europe's transformative power. The articles caution against assumption about unidirectional flows and also highlight the importance of specifying the ways in which European integration can empower some actors and weaken others with clear implications for rights, for the boundaries of inclusion and exclusion and for citizenship. The article all add something new and distinctive to the roles played by issues such as extradition, migration, mobility, visas, social rights, welfare and education and demonstrates both the impacts of Europeanisation, as well as some of its limits.

Third, the articles all engage with the governance of citizenship practices and encourage reflection on the meaning of the word itself rather than the attachment of various adjectives to it. By doing so, the articles highlight the importance of conceptualising underlying social systems and relationships before then thinking about the adaptive capacities of these systems and recognising the potential for maladaptation to occur that might exacerbate rather than address systemic vulnerabilities. There is rich potential for research in the direction opened by the articles in this collection that place the practices of governance at the heart of their analysis and prompt research that is sensitive to context, but that also engages with concepts and ideas that resonate beyond the borders of south east European countries.

THE EUROPEANISATION OF CITIZENSHIP GOVERNANCE

Disclosure statement

No potential conflict of interest was reported by the author.

References

Adger, W. N. (2006) Vulnerability, *Global Environmental Change*, 16(1), pp. 268–281.
Adler, E. & Pouliot, V. (2011) International practices, *International Theory*, 3(1), pp. 1–36.
Barnett, J. & O'Neill, S. (2010) Maladaptation, *Global Environmental Change*, 20(1), pp. 211–213.
Geddes, A. & Taylor, A. (2013) How EU capacity bargains strengthen states: Migration and border security in South-East Europe, *West European Politics*, 36(1), pp. 51–70.
Green-Cowles, M., Caporaso, J. & Risse-Kappen, T. (Eds) (2001) *Transforming Europe: Europeanization and Domestic Change* (Ithaca: Cornell University Press).
Mann, M. (1984) The autonomous power of the state: Its origins, mechanisms and results, *European Journal of Sociology*, 25(2), pp. 185–213.
Mattli, W. (1999) *The Logic of Regional Integration: Europe and Beyond* (Cambridge: Cambridge University Press).
Nelson, D., Adger, W. N. & Brown, K. (2007) Adaptation to environmental change: Contributions of a resilience framework, *Annual Review of Environment and Resources*, 32(2), pp. 395–419.
Pierre, J. (Ed.) (2000) *Debating Governance: Authority, Steering, and Democracy* (Oxford: Oxford University Press).
Taylor, A., Geddes, A. & Lees, C. (2013) *Political Change in South East Europe: The Dynamics of Multi-Level Governance and Europeanisation* (London: Routledge/UACES).
Weiss, L. (1998) *The Myth of the Powerless State* (Ithaca: Cornell University Press).
Wenger, E. (2010) Conceptual tools for CoPs as social learning systems: Boundaries, identity, trajectories and participation, in: C. Blackmore (Ed.) *Social Learning Systems and Communities of Practice*, pp. 125–143 (Dordrecht: Springer).

Index

accommodating approach: comparisons of 47; in Croatia 43, 46–7, 50–1
acquis 4–6, 12, 15, 28–32, 71, 87, 116
adaptation 111, 114–17
Agreement on Extradition 18, 22
anti-discrimination laws 28, 31–3, 38
anti-discrimination policy 28–33, 76–7
asylum seekers 34–8

Bauböck, Rainer 24
belonging, ideas of 2–3
black list 27, 34
Bosnia: extradition policies in 21–2; visa liberalisation 27; wars in 64–5, 94–5

'capacity bargain' 112
citizenship: civic citizenship 78–9; civic dimensions of 77; concepts of 76–7, 79–80, 83, 86, 89; in Croatia 59–72; definition of 15; education and 75–90; ethnicization of 96–9; ethnocentric dimensions of 8, 75–82, 88–9; Europeanisation of 1–9; exclusive concepts of 76–7, 79–80, 83, 86, 89; extradition policies and 14–23; in 'family state' 77–8; future research on 117; governance of 1–9, 111–18; identities and 77, 86–8; impact on 1–9; inclusive concepts of 76–7, 79–80, 83, 86, 89; independent citizenship 5; language policies and 83–6; 'lived citizenship' 5, 94, 108, 111–12, 114; minorities and 77–9; in Mostar 93–109; multicultural dimensions of 77–8; political economy of 64–7; in post-Yugoslav states 1–9, 43–55, 75–90; social citizenship 7–9, 43–9, 59–61; in South-East Europe 111–18; in 'state of families' 77–8; in 'state of individuals' 77–9; understanding of 117
citizenship policies: in post-Yugoslav states 1–3; in South-East Europe 112, 117
citizenship regimes: independent citizenship 5; in post-Yugoslav states 1–8, 75–9; in Western Balkans 28–30, 37–8
CITSEE 2, 4, 24, 111

civic citizenship 78–9; *see also* citizenship
civic education 78–9; *see also* education
clientelism: concept of 59–64; in Croatia 59–72; elements of 63–4; explanation of 59–64; institutional particularism 63–4; political economy of 64–7; rethinking 62–3; social welfare and 59–72
communism, collapse of 14, 43–4
Constitutional Act on the Rights of National Minorities 83
Constitutional Law on the Rights of National Minorities 87
construction process 3–4, 60, 114–16
Council of Europe (CoE) 4, 5, 23, 37
Criminal Codes 17, 22, 35
criminal law 19–20, 35–7
criminal matters 11–12, 17–20, 35–7
Criminal Procedure Code 22
Croatia: accommodating approach in 43, 46–7, 50–1; citizenship practices in 59–72; clientelism in 59–72; Europeanisation in 59–72; extradition policies in 17–18; social welfare in 59–72; state-building process 62–5; wars in 64–70
Croatian Democratic Community 64
Croatian Pensioners Party 50
Croatian war 64–70
cultural rights 75, 78–89; *see also* rights

Dayton Peace Agreement 22, 95
Democratic Party of Socialists 20
Democratic Serbian Party 66
diffusion process 3, 18, 60
Djindjic, Zoran 18
Dukanovic, Milo 20
Džankic, Jelena 1, 6–7, 11, 112–14, 116

economic crisis: global economic crisis 51–5; political economy and 64–7; in post-Yugoslav states 43–55; welfare state and 43–55
economic growth rate 54
economic indicators 43–5, 48–54

INDEX

economic progress 48–54
education: citizenship and 75–90; for civic citizenship 78–9; civic education 78–9; cultural rights 75, 78–89; ethnic group dominance and 75–6, 82–3, 88; ethnocentric dimensions of 77–8, 89; free education 78; governance of 86–8; language policies 83–6; linguistic rights 75, 78–89; multicultural education 8, 78–80, 84–6, 89; for nation-building 82–3; policy level of 77, 86–8; in post-Yugoslav states 75–90; role of parents 100–1; role of teachers 99–100; social changes and 99–108; spatial governmentality of 94–8, 108; transformation of 99–108; *see also* teachers
education systems: consociational systems 75, 80–2; in post-Yugoslav states 75–82; reform of 87–8; universal systems 75, 78–80
Employment Policy Priorities 51
Erdut Agreement 65, 83
ethnic engineering 65, 75–6, 82
ethnic governance 9, 89, 96–9; *see also* governance
ethnic groups: dominance of 8–9, 75–6, 82–3, 88; teachers' strike and 98–100, 105; war and 95
ethnocentric citizenship 8, 75–82, 88–9
ethnonational belonging 94–5
ethnonational governance 8, 93–109
EU *acquis* 4–6, 12, 15, 28–32, 71, 87, 116
European Arrest Warrant and Surrender Procedures (EAWSP) 17
European Arrest Warrant (EAW) 6, 11–24
European Charter for Regional and Minority Languages 4
European Convention on Human Rights (ECHR) 4, 5, 18
European Court of Human Rights (ECtHR) 4, 23, 33
'European norms' 76, 87, 89
'European social model' 44, 60–1
Europeanisation: changing nature of 13–14, 22–3; of citizenship practices 1–9; concept of 3–5, 13–14, 23, 60–2; construction process 3–4, 60, 114–16; in Croatia 59–72; defining 3–4, 13; diffusion process 3, 18, 60; erosion of sovereignty and 11–24; extradition policies and 11–24; impact of 1–9; influences of 87–9; institutionalisation process 3, 29, 60, 63; limits of 59–66; in post-Yugoslav states 1–9, 11–24, 43–55; processes of 3–4, 18, 29, 60–3, 114–16; securitisation and 28–9, 37–8; sovereignty and 11–24; transformative power of 4, 11, 20–1, 112, 114, 117; in Western Balkans 27–41

Europeanisation of Citizenship in the Successor States of the Former Yugoslavia 2, 111
Extradition Agreement 18, 22
extradition policies: in Bosnia 21–2; citizenship and 14–23; in Croatia 17–18; in Kosovo 21–2; in Macedonia 18–21; in Montenegro 18–21; in post-Yugoslav states 11–24; in Serbia 18–21; in Slovenia 17–18

'false asylum seekers' 36, 38; *see also* asylum seekers
'family state' 77–8
Federal Republic of Yugoslavia (FRY) 18–20
Framework Convention for the Protection of National Minorities (FCNM) 4, 8, 76, 85
Framework Law on Primary and Secondary Education 85
'freedom of movement' 5, 28, 30, 36–8
fundamental rights: impact on 27–38; in post-visa liberalisation period 34–8; requirements on 29–30, 37–8; side-lining of 27–8; in Western Balkans 27–38; *see also* rights

Geddes, Andrew 9, 111
global economic crisis 51–5; *see also* economic crisis
governance: adaptive features of 111, 114–17; of citizenship practices 1–9, 111–18; defining 3, 115; of education 86–8; ethnic governance 9, 89, 96–9; ethnonational governance 8, 93–109; future research on 117; hard governance 5; modes of 5–7, 62, 67, 111, 115–16; multi-level governance 4–5, 31, 114–15; politicisation of 8; practice of 71, 111–17; soft governance 5; spatial governmentality 94–8, 108; understanding of 117
gross domestic product (GDP) 48, 68–9

Homeland War 67–9
Hromadžic, Azra 8–9, 93, 114

identities: citizenship and 77, 86–8; collective identities 77; individual identities 77; rights and 77
identity documents 28–30
illegal immigration 27–9, 35
independent citizenship 5
Independent Democratic Serbian Party (SDSS) 66
institutional particularism 63–4
institutionalisation process 3, 29, 60, 63
Interim Agreement on Satisfying Special Needs and Rights to Returnee Children 83
International Criminal Tribunal for the Former Yugoslavia (ICTY) 18–19, 22

INDEX

International Financial Institutions (IFIs) 44, 47, 51–4
International Labour Organization (ILO) 44

Kacarska, Simonida 1, 7, 27, 112–15
Kalinic, Srecko 18
Kosovo: extradition policies in 21–2; neo-corporatist approach in 53–4; neoliberal approach in 43, 46–7, 53–4; visa liberalisation in 34–5; wars in 52
Kurtovic, Larisa 108

Labor Code 51
language policies 83–6
Law on Education 86
Law on International Legal Assistance in Criminal Matters 19–20
lex Perkovic 12, 18
linguistic rights 75, 78–89; *see also* rights
'lived citizenship' 5, 94, 108, 111–12, 114

Macedonia: asylum seekers from 34–8; extradition policies in 18–21; neo-corporatist approach in 53–4; neoliberal approach in 43, 46–7, 53–4; visa liberalisation 27
maladaptation 111, 114–17
Manevski, Mihajlo 21
Marshall, T. H. 44–6, 61
Merkel, Angela 11
Milošević, Slobodan 19–20
minorities: citizenship and 77–9; education for 8, 78–80, 84–6, 89; protection of 28–31
Montenegro: extradition policies in 18–21; paternalistic approach in 43, 46–7, 51–2; visa liberalisation 27
Mostar, Bosnia–Herzegovina: citizenship in 93–109; dissatisfaction in 93–109; ethnonational governance in 93–109; post-war governance 94–6; solidarity in 93–109; teachers' strike in 93–109, 114; war in 94–5
Mostar Gymnasium 9, 86, 89–90, 93–100, 107–9, 114
multicultural citizenship 77–8
multicultural education 8, 78–80, 84–6, 89; *see also* education
multi-level governance 4–5, 31, 114–15; *see also* governance

nation-building 79, 82–3, 89
neo-corporatist approach: comparisons of 47; in Kosovo 53–4; in Macedonia 53–4; in Slovenia 43, 46–7, 49–50
neoliberal approach: comparisons of 47; in Kosovo 43, 46–7, 53–4; in Macedonia 43, 46–7, 53–4

Ohrid Framework Agreement 53, 83
Organisation for Security and Cooperation in Europe (OSCE) 4, 9, 96–7

Pantic, Nataša 1, 8, 75, 114
paternalistic approach: comparisons of 47; in Montenegro 43, 46–7, 51–2; in Serbia 43, 46–7, 51
Peace Agreement 22, 95
pension system 50–2, 68
Perkovic, Josip 12
political economy 64–7
political transformations 11, 44–5, 48–9, 54
post-Yugoslav states: changing citizenship in 48–9; citizenship policies in 1–3; citizenship practices in 1–9, 43–55, 75–90; citizenship regimes in 1–8, 75–9; economic crisis in 43–55; economic growth rate in 54; economic indicators in 43–5, 48–54; economic progress in 48–54; education in 75–90; erosion of sovereignty in 11–24; Europeanisation in 1–9, 11–24, 43–55; extradition policies in 11–24; governance of citizenship in 1–9; ideas of belonging in 2–3; impact on 1–9; political transformation in 11, 44–5, 48–9, 54; social citizenship in 43–55; socioeconomic indicators 43–5, 48–54; state-building process 14, 23, 47–9, 62–5; welfare state in 43–55
poverty rates 48, 53–4, 70–1, 79–81
privatization 47–53

regime theory 60–2
Republika Srspka Krajina 64, 85, 95
Riddle, Heather M. 108
rights: cultural rights 75, 78–89; fundamental rights 27–38; identities and 77; linguistic rights 75, 78–89; losing 27–41

Schengen black list 27
Schengen Convention 35–6
Schengen visa liberalisation 5, 7, 30; *see also* visa liberalisation
securitisation 28–9, 37–8
Serbia: asylum seekers from 34–8; extradition policies in 18–21; paternalistic approach in 43, 46–7, 51–2; visa liberalisation 27
Shaw, Jo 1, 24
Slovenia: crisis in 49–50; extradition policies in 17–18; neo-corporatist approach in 43, 46–7, 49–50
social citizenship: concept of 7–9, 43–9, 59–61; in post-Yugoslav states 43–55; welfare state and 43–9, 54–5, 113–16
'social model' 44, 60–1

121

INDEX

social welfare: clientelism and 59–72; in Croatia 59–72; economic crisis and 43–55; in post-Yugoslav states 43–55; social citizenship and 43–9, 54–5, 113–16; *see also* welfare state

Socialist Federal Republic of Yugoslavia (SFRY) 1–2

socioeconomic indicators 43–5, 48–54

solidarity: among teachers 93–109; generational dimensions of 94; moral dimensions of 94; in Mostar 93–109; socioeconomic dimensions of 94

South-East Europe: citizenship policies in 112, 117; citizenship practices in 111–18; governance of citizenship in 111–18

sovereignty: erosion of 11–24; porousness of 14–16; transformation of 16–23

'sovereignty bargain' 112

spatial governmentality 94–8, 108

Stambolieva, Marija 7, 43, 113

Stara Gimnazija (Old Gymnasium) 96, 102–3; *see also* Mostar Gymnasium

'state of families' 77–8

'state of individuals' 77–9

state-building process 14, 23, 47–9, 62–5

Stubbs, Paul 7–8, 59, 112–14

teachers: accusations against 100–1; code of conduct for 86; parents and 100–1; role of 99–100; strike in Mostar 93–109, 114; union of 103–4

teaching: role of parents 100–1; role of teachers 99–100; social changes and 100–8; social poetics of 99, 105; teachers' strike and 93–4, 98–100, 103–8, 114; *see also* education

trade unions 45, 49–52

transformative powers 4, 11, 20–1, 112, 114, 117

Tuzla Canton Law on Minorities 85

Use of Languages in Kosovo Act 85

visa liberalisation: anti-discrimination laws and 28, 31–3, 38; in Bosnia 27; fundamental rights and 27–38; in Kosovo 34–5; in Macedonia 27; in Montenegro 27; Schengen visa liberalisation 5, 7, 30; in Western Balkans 27–41

war crimes 17–19

wars: Bosnian war 64–5, 94–5; Croatian war 64–70; Homeland War 67–9; in Kosovo 52; in Mostar 94–5; Yugoslav wars 17–20, 50

'weak power' 94, 107

welfare models 44, 47, 52–4

welfare outcomes 46–7

welfare policies 43–4, 55

welfare reform 43–55

welfare regimes 44, 47, 60–2

welfare state: changes in 43–55; economic crisis and 43–55; outcomes of 46–7; post-Yugoslav states 43–55; restructuring 43–55; social citizenship and 43–9, 54–5, 113–16; *see also* social welfare

Western Balkans: asylum seekers from 34–8; citizenship regimes in 28–30, 37–8; Europeanisation in 27–41; fundamental rights in 27–38; illegal immigration in 27–9, 35; losing rights 27–41; securitisation in 28–9, 37–8; visa liberalisation in 27–41

World Bank 4, 51–2, 69, 71

Yugoslav: disintegration of 17–20, 95; secession of 50–2; succession of 61–5; wars of 17–20, 50; *see also* post-Yugoslav states

Zrinšcak, Siniša 7–8, 59, 112–14